THE

MATUSOW

AFFAIR

MEMOIR OF A NATIONAL SCANDAL

Books by Albert E. Kahn:

*Sabotage!**
*The Plot Against the Peace**
*The Great Conspiracy**
High Treason
The Game of Death
Days with Ulanova
Smetana and the Beetles
The Unholy Hymnal

Joys and Sorrows by Pablo Casals
as told to Albert E. Kahn

*In collaboration with Michael Sayers

THE
MATUSOW
AFFAIR

MEMOIR OF A
NATIONAL SCANDAL

ALBERT E. KAHN

Introduction by Angus Cameron

MOYER BELL LIMITED

MT. KISCO, NEW YORK

Published by Moyer Bell Limited

First Edition

Library of Congress Cataloging-in-Publication Data

Kahn, Albert Eugene, 1912–1979.
    The Matusow affair.

    Includes index.
    1. Matusow, Harvey, 1926–   . 2. Matusow,
Harvey, 1926–   . False witness.   3. Communism—
United States—1917–   .   4. United States—Politics
and government—1945–1953.   5. False testimony—
United
States.   I. Title.
E743.5.M36K34   1987   973.92'092'4   87-22136
ISBN   0-918825-38-5

Printed in the United States of America

The country will swarm with informers, spies, delators, and all the odious reptile tribe that breed in the sunshine of despotic power. The hours of the most unexpected confidence, the intimacies of friendship, or the recesses of domestic retirement, will afford no security. . . . Do not let us be told that we are to excite fervor against a foreign aggression to establish a tyranny at home; and that we are absurd enough to call ourselves free and enlightened while we advocate principles that would have disgraced the age of Gothic barbarism.

—Congressman Edward Livingston, speaking in the House of Representatives on the Sedition Act of 1798

CONTENTS

viii

PREFACE

Bizarre and unlikely as many of the events in this book may seem, they all occurred. None are fictional.

Some are of course a matter of public record. In recounting others I have relied largely on journals I kept at the time. I have supplemented my own records with tape-recorded interviews and memoranda of other participants in the Matusow affair.

The dialogue throughout is based on my contemporaneous notes or on records of court proceedings, transcripts of congressional hearings and similar documentary sources.

I regard total objectivity as a mythical virtue in both journalists and historians. In any event, I could not claim impartiality as author of this book. I have a certain prejudice, for example, against government authorities who—no matter how highly motivated—sought to curb my dissent or slap me in jail. I've done my best, however, to prevent such personal bias from coloring my account of the actual facts.

I wrote a draft of the book in the late 1950s and submitted it to several former publishers of my works. Though their comments were favorable, their rejections were unanimous. The head of one distinguished firm, a friend of mine, told me: "Sure, it's a hell of a yarn. But why beat around the bush? Nobody will publish it. The FBI is still a sacred cow, you know. Maybe in twenty years. . . ."

Well, more than twenty years have passed.

A.E.K.

IN APPRECIATION

My husband, Albert E. Kahn, was revising *The Matusow Affair* at the time of his death in 1979. It is a true fulfillment to see it in print. The book marks not only a signal period in the history of this country, but in the lives of our family and friends as well. Now we are gathered together again in these pages, after a separation of more than thirty years. It is a warming reunion.

We came together in 1955, combining our energies to help in the publication of Harvey Matusow's *False Witness*—the catalyst that would expose the full corruption of the government's paid witness system. We were a small and disparate group, but each one contributed his best effort to bring an end to that virus, fed by ignorance, demagoguery and fear, that blighted the country.

As I read *The Matusow Affair*, familiar faces and qualities come to me again—qualities of courage, conviction, dedicated work, steadiness—and much more. The times required all of these. I remember the period as a kaleidoscope of daily challenges, uncertain sleep, exhilarating victories, major setbacks and a massive amount of complex work to be done at breakneck speed on a score of levels. And all of this was interwoven with an irrepressible, rollicking humor that helped us keep things in perspective.

Did we shake the walls of Jericho? Yes, indeed we did! And though the walls did not tumble down completely, we made some mighty good cracks in them that could never be repaired.

I do not mean to imply that we were heroic, nor do I intend to romanticize what was, in fact, a difficult and at times hazardous experience. But for me it is most meaningful to relive that significant time we spent together, and to have this opportunity—as Albert intended when he wrote the book—to convey to you my respect and affection.

I deeply appreciate Angus Cameron's Introduction, which brings to the story his unique and encompassing view of the period. To author and longtime friend, Arthur D. Kahn, and to my sons Brian and Steven, who gave me immeasurable assistance in the responsible task of editing this book, my lasting gratitude.

Riette Kahn
August, 1987

INTRODUCTION

Angus Cameron

Today's reader may question the relevance to contemporary America of a thirty-year old national scandal. In the intervening period, after all, our country has changed dramatically. Having lived through the "scandals" of Viet Nam, Watergate and the Reagan years, we've become accustomed to corrupt public officials and lying presidents. By comparison, the perjury-based framing of a leftist labor leader, the criminal prosecution of American communist leaders, the attempt by the FBI and Justice Department to block publication of a book might well seem part of a tame and distant past.

There is, perhaps, something to be said for this view of a memoir which deals with the McCarthy period, an era as far away in time to many young people as the Alien and Sedition Acts, and which concerns itself with public figures unfamiliar to many contemporaries. McCarthy himself, after whom the witch hunt era was named, is a dim figure to most, and wholly unknown to many.

Yet the politics of those days lay a heavy hand on the present. To take only one example, our horrendous public debt, so largely military, dates back to decisions Truman made in the late 1940s to come to the rescue of a bankrupt and beleaguered Britain by assuming the military policing of Greece, Turkey, Iran and the Middle East.

But first a bit of background.

By 1944, Franklin D. Roosevelt had been president for nearly three full terms. During those years of his administration, under the tremendous impact of the Great Depression and the Second World War, the American political landscape had undergone profound changes. Tens of millions of Americans felt, for the first time, that the federal government had a vital role to play in protecting the nation's citizenry from the terrible consequences of concentrated, private economic power—depression, farm foreclosures, boom and bust economics, unemployment, poverty and hunger. A powerful, class conscious trade union movement had developed; socialist and communist movements, building on the traditions of American socialism initiated by Eugene Debs and others, had become a significant, if still minority, force in state and national politics. In foreign policy, Roosevelt had rejected the legacy of imperialism, establishing a "good neighbor policy." He resisted the call in corporate circles to intervene militarily when Mexico nationalized American banks. He established diplomatic relations with the Soviet Union and eventually forged a vital American-Soviet-British alliance to fight the fascist Axis powers. His vision for the post-war world was based on a continuation of unity between the major powers and the formation of a cooperative, multinational organization, the United Nations, to address the world's pressing problems of poverty, deprivation and keeping the peace.

These profound changes, though supported by the large majority of Americans, were not without violent opposition. The dominant business interests vehemently opposed FDR's evolving efforts to use government to both stimulate the economy, impose order on laissez-faire business practices, and establish legal protection for the organizing of industrial unions. Despite the political reality that FDR's reforms very probably saved the capitalist system from total collapse, he was called "a traitor to his class," a label reflecting appropriately on the prevailing mentality of his class peers. In the area of foreign policy, Roosevelt's policies were similarly villified by a wide-ranging coalition of isolationists, fascist sympathizers, pan-Germans and imperialist-oriented international business interests. (Many, perhaps most, contemporary readers are not aware of the strong fascist movements which existed in pre-war America.)

The anti-Roosevelt coalition formed around the Republican Party. But serious opposition existed within the Democratic Party as well, particularly in the conservative Southern wing. When FDR sought election to an unprecedented fourth term, this conservative wing brought intense pressure to bear. Prior to the Democratic convention, they made it clear that, in exchange for their continued support, Roosevelt must set aside his staunch New Deal supporter, ally and vice-president, Henry A. Wallace, and select instead as his running mate Senator Harry S. Truman of Missouri. Senator Truman had made a minor reputation as chairman of a senate committee on small business during the early part of World War II, but some felt he was essentially Boss Pendergast's man in Washington, a small-minded product of Pendergast's machine and hardly a man to carry on President Roosevelt's progressive policies. Roosevelt gave in to pressure and named Truman as his running mate.

When Roosevelt died in April of 1945, Truman succeeded to the presidency and very soon the leadership's political outlook changed. Shortly after he was sworn in, Truman set about to eliminate the old New Dealers from the administration. To appease those who had supported Roosevelt's progressive foreign policies, including positive relations with the Soviet Union, Truman did appoint Henry A. Wallace as Secretary of Commerce. Wallace's service was short-lived; his strong opposition to the Truman foreign policy eventually forced him to resign.

That new foreign policy took shape as conservative opposition to the wave of democratic movements throughout the world that followed the defeat of fascism, the end of World War II and the impending demise of colonialism. The ferment of people's movements in France, Italy, Turkey, Greece, Iran, China, the Philippines and Vietnam, dubbed "Soviet-inspired communist expansion" by conservatives in both the United States and Britain, spurred Truman to abandon a policy of conciliation with our wartime ally, Russia, and to initiate the policy of "containment" of expanding communism. Prior to this new Truman policy, the policing of leftist peoples' movements in Greece, Turkey and the oil lands of the Middle East had been done by Britain. Now Truman proposed a program of economic and military assistance to these "threatened" countries to permit them to take a firm stand against what became known as communist aggression. In reversing America's anti-colonial policy, Truman had the ardent help of that doughty old Red hater and unreconstructed imperialist, Winston Churchill. (Few readers will likely recall Churchill's unflagging efforts, in his own words, to "strangle the Soviet infant in his crib," or his vehement opposition to post-war independence for India.) In March, 1946, in a famous speech at Fulton, Missouri, attended by

President Truman, Churchill called for an alliance between Great Britain and the United States against "the growing challenge and peril to Christian civilization from Russian Communism." The Cold War was formally declared and the phrase, "the iron curtain," used by Nazi Propaganda Minister Goebbels, became part of the American lexicon.

The Truman Doctrine brought many changes: it cast our wartime ally as our mortal enemy and classified serious critics like Henry Wallace as supporters of the Reds. To obtain congressional appropriations for his new objectives Truman had to demonstrate an outside threat—"monolithic, Soviet-inspired communism" sufficed; to silence domestic critics—among whom liberals, socialists, communists and organized labor formed a potentially powerful coalition—and Truman initiated the witch hunt by instituting his "loyalty oath" program. Senator Joseph McCarthy, the junior senator from Wisconsin, soon became the master of ceremonies. The McCarthy Era came on, one may fairly say, when critics of the new policy were answered by the accusation that *they* were communists or communist dupes. There could be, under such a policy, no *loyal* opposition; all opponents of the Cold War were labelled disloyal and subversive.

Ironically, the leadership of the American Communist party had played into the hands of the witch hunters: during the 30s and 40s they consistently followed the Soviet policy line on all foreign and many domestic policy issues. Because of this, government inquisitors found it an easy step from labelling communists as "agents of a foreign power" to tarring all dissenters with the same brush.

Congress itself was passing repressive legislation such as the Taft Hartley Act and the McCarren-Walters Act under the guise of preventing communism, but actually to silence any criticism of government policies. Soon committees of Congress like the so-called House Un-American Activities Committee, the Senate Internal Security Subcommittee and McCarthy's own committee were hauling dissenters in for public "hearings."

The purpose of these committees was the same and so were their methods. The committee hearing rooms became, in effect, kangaroo courts where reputations were smeared and guilt of some sort imputed without benefit of the right to cross examine or call witnesses against the witch hunters. The victims of these hearings were sometimes imprisoned for contempt of Congress if they invoked the First Amendment in protection of free speech; more often, once smeared, they were blacklisted by employers who feared that, by hiring someone dubbed as "subversive," they themselves would be similarly labeled. Many victims of the committees lost positions in business, teaching, government and the arts.

In this atmosphere of incipient political terror the famous Hollywood Ten screenwriters were jailed, as were the leaders of the American Communist party. Future luminaries, Congressman Richard Nixon and actor Ronald Reagan, earned their spurs with anti-communist crusades. Simultaneously, there emerged a small army of former radicals, turncoats who had seen the light and who, for a consideration, made a profession of appearing as friendly witnesses for the committees, naming names and smearing political critics as disloyal.

In the mid-50s, however, the interests which had developed the political tool of character assassination and blacklisting lost their chief ringleader. Senator McCarthy, who ironically accused the Truman Administration of harboring disloyal Americans and stifling the effort to expose them, was foolish enough to carry his attack to the Army. As a result, he was himself investigated and "censured" by his fellow senatorial inquisitors. But though McCarthy himself was discredited, "McCarthyism" continued to flourish. The witch hunt had become institutionalized.

In 1952, with the witch hunt at its height, the publishing firm of Cameron & Kahn was founded by two of its earlier victims. Albert E. Kahn, an author of best-selling political exposés, had been blacklisted by major publishers. And I, a vice-president and Editor-in-Chief at Little Brown & Company, had been forced to resign that position in 1951. In addition to friendship, Albert and I shared the belief that the public interest demanded a publishing outlet for blacklisted writers and progressive books.

In 1954, Cameron & Kahn learned that one of McCarthy's and the Department of Justice's foremost professional witnesses was having second thoughts. Harvey Matusow had testified falsely in hearings and trials, ruining careers and sending people to jail. However, having undergone a religious experience, Matusow felt compelled to attempt to make retribution for the harm he had done. Cameron & Kahn published his confession in the celebrated book, *False Witness*. *The Matusow Affair* is an account of the story of how Matusow's confession of perjury came to be written, the fight to get it published despite attempted suppression by the federal government, and the eventual impact the book had on the practices of witch hunting.

These, in brief, are the basic political realities which set the stage for the story told in *The Matusow Affair*. But to return to the observation that in the light of present day scandals, this book might be viewed by contemporary readers as a period piece: it must be emphasized that the "period" in question is one with profound implications for the America in which we now live. Its basic parameters have become institutionalized: a militarized foreign policy and domestic economy; a forty-year legacy of opposition to popular, indigenous peoples movements for revolution and reform—Viet Nam, Guatemala, Cuba, Congo, Dominican Republic, Chile, El Salvador, Honduras, Angola, Nicaragua; the destruction of the American left as a viable political alternative; the association in the public mind of socialist and communist views with disloyalty; the destruction of class consciousness as a meaningful element of the trade union movement. In sum, the shift from Roosevelt's anti-colonial, peaceful coexistence policies to those aimed at acquiring imperial economic power, has been achieved. And part and parcel of the shift is the legacy of the stifling of substantive dissent—an action which corrupted the processes and attitudes critical for the functioning of democratic society. That corruption, spawned during the post-war period described in this book, is still with us, albeit dressed in less crude and garrish trappings.

The politics of those days lay a heavy hand on the present.

THE

MATUSOW
AFFAIR

MEMOIR OF A NATIONAL SCANDAL

CHAPTER ONE

THE INFORMER

1. *Call from Taos*

A telephone call reached me on a bright autumn morning at my home at Croton-on-Hudson, New York. The operator said the call was collect from a Mr. Harvey Matusow in Taos, New Mexico. She asked if I wished to accept it.

I said yes. It was an understatement. I had been looking for Matusow for almost a month.

Matusow came on the line. Though two thousand miles of plain and mountain stretched between us, something about his voice made him sound unpleasantly near. "I understand you've been trying to reach me," he said. "I'm not easy to get hold of these days. I've been moving around a lot."

I started to reply but he cut me short.

"You know, we've met," he said. The claim seemed modest enough since Matusow had testified under oath as a government witness that we'd once been close friends and fellow members of the Communist party.

"I don't recall our ever meeting," I said.

"Oh, yes," he said breezily, with no trace of embarrassment. "I used to work at the Jefferson School bookshop in New York, and you once bought some books from me."

I acknowledged that was possible—I had occasionally bought books there.

"Know what I've been doing?" he asked with sudden enthusiasm, as if we were old friends.

"No, what?" I dutifully replied.

"Having a fabulous time! Bicycling around with a pack on my back! I've traveled more than eight hundred miles in Texas and New Mexico, picked cotton in Lubbock and harvested grain in the Panhandle. One thing you learn on a trip like this. You don't need more material possessions in life than you can carry on your back. All I've got in my pack is a small typewriter, change of clothes, two blankets, cooking utensils, a trench knife, two harmonicas and a flute. I've been sleeping in the open under the stars, living off the land like a pioneer, just losing myself in nature."

As he plunged ahead with his effusive travelogue, I had difficulty visualizing this youthful ex-aide of Senator Joseph McCarthy and FBI informer as a vagabond nature-lover.

He finally concluded: "Say what you want—there's nothing like the Southwest!"

At least, I thought, that gives us something in common. "New Mexico," I told him, "is my favorite state. When I get to the Sangre de Cristo Mountains I feel. . . ."

"You know, of course, that's Spanish for 'Blood of Christ,'" he interrupted. "But do you know how the mountains got the name? The conquistadors named it in the sixteen hundreds. They said that at sunset the mountains glowed as if they were covered with the blood of Christ. I know every inch of the terrain. I first camped there in 1951. Most of it really belongs to the Indians—the Pueblos of Taos." He paused for breath.

I took advantage of the momentary lull. "Let me tell you why I want to talk to you."

"Go ahead."

"A couple of years ago my friend Angus Cameron and I started a publishing firm,[1] and. . . ."

"I know you did." His tone managed to imply familiarity with all our activities.

"Anyway, we've heard that you're having second thoughts about your work for the government and that you're thinking of writing a book which. . . ."

He broke in again. "I've already started the book. I call it *Blacklisting Was My Business*. I may change the title."

"Well, Cameron and I would like to talk to you about the possibility of our publishing it, if you're interested."

"I'm interested."

"Could you come to New York? We'd provide the plane ticket."

"I was planning on heading up to Salt Lake City," he said.

Now that I'd found him I didn't intend losing him. "I can come to Salt Lake if you like," I told him. "We could discuss the book there. Though I'd much prefer having Angus in on the meeting."

"I would too," he said. "I know his reputation as an editor."

"Then why not make it New York? It's only a few hours flight from Albuquerque."

"Okay—New York it is. Name the time."

"The sooner the better. Today's Saturday. Could you fly in tomorrow? We could get together on Monday."

"Suits me fine."

I told him I'd make the plane reservation. "Where can the airline reach you to let you know the flight you're booked on?"

"At the Taos Inn." He chuckled. "Young Lochinvar is coming out of the West," he said.

The receiver clicked.

Afterward, I sat for several minutes by the phone in my study looking out at the nearby woods, flamboyant in their autumn foliage. I could still hear the obnoxious inflections of Matusow's voice, but our conversation now had a strangely nebulous and unreal quality, almost as if we hadn't talked at all. Perhaps it was because everything seemed to have gone much too easily.

I made a short memorandum of the conversation. It concluded: "At least, I've found him and we've talked. I wonder if he'll actually come."

The memorandum was dated October 23, 1954.

2. *The War Within*

Nothing had been further from my mind than the thought of any future collaboration between us when, in the spring of 1952, I'd added to my research files in a section headed *Government Intelligence: FBI Informers, CIA Agents, etc.*—a folder labeled "Harvey M. Matusow."

My interest in intelligence activities dated back to World War II, when as editor of *The Hour* newsletter and also in two books, I had focused on exposés of Nazi espionage, sabotage and propaganda operations in the United States.[2] I hadn't contemplated making a literary career of investigative journalism; in fact, at the war's end I was thinking of getting back to work on a novel on Dante I had begun on graduating from Dartmouth. But man proposes and God disposes. Whether the intervention in this case was divine or not, my novel never got written. Instead of peace, the Cold War came.

And as one of its lesser consequences, I found myself still preoccupied with the subject of political intrigue and, in particular, intelligence activities. The latter, however, differed in a singular respect from those on which I had previously concentrated. The undercover operations on the home front that now seemed most noteworthy to me were no longer directed by intelligence agencies in Berlin. They were directed by intelligence agencies in Washington, D.C.

Regardless of one's politics, one had to admit there was little of the dull or commonplace about the postwar years in the United States. They were, in fact, remarkable in many ways and full of startling surprises.

Who, for example, would have predicted that almost as soon as World War II had ended, the nation would be haunted by the spectre of an even more fearsome global conflict? Yet barely two years after the surrender of Japan, the Gallup Poll reported that 73 percent of the voting population thought a third world war inevitable—this time, with the Soviet Union; and the Alsop brothers observed in their column: "The atmosphere in Washington is no longer a postwar atmosphere. It is, to put it bluntly, a prewar atmosphere . . . it is now universally admitted that war within the next few months is certainly possible."

And who would have believed that with the fascist powers crushed, the very freedoms in whose name we had fought overseas would be imperiled within our own borders? Yet such was the state of affairs by 1947 that a group of Yale University Law School professors warned in a public letter addressed to President Harry Truman: "A pattern of suppression is today evolving at the highest level of Federal

Government . . . in disregard and in defiance of the Constitution of the United States. . . . There are alarming signs that persecution for opinion, if not curbed, may reach a point never hitherto attained even in the darkest period of our history."

At the war's end, millions had hoped for the dawn of a new era—an era of peace among the nations. That grand illusion was short-lived. The Cold War brought a bizarre sort of war in peace. With our recent Soviet ally suddenly regarded as our main foe, and our recent Axis foes viewed as our vital allies, the Cold War was waged not only abroad but at home. And the first major casualties on the homefront were the domestic and foreign policies of the New Deal.

"The crusading days of the New Deal . . . are over," reported the *Wall Street Journal* a few months after the death of President Franklin D. Roosevelt. The *New Republic* noted: "Into the vacuum created by the exodus of the New Dealers, two groups have moved—the Brass Hats and the Wall Streeters." Though not yet a term in the political lexicon, the military-industrial complex was emerging as a potent force in the nation's affairs.

As U.S.-Soviet antagonisms mounted, a profound metamorphosis occurred within the United States.

With the outbreak of the Korean war in the summer of 1950, public apprehension reached a peak. Over the whole nation, shadowing every aspect of its life, there hung a pall of fear—fear of an atomic war, fear of Russian spy rings, fear of controversial views, fear of being dismissed from one's job on charges of disloyalty. Millions of Americans were now required to sign loyalty oaths.[3]

"Everyone who does not follow the military policymakers is suspect," wrote Supreme Court Justice William O. Douglas. "Fear runs rampant."[4]

Summing up the "dangerous developments . . . in our national life" by 1953, the general council of the Presbyterian Church declared:

> The shrine of conscience and private judgment is being invaded. . . . These inquisitions find their pattern in medieval Spain and the tribunals of modern totalitarian states. . . . The demagogue who lives by propaganda alone is coming into his own on a national scale.

By far the most notorious demagogue to have come into his own—emerging from the murky climate of the times like the incarnation of all the repression and fear in the land—was Senator Joseph R. McCarthy. His sensational investigations of "Communist conspiracies," his lurid denunciations of high-placed "Soviet spies," his flamboyant rhetoric and swashbuckling mannerisms were familiar to countless millions not only in America but on every continent. As the undisputed leader of the nation's anti-Communist crusade, the junior senator from Wisconsin had added a new word, "McCarthyism," to all languages.

Never before had any American politician gained such extensive power in so short a time. "Sometimes," former Prime Minister Clement Attlee stated in Parliament, "one wonders who is the more powerful—the President or Senator McCarthy." Perhaps no other American wielded so great an influence over the affairs of the nation as this burly mountebank whose brief congressional career included shady financial dealings and the use of forged documents against his political opponents.[5]

Such were some of the strange circumstances forming the background to the Matusow affair.

3. *Origin of a Species*

One other development—no less bizarre—had a special relevance. A new and remarkable political species had evolved in the era of the postwar witch-hunt.

The paid political informer had undergone a startling mutation. Long classified as a pariah, the informer was now acclaimed as a patriot. The climate of the times, as author Alan Barth put it, "had elevated him to the status of a national hero and transformed his role into that of a profession."

Few professions, in fact, enjoyed comparable influence and prestige. The testimony of informers appearing before congressional committees and at federal trials as "expert witnesses" on Communism made front-page news from coast to coast. Their sensational revelations of Moscow plots, Communist subversion and Kremlin agents in high places were cited by government dignitaries as a major factor in determining foreign policy and domestic laws.

The exploits of FBI informers were celebrated in motion pictures, TV serials, books and magazine articles. Informer-witnesses were feted at testimonial dinners, featured as speakers at town hall meetings, awarded citations for "Americanism." One renowned member of the profession, the ex-Communist Louis Budenz, was appointed professor at Fordham University and presented with the keys to the City of Boston. A special day was set aside by the State of Pennsylvania to honor the former FBI informer Matthew Cvetic. The State of Massachusetts paid similar tribute to ex-informer Herbert Philbrick, and the *New York Herald Tribune* featured him as a regular columnist.

The informer-witness profession became highly lucrative.[6] Special legislation was enacted, unprecedented in the annals of American jurisprudence, whereby informers received regular fees from the government for their services as expert witnesses. Leading members of the profession supplemented their income with generous lecture fees, royalties from best-selling autobiographies, and radio, TV and film rights to their harrowing personal exposés of the Red Menace. Despite such fringe benefits, professional witnesses bargained forcefully for higher government pay. "We have to negotiate with them and shop around," complained Assistant U.S. Attorney General S. A. Andretta, seeking more funds for witnesses, at a closed session of the House Appropriations Committee. "That expert witness business is really killing when you consider the rates these fellows charge today."

Such complaints in government circles, however, were generally muted and made in private. For the most part, government officials publicly echoed the high praise of FBI Director J. Edgar Hoover for the informer-witnesses. "These people deserve the Nation's respect," he declared in an article in *This Week* magazine. "The informant is an institution, an indispensable part of all walks of life."[7]

The institution was one in which Hoover had special personal interest, and nobody had contributed more to its creation. Under his diligent supervision, the FBI's informer network had assumed the proportions of a private army. The country swarmed with its secret legions, spying on countless citizens. FBI informers had become so ubiquitous that quite often their reports to Bureau headquarters dealt unwittingly with the "subversive activities" of fellow undercover operatives. Even so, Hoover constantly called for new recruits from the public. In this field, if none other, he took an unequivocal stand against discrimination. All citizens, he stressed, regardless of color, creed, sex or occupation, were qualified to serve as Bureau spies—if only as amateurs and on a "part-time basis."[8]

Considering the far-reaching impact of the professional witnesses on national affairs, these government employees had rather peculiar qualifications for the services they performed.

My data on government informer-witnesses, though dealing with an inevitably limited cross-section, indicated that a significant percentage of these public servants were ex-convicts, labor spies, petty racketeers, psychotics, and habitual perjurers.

Typical of the notes my files contained were the following:[9]

WILLIAM O. NOWELL—labor spy expelled from United Automobile Workers Union, former confidential adviser to notorious right-wing extremist and anti-Semitic propagandist Gerald L. K. Smith (ex-Silver Shirter No. 3223);

MORRIS MALKIN—obtained citizenship fraudulently, convicted of criminal perjury, served prison term for "particularly brutal, felonious assault";

CECIL SCOTT—served prison term for forgery, temporarily committed to mental institution;

PETER J. INNES—labor spy expelled from National Maritime Union for theft of union funds, sentenced to eight years imprisonment for attempted rape of child;

MATTHEW CVETIC—former labor spy, chronic alcoholic periodically institutionalized for psychiatric care (author of the highly publicized book, *I Was a Communist for the FBI*);

LOWELL WATSON—self-admitted perjurer, whose criminal record included jail sentences for contributing to the delinquency of a minor and for petty larceny;

MANNING JOHNSON—former labor spy testified on the witness stand that he would lie under oath "a thousand times" if instructed to do so by the FBI.

Such was the calibre of the informer-witnesses who had come to play such a vital role in the life of the nation.

Nor was there a more active member of the species than Harvey Matusow.

4. *Pilgrim's Progress*

Expelled from the Communist party in 1951 as an FBI informer, Matusow had promptly moved into the ranks of the government's professional witnesses. Though only twenty-six, he met with immediate success. In his first appearance on the witness stand—it was at a hearing of the House Un-American Activities Committee—he was billed as an "authority on the Communist conspiracy to penetrate the youth of America." Overnight, his name was in the headlines.

It stayed in the headlines as he traveled the professional witness circuit, giving star performances at congressional hearings, deportation proceedings, and federal trials. From the outset, he exhibited a special flair for hyperbole. At one congressional hearing he stated that he knew "by sight probably more than ten thousand Communist party members in New York." (The party doubtless would have been delighted to have had that many members in the city.) On another occasion he declared there were "well over one hundred dues-paying Communists on the staff of the Sunday edition of the *New York Times*." (The total staff of the Sunday *Times* then numbered in the eighties.) "Harvey Matusow," reported columnist Danton Walker in the *New York Daily News*, "claims he was personally responsible for recruiting three thousand New York school children into the Red ranks."

In other times, such claims might have raised certain doubts. Matusow's credibility, however, went unquestioned by the congressional committees employing him as an expert witness, and by the FBI, which vouched for his reliability in Justice Department trials and other federal proceedings. Sensational revelations were, after all, the stock-in-trade among professional witnesses.

If there was any distinguishing feature to Matusow's career as a witness, it lay in the diversity of his extracurricular activities. He made news as a special investigator uncovering "subversive trade unionists" for the Ohio State Un-American Activities Committee. He became associate editor of *Counterattack*, a blacklisting newsletter that specialized in denouncing "Reds" in the entertainment world. In September 1952 he went to work for Senator Joseph McCarthy, campaigning for the senator's reelection in Wisconsin and for McCarthy-endorsed candidates in several other states. Soon after, appearing as a star witness before the McCarthy Committee, he was assigned by the senator to the "monumental task" of compiling "a list of Communists who have infiltrated newspapers, periodicals, radio and television in New York City."

Early in 1953 Matusow startled Washington society by marrying the millionairess, Mrs. Arvilla Bentley, former wife of Representative Alvin Bentley, and a contributor of sizable sums to Senator McCarthy's private fund to "fight Communism." This romantic inter-lude, however, was short-lived. Within a few months, after enlivening the gossip columns with a series of marital brawls, the newlyweds were divorced. They were remarried briefly and then divorced again.

Prior to 1954 the clippings in my Matusow file, though showing him as one of the more colorful and enterprising members of the informer-witness profession, contained little to differentiate him significantly from his colleagues. That summer, however, the press carried several news items that aroused my curiosity.

At a Baltimore conference of the Methodist church, reported the June 7 issue of the *Washington Evening Star*, the well-known libertarian Bishop G. Bromley Oxnam had related that Harvey Matusow had recently visited him and made some startling admissions. According to the bishop, Matusow had stated that he had repeatedly lied as a government witness and that he had come to apologize personally to Oxnam for having denounced him as a "supporter of Communist causes." Matusow explained he had had a religious experience and wanted to undo the harm his lies had caused. He planned similar pilgrimages to other persons he had vilified. (He was, I reflected, going to be a busy traveler.) He was also, he said, contemplating writing a book on his blacklisting activities.

Shortly after the Methodist Church Conference, the House Un-American Activities Committee convened a special session in Washington and summoned Matusow for questioning regarding Bishop Oxnam's statement. Matusow claimed the press accounts of their meeting were inaccurate. "If the bishop was correctly quoted by the newspapers," said Matusow, "then he is a dishonest man. I did not say then and I do not say now that I ever lied under oath."

It seemed to me, however, reasonable to assume that the bishop's honesty was less open to question than Matusow's.

In addition, the Washington attorney Russell Brown—a law associate of former U.S. Attorney General Howard McGrath—now made public the fact that Matusow had visited him, too; and had told him substantially the same story the bishop had recounted.

Obviously, despite his indignant protestation to the House committee, *something* was troubling Matusow. And I began wondering just how troubled he was and how much of the truth he might ultimately be willing to reveal about his career as an FBI informer and professional witness.

Especially provocative was the thought that Matusow had been a key prosecution witness in two federal trials in which the defendants had been found guilty and sentenced to imprisonment.

One was the trial of thirteen alleged Communist leaders, convicted on charges of violating the Smith Act and given prison terms ranging from one to five years, in the so-called Flynn case (one of the defendants was the veteran radical, Elizabeth Gurley Flynn, once the fiery young labor organizer of the early 1900s called the "Joan of Arc of the Working Class").

The sole defendant in the other trial, a close personal friend of mine, was Clinton Jencks. An official of the Mine, Mill and Smelter Workers Union, Clint had been convicted on charges of violating the Taft-Hartley Law and sentenced to five years imprisonment.[10]

What if Matusow now admitted he had testified falsely at both these trials?

Such speculations on my part would probably have remained mere speculations if Jencks, who was free on bail and on a trip raising funds for his case, hadn't paid me a visit early in September.

When I first met Jencks during a protracted strike he was leading in a small mining community in New Mexico, he struck me as one of the most cheerful persons I had ever known. The threat of his trial hadn't changed him. He gave a booming laugh as I opened the front

door, his eyes crinkling in his youthful craggy face, and threw his
arms around me in a bear hug. "Goddamn, you're a sight for sore
eyes!" he said. "Where's Riette and those three young hellers?"

I told him Riette had taken the boys to the dentist. "Mass production—they'll be home in a couple of hours."

"Hell, I'll miss them," he said. "I'm due back in New York for a
four o'clock meeting. This trip's been wild."

Over lunch on the patio, I asked Clint how things looked on the
appeal in his case. He shrugged. "The cards are stacked, but that's to
be expected." He munched on his sandwich, looking around the garden. "How much do you know about the details of the case?" he
asked.

"Just what I've read in the papers. They didn't carry much here."

"Well, the thing really started with the strike. The company
charged it was staged by Communists to sabotage war production for
Korea. I got indicted right after that on the Taft-Hartley charge. The
actual frame-up was pretty crude, even by government standards."

"In what way?"

"Hell, there was only one witness who claimed to have first-hand
knowledge I'd been a party member when I signed the Taft-Hartley
non-Communist affidavit. It was that creep Matusow! It was obvious
the bastard was lying. And anyway it was just his word against
mine."

"Did you actually know him?"

"I met him a few years ago when Virginia and the kids and I were
vacationing at the San Cristobal ranch. He was still an FBI informer
in those days. Of course I didn't know that then, but I did think him
nuts. He had a little station wagon full of Marxist literature out there
in the goddamn desert. He testified at the trial I told him I was a
Communist and planned to sabotage war production. Christ, can you
imagine anyone crazy enough to say something like that?"

"Well, it looks like his conscience is bothering him now," I said.

"You mean because of what he told Bishop Oxnam?" he asked
pointedly.

I nodded, realizing then that it was Matusow he had come to talk
about.

He leaned back in his chair, his thick fingers clasped in his tousled
ash-blond hair. "Look, Albert," he said, "you've broken stories like

this before. What would be the chance of your getting Matusow to give an affidavit saying he lied against me?"

"About one in a hundred."

"He told Oxnam he lied against people, didn't he?"

"Sure. But telling Oxnam is one thing. A formal admission of perjury is another. He could go to jail for that. I doubt his conscience is bothering him that much. Look at his latest testimony before the Un-American Activities Committee."

"Even if there's only one chance in a hundred, it's worth trying, isn't it?"

"I can't see him risking jail, Clint, just to set things straight in your case. From what I've read about him, he loves the limelight so much that if he ever were to incriminate himself, he'd want to do it on a grand scale." I tamped some tobacco into my pipe and lit it. "He told Oxnam he's planning a book on blacklisting. Maybe he'd consider another book if he thought it would make a big enough sensation. A book in which he told everything he'd done. You might conceivably get an affidavit that way."

"Then how about getting him to write it?" urged Clint. "Cameron & Kahn could publish it."

"The firm's practically broke," I told him. "We've been operating on what Angus calls a frayed shoestring with several knots in it. Angus is trying to reorganize things, and I'm going back to full-time writing." I didn't sound too convincing, even to myself. "A project like you're proposing would be a major job."

Clint grinned. "Here's an idea. Why don't you give Nat Witt a ring and tell him you'll drop by? He's the Mine-Mill counsel, you know, and he's handling my case. Maybe the union can order enough copies of the book in advance so you can swing the thing financially. I'll bet they'll be interested."

"They should be damn interested, but that doesn't mean they'll put up any money on such a long shot. But all right, I'll see Witt," I told Clint with a laugh, knowing he had sensed I had been sold on going after the Matusow story from the moment we started talking about it.

I phoned Angus afterward and told him about my talk with Jencks. I asked him how he would feel about our publishing a full confession by Matusow.

"That's a sort of superfluous question, isn't it?" he said. "You don't need me to tell you what a book like that would do. You know that if Matusow ever told his story . . . hell, it could really be a body blow to these bastards running their witch hunt." He paused. "But it would have to really be his whole story, you know."

"I don't understand."

"I mean there couldn't be anything half-assed about it. He'd have to tell the whole truth—everything."

"That's what I have in mind."

"I realize that. But it's a question what *he* will have in mind. Assuming he could ever be gotten to write it."

Next day I saw Nat Witt at his office in New York.

The well-known labor lawyer, who formerly had been a member of the National Labor Relations Board in the Roosevelt Administration, said he'd been closely following the recent press reports about Matusow.

"Not just because of the Jencks case, mind you," Witt told me. "Nobody's done the Mine-Mill union more harm than that character. When he testified at the Senate Internal Security Subcommittee hearings in El Paso, he splashed all over the front pages the yarn that the union is run by Reds who are out to cripple defense production. The union would certainly be interested in a book telling who cooked up that one."

"Would they be interested enough," I asked, "to place an advance order for the book? Angus and I couldn't possibly tackle it otherwise."

Witt said he'd have to check with Mine-Mill headquarters in Denver.

Later that week Witt telephoned me. "They're willing to speculate on an initial order for two thousand copies," he said. "They'll probably increase the order if the book materializes."

The firm of Cameron & Kahn had its first order for a book by Matusow.

Now all we had to do was get the book.

5. *Search for a Witness*

Before attempting any direct negotiation with Matusow, I decided to learn more about him. First I obtained the published transcripts of congressional hearings at which he had appeared as a witness.

Though familiar enough with the widely publicized tales of the government's professional witnesses in recent years, I had never before read any witness' entire testimony at a series of hearings. To do so was a strangely disquieting experience. It was like entering another world, a world of grotesque fantasy, a world without reality. As I read through hundreds of pages of Matusow's testimony, containing one wanton allegation after another, I was constantly reminded that not only had such lies and lunacies been foisted on the public as news of national import but that they had also served as the grounds on which countless citizens had been stigmatized, persecuted, ruined. If the Congress had deliberately sought to compile for future historians a sweeping indictment of its inquisitorial practices in the postwar years, it could not have done so more effectively than through the records of these hearings.

I did learn certain miscellaneous facts about him. He had grown up in the Bronx, served in the army from 1944 to 1946, and briefly reenlisted during the Korean War. He had worked as an obscure professional entertainer in radio and television. He joined the Communist party in 1947, became an FBI informer in 1950 and was expelled by the Communists a year later. But such biographical data contributed little to my perception of Matusow as a person. After I'd spent several days wading through his testimony, he remained a shadowy automaton who, when asked a question, answered mechanically with a lie.

From Bishop Oxnam, however, I obtained some material which showed Matusow in a much more vivid light: notes which Oxnam had dictated after his meeting with Matusow.

The bishop's notes read in part:

> I do not know how to estimate this man. He may be a genius; he may be a charlatan. He is at least in part what he says he is. He may be a poet of unusual ability; he may be a panhandler. . . .

I said, "And why do you want to see me?" He replied that he had
had a religious experience of a considerable sort and was a completely changed man. He said, "I have lied again and again in my
statements to these committees and in my reports, and I want to go
to each individual about whom I have falsified to ask his forgive-
ness. . . .

I asked him why he had done such things, and he said he hardly
knew, but that one fabrication led to another and there was a thrill
in being involved in such revelations.

Matusow, the bishop went on to say, had told him he was planning
to publish not only a book about his blacklisting activities but also a
volume of poetry. As a sample of his work as a professional entertainer, Matusow had acted out some "skits with . . . pipe cleaners":

He then gave me a copy of most of his poems . . . I must say the
first one was a striking creation of mood, and, I think, of considerable value. . . .

He was in the Second World War, so he states—in the infantry.
His only brother, in the air corps, was shot down and killed . . . he,
himself, discovered his brother's grave. . . . He had a picture also of
his kneeling over the grave.

Bishop Oxnam summed up his impressions of Matusow with this
comment:

What does it all add up to? I don't know. . . . Maybe this man is
all he says he is. Maybe he's a psychiatric case. . . .

I really can't fathom the fellow, but whatever the facts are, here
is an individual whose testimony has been published by the House
Un-American Activities Committee. . . .

After reading the bishop's notes, I felt convinced of at least one
thing—the problems of dealing with Matusow would be even more
complex than I had expected.

That conclusion was confirmed when I read a letter which former
U.S. Attorney General J. Howard McGrath had sent to Bishop
Oxnam's lawyer. McGrath's letter stated:

I thought you might be interested to know that Matusow was
interviewed late in April of this year by Russell Brown and Robert

Norvell of my office; Matusow told them substantially the same thing as he apparently told the Bishop. I don't mean to say that the bishop was mentioned, but Matusow did indicate that he had lied about many people concerning their connection with Communism. . . .

In . . . a memorandum dictated after the interview, Brown states: "He [meaning Matusow] said in so many words, 'You should know that I am not to be trusted under any circumstances. I have betrayed everybody who ever befriended me. If I give you some information which is helpful, you check it one hundred percent because I don't even trust myself.'"

Early in October I began trying to locate Matusow. It proved a good deal more difficult than I had anticipated.

When he had appeared before the House Un-American Activities Committee in July—to challenge Bishop Oxnam's account of their recent meeting—Matusow stated he was living in Dallas. He had, however, given no street address. On checking with Dallas telephone information, I was told his name was not listed in the directory and he had no unlisted number. One of my press clippings on his Oxnam testimony mentioned he was employed at a Melba Theatre in Dallas. I called the theatre and learned he had recently quit his job. They suggested trying the White Plaza Hotel. I phoned the hotel. The hotel operator informed me Matusow had moved a couple of weeks before —she gave me his new number. I called the number. Matusow, I was told, had already moved again—the previous day. This time he had left no forwarding address.

Trying a long shot, I placed a person-to-person call to Matusow at the staff offices of the House Un-American Activities Committee in Washington. I told the operator to say the call was urgent. To my surprise, a woman's voice offered to give me his current number—at the White Plaza Hotel.

I called the city editor of the *Dallas Times-Herald*. I said I was having difficulty locating Harvey Matusow and asked if he had any idea where I could reach him. I mentioned the places in Dallas I had tried so far.

"Curious you should call today," he said. "We ran a story on him this morning."

"In what connection?"

"He released a statement to Attorney General Brownell. Says he won't testify anymore as a government witness."

"Did he give a reason?" I asked.

"Says he's protesting Corporal Batchelor's sentence. You know, the guy that just got life imprisonment for his peace propaganda as a Korean POW."

"Was there any address with Matusow's release?"

"No, just called it in on the phone—yesterday. We've been trying ourselves to get hold of him today for an interview. He's not where he was staying. Gone bag and baggage. Looks like he left town in the last twenty-four hours."

I cursed my luck, thanked the editor for his help, and said I would appreciate his sending me a clipping of the Matusow story.

"No sweat," he said. He added: "Incidentally, you're not the only one looking for him. We had a couple of visitors today. Thought you might like to know."

Since he didn't volunteer the information, I didn't ask who the visitors were.

My transcripts of Matusow's testimony at public hearings indicated that during the last two years he'd lived in four other cities—New York, Dayton, Santa Fe and Washington. (He never gave a street address—he said that if he did his life would be endangered by Communists.) I checked with newspapers in each city for possible leads as to his present whereabouts. No luck.

Two days later the *Dallas Times-Herald* clipping arrived in he mail. Headlined "Dallas Ex-Red Protests Term Given Batchelor," it read in part:

> A protest against the Army court-martial life sentence given Cpl. Claude Batchelor, returned Korean war prisoner, was sent to Att. Gen. Herbert Brownell Thursday by Harvey M. Matusow of Dallas.
>
> Mr. Matusow, who joined the communist movement when he was 18, broke with the party and has since testified at many government investigations, said he would not appear at six hearings where he was scheduled to be a witness.
>
> "The reason for this is my conscience will not let me be a party to any future Claude Batchelor cases," he wrote.

My response was mixed. While Matusow's latest action heightened my eagerness to talk with him, it also increased my concern over the problem of reaching him. Even before the Dallas city editor had mentioned the recent visitors to his newspaper I suspected that the FBI, like me, might also be wanting to chat with Matusow. If so, their motive doubtless differed from mine. The Justice Department had cause to be uneasy about the indiscreet talking Matusow had been doing lately—his present defection would naturally have made them more so. Whereas I wanted to keep him talking, they had ample reason for wanting to keep him quiet.

The problem was how to get to Matusow before they did. He seemed to have dropped completely out of sight.

Possibly, I decided, the most effective way to contact Matusow was to arrange for him to contact me. I knew from testimony of Matusow's that his parents still lived in the Bronx. I had not wanted to involve his parents, but I felt I now had no choice. Their number was listed in the telephone book, and I called them.

Mrs. Matusow answered the phone.

I introduced myself and said I had been trying to reach her son for over a week. "I'm very sorry to bother you," I told her, "but I'm a publisher and I'm interested in a book I hear he wants to write. I was wondering if you could possibly have him call me."

"I'm afraid I don't have any way of reaching him myself, Mr. Kahn. He's traveling now." Her voice had a gentle, singsong cadence. "But he does call me sometimes, and I'll be glad to give him your message."

I thanked her.

Ten days went by without any word from Matusow.

I was wondering what my next move would be when, on October 23, Matusow phoned from Taos and agreed to come east.

Twenty-four hours after he called, FBI agents arrived in Taos looking for Matusow.

They arrived too late.

Matusow was already on a plane headed for New York.

CHAPTER TWO

ENTER MATUSOW

1. *Strange Conference*

There was a distinct incongruity to the meeting which took place in New York City on October 25, 1954, between Harvey Matusow, Angus Cameron and me.

Three years before, when Angus was still Editor-in-Chief and vice-president of Little, Brown & Company, Matusow had gone to work for the blacklisting newsletter, *Counterattack*.[11] Soon after, the newsletter published a lengthy article denouncing Cameron as "one of the most sinister influences in U.S. book publishing circles." Under his dark aegis, the article charged, the venerable Boston firm with which he was associated had been converted into a "Communist-front" publishing house. As proof, the article cited Cameron's having contrived the publication of works by such writers as Lillian Hellman, James Aldridge, Owen Lattimore, Albert Maltz, and myself. The *Counterattack* charges, published in a syndicated column in the Scripps-Howard press, caused widespread comment in the book business —and consternation at Little, Brown. Commenting on these developments, *Time* magazine characterized Cameron as "the leading book editor in the country."

Other considerations, however, prevailed among Angus's colleagues on Little, Brown's board of directors. Panicked by *Counterattack*'s smear and intimidated by the growing climate of repression, these men who had heretofore stood up well against the attacks on their editor and their books, made such conditions that no free editor could conform to them. Angus was obliged to resign.[12]

Matusow's and my path had crossed, even if at a distance, on previous occasions. At various congressional hearings he had credited me with being a wellspring of "Moscow-inspired propaganda" (including in that category my book, *Sabotage!*, a bestseller during World War II, which was reprinted by that less than revolutionary magazine, *Reader's Digest*). And as recently as June 1954 he had testified under oath before the Subversive Activities Control Board that he and I had "worked closely together . . . on many, many occasions" as fellow conspirators in the Communist party.

And now here Angus and I were about to sit down with Matusow to discuss the possibility of our becoming his publishers.

It promised to be an interesting encounter.

Matusow had telephoned me on his arrival at LaGuardia Airport, and I had suggested he meet Angus and me for lunch the following day at the Delmonico Hotel at 54th and Park Avenue.

As I entered the hotel lobby to keep the appointment, an authoritative voice informed me, "You're Albert Kahn."

I admitted I was.

I wouldn't have recognized Matusow if he hadn't spoken first. In his news photos and the few times I'd seen him on TV, Matusow had been a dapper, well-groomed young man with close-cropped black hair and a bow tie. Now, despite his recent bicycle trip, he was grossly overweight; his stocky figure bulged out of his clothes. His skin was sallow and his eyes were ringed with dark circles. He wore a tweed jacket, black turtleneck sweater, jeans, and cream-colored buckskin moccasins. Under one arm he carried a bulky briefcase. I felt an immediate aversion to him.

Since Angus had called at the last minute to say he would be late, I suggested to Matusow that we start lunch.

"Suits me," he said. "I'm starved. The food's good here." His manner was both aggressive and ingratiating.

We went into the quiet, luxurious dining room, where the head-waiter—warily eyeing Matusow's attire—led us to the table I had reserved. As soon as we had ordered, Matusow leaned forward with his elbows spread on the table and said, "Let's talk about my book."

"Why not wait for Angus?" I suggested. "Otherwise, we'll only be going over the same ground."

He nodded. "Agreed." He picked up his briefcase, extracted a looseleaf notebook and thrust it before me, pushing aside my plate in the process. "Take a look at these. They're some of my poems."

I had the feeling that this had happened before, and then remembered that it had—in Bishop Oxnam's memorandum describing his meeting with Matusow.

The notebook contained about a hundred typed poems. Though hardly in the mood for verse, I read the first few. To my surprise, though somewhat trite and sentimental in content they showed an inventive use of language and an unusual sense of imagery. As I read I was uncomfortably conscious of Matusow's eyes pinned on me. Once as I was about to turn a page, he stopped me, pointed to a line and demanded, "Did you notice this metaphor?"

I sensed his dissatisfaction when I said simply yes.

Before long he asked impatiently, "Well, what do you think of them?"

"I'd have to read them more carefully before—"

He interrupted me. "But what's your initial reaction?"

"I'd say parts are good."

His dark eyes glowed with pleasure. "You once had some poetry published yourself, didn't you?"

"A long time ago." I wondered where he'd picked up this piece of trivia.

"Anyway, I want your full criticism," he said. "From a purely literary viewpoint, that is. Leave out politics. Are they or aren't they poetry? As a professional writer, do you think they're publishable? I know you can't concentrate on them properly here. You need to read them in private. Take them home with you. Then give me your opinion." It was more an order than a request. He added with a certain condescension: "You know, I've read some of your books. *The Great Conspiracy* had a real influence on me."

I couldn't resist observing, "That's a rather dubious compliment."

His teeth flashed in a mechanical grin.

As the meal progressed, my aversion to him grew. He radiated arrogance and conceit. He was as brash as he was glib, as opinionated as he was boastful. Above all, he was inordinately garrulous. Words poured from him in a torrent, buffeting and engulfing me. When I tried to interject some remark in sheer self-defense, he invariably broke in before I could complete it. Only one subject interested him: himself.

He took another notebook from his briefcase. "This is my prospectus as a nightclub entertainer," he told me briskly. "When you apply for jobs, you want to give a quick, graphic presentation of your talents. The market is glutted with entertainers. Most of them third-rate amateurs. They just don't know show business. They lack imagination. Their acts are usually cheap imitations of some really gifted star, like Zero Mostel—before he was blacklisted, of course." (I wondered what part Matusow had played in Mostel's blacklisting.) "My prospectus highlights the originality of my acts. I designed the whole thing myself. Made the drawings, too."

He handed me the notebook, a conglomeration of materials concerning his "unique, delightful and versatile artistry"; photographs of him working with puppets and marionettes; and press notices about his performances. Each page was bordered with hand-drawn figures of rabbits, dogs, monkeys, and other animals. It was pathetically pretentious and tawdry. It embarrassed me.

Centered on one page was a newspaper column describing a technique Matusow had devised for making miniature animals out of pipe cleaners—he was, it declared, "the pioneer and sole practitioner" of the craft. As I finished reading the column, Matusow ordered, "Wait a minute!"

He suddenly reached into a pocket, brought out a fistful of pipe cleaners and started twisting several of them together with startling swiftness. As he did so, he kept up a running patter, interspersed with grimacing smiles: "There was once a French poodle named Pierre Duma. His father was André Duma and his mother Madeleine Du-*mama*. He was a true patriot—his blood was red, white and blue. He joined the underground when the German police dogs occupied France. He operated out of the Paris metro. He performed dangerous missions like smuggling anti-fascist poodles over the Pyrénées. Once he disguised himself as a German schnauzer, penetrated Nazi headquarters and stole secret documents, which he smuggled to the Free French by flea couriers. At the war's end, General de Gaulle himself decorated Pierre Duma for his heroism. The general licked him on both cheeks, shook his four paws, and bestowed on him the Croix de Grrrr."

Matusow never once looked at the pipe cleaners he was deftly manipulating during the recitation. His eyes remained focused on me, eagerly watching my reactions. With a flourish as he finished his tale, he set before me on the table a precisely formed little poodle.

"That's really ingenious," I said. "It must take a lot of practice."

He grinned delightedly and, without pausing, proceeded to model more animals, reciting anecdotes for each member of his growing menagerie. Soon, neatly arrayed on the tablecloth alongside the poodle, were the tiny figures of a monkey, bear, kangaroo, and jack rabbit. The last two he shaped with his hands behind his back.

I had to reposition the animals when my salad was served. "Keep them," Matusow said, "They're yours." I thanked him and pocketed the collection.

"My favorite hobby," he informed me, gulping his food, "is entertaining children."

He picked up his prospectus and, leafing through it, pointed to photos of himself performing with puppets before clusters of wide-eyed youngsters. "We get along famously," he said. "We understand each other. It's something intuitive."

For lack of anything better to say, I remarked, "You must use a lot of pipe cleaners."

"About ten or twelve thousand a year," he briskly replied. "I get them wholesale, of course."

"Is your repertoire mainly puppets and pipe cleaners?" I asked with a feeling of inanity.

"Name an international celebrity," he said.

"Why?"

"Go ahead. Just name one. Any one."

"Winston Churchill," I said somewhat apprehensively.

Matusow sank back in his chair, his chin resting heavily on his chest, and scowled up at me. In a voice startlingly like Churchill's, he declaimed sonorously, "My fellow countrymen, comrades in arms and gastronomy, we gather in this garrison of the Delmonico to make, if need be, a final stand against the assault of fish and fowl and mammal foe. We shall not flag or fail, no matter by what devilish device they test our powers of digestion. We shall endure undaunted through soup and salad and dessert, meeting with stout hearts each morsel that may come our way. In distant years a newborn breed of gluttons and gourmets will say, 'This was their finest hour!' "

He obviously relished my laughter, though his high-pitched chuckle seemed chiefly in delight at his performance.

"Generally," he told me with a brisk professional air, "I prefer to impersonate characters I create myself. It's more of an artistic challenge. You didn't get to that part of my prospectus." He opened it to a page headed, "The Man with a Thousand Voices," and pointed to a lengthy list of folksy names. "They're just a few of the characters I've created. I act out all of them—men, women, children. Different backgrounds, different personalities, different nationalities. Nothing racist, of course. And they've all got one thing in common. They're all cheerful eccentrics," he grinned, "like me."

I anticipated what was about to happen but saw no way of preventing it. As the rest of the meal was served, Matusow promptly launched into a series of impersonations, interpreting in swift succession the roles of a drunken minister, a backwoods judge, a wealthy German widow, and an Italian explorer.

He took a sip of water. I was hoping he'd finished, but he added, "I vocalize the sound effects, too." He proceeded to imitate the sounds of a train, a boat whistle, a baby crying, a chain saw, and tropical birds in a zoo.

Our table had become the center of attention in the dining room, and I sensed a spreading doubt among the diners about Matusow's (and my) sanity. I was beginning to entertain certain doubts on this score myself and to wonder if I hadn't embarked on a wild goose chase. It was with decided relief that I finally saw Angus's portly figure approaching. There was a homespun quality about Angus's appearance which always gave me a warm and pleasurable feeling, but I'd never found the sight of him more gratifying. The effusiveness with which I greeted him, however, went unreturned. His plump, usually affable face was set in a dour mask. He muttered some monosyllabic excuse for his tardiness, acknowledged my introduction to Matusow with a curt nod, and startled a nearby waiter with his belligerence in demanding a menu.

I didn't need to be told what was troubling Angus. Despite his encyclopedic knowledge and the diversity of his experience, he had never socialized before with an informer. And though Angus took a quiet satisfaction in his catholic tastes, he considered certain circumstances an innate affront to his dignity.

Matusow waited with ill-concealed impatience while Angus scrutinized the menu and interrogated the waiter about the composition of the ragout. The moment Angus had ordered, Matusow reached into his briefcase. "Here, take a look at this," he said. "It's the outline of my book." He handed each of us a copy of the outline. It was headed, *"Blacklisting Was My Business* by Harvey M. Matusow." Two pages in length, it summarized thirty chapters dealing with his career as an FBI informer, professional blacklister, and aide to Senator Joseph McCarthy. Some of the chapter titles were: "Sidewalks of New York," "Reds in Khaki," "Dude Ranch for Comrades," "I'm Here to Talk for Joe," "Newspapers are Red," and "Blacklists for Dollars."

Matusow rummaged in his briefcase again. "I've got a couple of sample chapters with me," he declared.

"We'll read them after lunch," said Angus brusquely, focusing his attention on buttering a French roll.

"Exactly—after lunch," said Matusow, as if that had been his own intention. He glanced at his watch. "You'll have to excuse me. I've got to make a phone call." He stood up and said with a sly wink. "Don't worry. It's kosher. I'm not reporting to the FBI these days." He sauntered from the table.

Angus grimly watched him go. "Jesus!" he muttered, shaking his head. After a pause, he added, "Well, what do you think?"

"I think you'd better start looking at him when you talk to him."

"God, is it as obvious as that?"

"It is to me, and whatever he is, he's no fool."

"Well, there is something shabby about it all," grumbled Angus.

"In what way?"

"You know as well as I do. Yesterday this guy was sending people to jail. Today he's peddling his confession."

"How come you didn't object before to the idea of publishing his book?" I asked.

He smiled knowingly. "You'd have gone after it anyway, wouldn't you?" he said. "You know how you are when you're set on doing something, Albert. Opposition just makes you all the more obdurate. It's like waving a red flag at a bull."

"Yes, I'd have gone ahead," I acknowledged. "But that isn't why you didn't object, is it? You were as keen as I was about getting his story."

Angus lit a cigarette and shook out the match with a preoccupied air. "Maybe it's a conditioned reflex to seeing him in the flesh."

I thought it best not to mention my own present doubts about Matusow. Leaning forward I said in a lowered voice, "Aren't you forgetting something, Angus?"

He raised his eyebrows. "Forgetting what?"

"The Christian ethic," I said deadpan. "It's the Old Testament that advocates an eye for an eye. Christ teaches you Gentiles to welcome the sinner that repenteth."

Angus snorted with exasperation. "Christ never met Matusow," he said.

"Seriously though, go easy on him. I'll tell you something, Angus. I wasn't ever sure I'd get hold of him—even though I said I was. I don't want to lose him now."

"I'll tell *you* something," said Angus. "I was sure he'd never come." His eyes twinkled. "But there wouldn't have been any purpose in my telling you that either, would there?"

When Matusow returned to the table, Angus stared resolutely at him each time he spoke to him. Before the end of the meal, he showed signs of relaxing and even laughed at several of Matusow's jokes. Angus's embracing curiosity was overcoming his indignation.

After lunch, in the welcome privacy of a small pleasantly furnished conference room in the hotel, Matusow produced the completed portion of his manuscript.

"I've done two chapters so far," he told us. "They aren't in sequence. I just knocked out what I felt like doing when the book first occurred to me. They may need a little brushing up, but they'll give you an idea of how I conceptualize the book. I've a short preface which gives some indication of that, too." He handed the pages to Angus and sprawled back in a leather chair, his hands clasped behind his head, his posture accentuating the bulge of his belly. He seemed drowsy, as he watched us under half-lowered eyelids.

Angus finished the first page of the preface and handed it to me.

As he did, I noticed some printing on the back of the typed page. The sheet was a letterhead. I read with astonishment: "Committee for the J. Edgar Hoover Foundation."

"You missed something, Angus," I said. I showed him the printed letterhead. Angus stared at it incredulously. He flipped through the sheets of Matusow's manuscript. They were all typed on the blank side of the same stationery.

"Where on earth did you get this paper?" Angus asked.

Matusow's sleepy look had vanished. He was grinning broadly. "I thought it the right paper for the confession of an FBI informer," he said.

"But where did you get it?" Angus repeated.

"I got it where I typed those pages," said Matusow. "In Drew Pearson's office—on Jack Anderson's typewriter." He paused for the information to have the desired effect on us. "Do you know them?" he asked.

I said I had known Pearson when I was editor of *The Hour*—he had helped publicize the newsletter and carried some of its anti-Nazi exposés.

"Drew and Jack are real people," Matusow went on. "I trust them implicitly. When I was working with McCarthy, I gave them a lot of stuff on Joe. They were the first ones I told when I got the idea of doing this book. I started typing it in their office. They were using this stationery as scrap paper. The irony of beginning my book on it appealed to me." He chuckled, shaking his head in amusement. "You should have seen your faces!"

"What was the J. Edgar Hoover Foundation?" I asked. "I never heard of it."

"I really don't know," he said. "Probably some sort of charitable outfit. Maybe a sanitarium for infirm informers." He laughed heartily.

This interlude concluded, Angus and I proceeded with our reading of Matusow's manuscript. The gist of the brief preface was that Matusow deeply regretted his "past of hate" and had found "a new purpose in life." His book, he wrote, was to be "a reflection of my past projecting itself, if possible, into a constructive future." That theme, I reflected, could lead anywhere. My misgivings as to where it actually did lead increased as I read the first chapter. Entitled "Sidewalks of New York," it was a prolix, disjointed account of Matusow's youth, his role as an FBI informer in the Communist party, and his first

appearance as a witness before the House Un-American Activities
Committee. The chapter was glibly evasive. It concealed much more
than it revealed: there were no significant disclosures concerning Matusow's work for the FBI and not a single reference to any lies he'd
told on the witness stand.

The other chapter, entitled "I'm Here to Talk for Joe," came as a
distinct surprise. Both in style and content it might have come from
another book. Swift and colloquial, it graphically described Matusow's first meeting with Senator McCarthy during the 1952 presiden-
tial election campaign and his role as a campaign speaker for the
senator in the Wisconsin primaries. The chapter was spiced with intimate anecdotes about McCarthy, who emerged as a boisterous mountebank devising his anti-Communist tactics in an undershirt in hotel
rooms cluttered with whiskey bottles. Matusow's self-portrait was
equally vivid. He came across as a sleek, young rabble-rouser basking
in the limelight of the campaign trail and savoring his camaraderie
with McCarthy as "hitting the jackpot." The chapter had an authentic
ring.

As I put down the last page, Matusow leaned forward tautly in his
chair. "Well, gentlemen, what's the verdict?" he demanded.

Angus lit another cigarette and, for the first time, offered the pack
to Matusow.

Matusow shook his head. "It's against my principles," he said.

Angus regarded him quizzically, but Matusow didn't smile.

Almost defensively he began, "The Church of the Latter-Day
Saints. . . ." He paused. "Mormons abstain from smoking."

So *that's* what he meant, I thought, when he told Bishop Oxnam
that he'd had a religious experience.

Angus looked down casually—a little too casually—at the manuscript and riffled its pages. "Tell me," he said, "how long ago did you
write this?"

Matusow thought for a moment. "About a year and a half ago. Last
summer."

"That long ago?" asked Angus in surprise.

Matusow nodded. "It was in August around the time of my divorce. From Arvilla Bentley."

"Arvilla Bentley?"

Matusow looked pleased at the chance to identify her. "The former wife of Congressman Alvin Bentley. She's a millionairess—known in Washington as the "Hostess of Fox Hill." She's a close friend of Joe McCarthy. That's how I got to know her. He asked me to smuggle her out of the country to avoid her getting a subpoena from the Hennings Committee, which was investigating McCarthy's finances at the time. She'd given him more than $75,000. Part was for what he called his fund to fight Communism. Actually Joe invested most of it in the market—in soybeans. He made a nice profit too." Matusow smiled at the recollection. "Anyway, I arranged to get Billie—that was Arvilla's nickname—out of the country incognito. I took her to the Bahamas. Nassau. We stayed at the Bahamas Country Club until the Hennings thing blew over. McCarthy asked me to do him that favor on November 27, 1952. I remember the exact date because it was Thanksgiving Day. We got married the next March. Billie and me, that is—I didn't marry McCarthy."

"That story should make an interesting episode in the book," I said.

He hesitated a minute. "I don't mind telling about the incident in the book. But I don't want to drag in personal details about my marriage to Billie. Maybe it would make the book more sensational, but I don't want to commercialize on my marriage to her. That's a private affair."

"You were saying you began the book at the time of your divorce," I said. "But you continued as a witness for the congressional committees and the Justice Department?"

"I was all mixed up at the time. I even wrote McCarthy and told him I wanted to get out of the witness racket and out of politics altogether. I was going through a whole reevaluation of myself. I'd started writing a lot of poetry and introspective notes. I guess you could say I was trying to find my identity. I thought a book might help undo the harm I'd done. That it might be sort of a catharsis too, you know. I decided to put something on paper to show to a publisher."

"And a year went by before you finally made the break with the government?" I said.

Matusow's voice took on a note of impatience. "It wasn't a simple process."

"Let's get back to the manuscript," Angus said, putting out his cigarette. He frowned thoughtfully, squeezing his lower lip between his thumb and forefinger. "In that opening chapter you really only skim the surface, don't you? I mean, when you mention your parents and those early years in the Bronx, you—"

"Look," Matusow broke in, "I'm not writing my life story. Like I said, I want the book to do some good. Period."

"That's not my point," Angus said. He got up, walked over to the window, and stood there jingling the coins in his pocket—a habit he had when he was concentrating. "I understand your reason for writing the book. But my point is that if the reader is going to accept that reason, if he's going to believe you're sincere, he needs to know you as a person. He has to know you well enough to believe what you say in the book. I don't mean you've got to go into elaborate detail about your youth. But I do mean you have to tell enough about yourself for the reader to understand why you became an informer in the first place and what made you change. It's not enough merely to reveal what you've done—you have to reveal yourself. You have to reveal the interaction between the outside world and your inner self. You're dealing with—"

"It was fashionable to be an informer and a witness against Communists when I became one. Louis Budenz, Elizabeth Bentley, Whittaker Chambers—they were national celebrities. I just joined the hit parade. Everyone was dancing to McCarthy's tune."

"I didn't finish what I was saying," Angus told him. "The acceptance of informers and paid witnesses is part of the national climate, right? That climate didn't start with McCarthy. It started with the Cold War. The loyalty oaths, the spy scares, the trial of the Hollywood Ten—all that was going on before most Americans ever heard of McCarthy. He's just the thuggish clown who became the apotheosis of the anti-Communist crusade and gave it a name. And he's superfluous to—"

"I don't see my book as a history book," said Matusow. He added with a grin, "I may have been a turncoat but I'm not a Toynbee."

Angus ignored the remark. "McCarthy's superfluous to the maintenance of the present climate. And don't think for a moment that the Army-McCarthy hearings have put a dent in that climate either, whatever they've done to McCarthy's standing. Most Americans are so brainwashed by now that they believe every Communist is a Moscow agent—and that probably most nonconformists are too. They think that everything you've said in the past about Communists or fellow travelers, or whatever, is gospel truth. So how are you going to persuade your readers to believe that what you said before was false and what you're saying now is true? They can't do that unless they see you as a living person. Not only that. They'll have to be able to identify with you in some way—I mean, with your motives and emotions. You've got to make them feel what you yourself felt when you informed on people who'd been your friends or got up on the witness stand and pilloried them." He peered intently over his glasses at Matusow. "It's not enough for you to reveal what you've done—you have to reveal *yourself*. What I'm talking about isn't a question of politics or history. It's a question of your writing a dimensional book in which you emerge as a flesh-and-blood human being. If your book is going to come alive, you yourself have to come alive in it. That's what I'm driving at. That's why you have to explore yourself in the book." He blew his nose heavily.

"You don't think there's any self-exploration?" Matusow asked. "That didn't come across in what I've written?" He looked crestfallen.

"I didn't say that. Some of it does. The part where you describe your relationship with McCarthy, for instance. You really bring him to life. You show your own feelings there, too. That has a genuine quality. That's good writing."

"So you *do* think I can write?"

"Yes, I think you can write."

Matusow beamed and slapped his thighs exuberantly. "That's all I need to know!"

"It's one thing to be able to write," said Angus, "and another thing to—"

"Don't worry. You underestimate me. You'll see how I handle the thing."

While I shared Angus's view that Matusow needed to reveal more about himself, I was still mainly concerned with how much he intended to reveal about his government operations. His outline, I had noticed, contained no mention of his role in the case of Clint Jencks or his testimony at the Flynn trial. "Your outline deals mainly with your blacklisting activities. Of course that fits in with your title, *Blacklisting Was My Business*. But there's comparatively little in it about your work with the government. I'm not saying the blacklisting stuff isn't important. It obviously is. But don't you think you have things to reveal about your work with the government that are even more important? And certainly more sensational."

"The government's in the blacklisting business too," Matusow asserted. "Every branch of the government. Their lists don't just include hundreds of names—they include thousands, tens of thousands." He added with a note of pride, "I know. I helped compile some of them."

"But I'm referring to some of your appearances as a witness for various congressional committees and the Justice Department." I didn't want to be too specific about the omissions in his outline.

"I drafted that outline months ago," Matusow protested. "Of course, it's not definitive. It's more a sketch than an outline. I plan to revamp the whole thing."

"What about documentation?" I asked. "In a book like this that's vital, you know."

"I can document everything," he said. "Wait till you see the documents I've got. I'm a walking Smithsonian Institute."

There was a more crucial matter that had to be considered. "One thing you've got to realize," I said. "If you write this book—that is, if you write a book that tells everything you've done—you're going to face certain risks."

"You mean perjury?" he asked.

"Yes."

"I never committed perjury." He spoke firmly, as if he actually believed what he was saying.

I felt this wasn't the time to argue the point, but I didn't want to drop it that casually. "Sometimes it's hard to remember everything you've said. When you read over your testimony, you may find—"

"I'm ready to take that chance," he interrupted with a trace of irritation. "I've made up my mind that the only way I can make up for what I've done is by telling the truth now."

He added emphatically, "I want to live with myself."

It was a phrase that had appeared in his preface.

The conversation turned to the question of a contract on the book. We asked Matusow how much of an advance he would need against royalties.

He began to enumerate, in copious detail, expenses he'd have to meet. His files and personal belongings, he said, were scattered around the country and would have to be brought to New York. Once they arrived, there would be secretarial expenses in sorting and cataloguing his research materials. And he had some pressing debts. "I'm going to need to rent a place," he continued, "where I can live while I'm writing the book. I'm staying a few days with my folks, but I'll have to have an apartment of my own to work in."

"How much do you figure it will total?" I asked, thinking about the depleted state of our firm's finances.

He squinted thoughtfully. "Well, I figure I'll need a minimum of fifteen hundred dollars."

I refrained from showing surprise; I'd expected the figure to be several times as high.

"And how long," said Angus, "do you think it would take you to write a full-length book—say, eighty thousand words?"

"Two or three months," he said without hesitation. "Not more."

"That's not as easy as it sounds," I said.

"It certainly isn't," Angus agreed. "I haven't had an author do that yet."

"I can do it," said Matusow.

I suggested that Angus and I draft a preliminary contract summarizing the general terms of our understanding.

"We're in business," Matusow said.

His next remark came as a surprise. "Tell me," he said, "could we work out some arrangement so that most of the royalties go to my folks? They're not very well off. I've never really done anything for them. I'd like to do something now."

It was late afternoon when we left the hotel.

As we stepped outside, Matusow stretched and breathed deeply. "There's nothing like fresh air!" he declared, seemingly immune to the gasoline fumes.

He glanced up at the hotel marquee and suddenly asked Angus, "Do you know the hotel in Moscow I recommend to people who are visiting Russia for the first time?"

Angus looked perplexed.

"I recommend the Comrade Hilton," said Matusow with a grin.

I laughed. "I'll remember that when the State Department returns my passport."

We shook hands.

"Call me when the contract is ready," he said. *"Arrivederci!"*

He strode off down the street with a springy step, his cream-colored moccasins twinkling as he went.

Angus and I walked a block in silence.

Then Angus said, "What the hell are we getting into, Albert?"

"Your guess is as good as mine. I see limitless prospects—including jail."

Angus shook his head. "What a character!"

"You missed his main performance." I described the pipe-cleaner skits and other acts from Matusow's repertoire to which I had been treated before Angus's arrival.

"I'm not sorry I came late," said Angus. "But you know—he's versatile."

" 'Infinite riches in a little room.' "

"Where's that from? Shakespeare?"

"No." I was gratified—I rarely came up with a quote whose source Angus couldn't identify. "You're close though. Christopher Marlowe —*The Jew of Malta.*"

"How old was Marlowe when he got knifed in that tavern, anyway?"

"Twenty-nine."

"Remember that business with Marlowe and the Un-American Activities Committee?" Angus asked.

"Vaguely." I felt that Angus, as usual, was topping my one-upmanship.

"Sure you do, Albert. The committee was questioning an actor who'd done a play by Marlowe, and one of the congressmen asked him if Marlowe was a member of the Communist party." Angus added: "If ever you write anything about Matusow, you ought to get that in."

"I will," I said.

We had stopped at a crosswalk and were waiting for the traffic light to change.

"He's bright, you know," Angus reflected. He chuckled. "And you've got to admit it, he can be damned funny."

"You were serious, weren't you," I asked, "when you told him he could write?"

Angus looked indignant. "Of course I was serious, but I didn't say it all—that he could write well enough to do this book."

"I think he's got a book in him, all right," I said. "In fact, I'm damn sure he has."

"Whether he'll write it is another thing." Angus looked at me curiously. "What odds would you give?"

When Clint had asked that same question six weeks before, I remembered, I had put the odds at a hundred to one. "About one in five."

"You think the chances are that good, eh?"

"I do."

Angus nodded soberly. "So do I," he said.

2. *An Evening at Home*

The preliminary contract between Matusow and the firm of Cameron & Kahn took the form of a letter addressed to him from Angus and me. I wrote a draft the evening after our meeting with him at the Delmonico.

It covered such standard details as the author's advance, royalty percentages, and date of delivery of manuscript. There was, however, one paragraph in the contract which was far from routine. It read:

> The book . . . is to deal primarily with your life and activities during the past few years. One of the fundamental purposes of this book—as you have put it—is to "undo some of the harm done" to other individuals by your activity and testimony, much of which, as you have pointed out, was not a true and complete reflection of the actual facts. It is understood also that the book will seek to reveal the nature of the complex pressures and social forces which caused an individual during these turbulent times to act as the author had.

When I showed Angus the draft of the letter the following morning, he questioned the advisability of including the paragraph.

"That's tantamount to his admitting in writing that he's committed perjury," he said. "Don't forget how he reacted when you brought up the subject yesterday."

"It doesn't say he actually perjured himself."

"You're splitting hairs, aren't you?"

"We've got to have as clear an understanding as possible as to what the book is about," I insisted. "If he objects to the paragraph, we can always take it out. Why not leave it for the time being and see what happens?"

"No harm in trying I suppose," said Angus dubiously. "You handle it with him though."

There was, I told Angus, something about which I was more concerned.

"Meaning what?" he said.

"We have to assume the Justice Department will find out Matusow is doing a book for us—if they haven't already. I can't believe they won't try to stop him."

Angus shrugged. "There's nothing we can do about that."

"Maybe there is."

"For instance?"

"We can make him hard to find."

"You mean hide him out?" demanded Angus.

"Why not?"

"Absolutely not!" Angus snapped. "There's going to be no cloak-and-dagger stuff!"

I had the feeling he was more outraged at the idea of having such an unorthodox relationship with an author, than at the thought of playing games with the federal authorities.

I agreed, reluctantly, to drop the proposal.

Considering subsequent developments, it was doubtless fortunate Angus's counsel prevailed.

I telephoned Matusow and told him we had drafted the contract.

"Why not come out to my place in Croton for supper tonight," I suggested. "We could go over the preliminary contract there."

He sounded surprised and pleased at the invitation. "Swell! I don't have any decent clothes with me though. The only stuff I brought east is what you saw me in."

"My God, how formal do you think we are?"

He chuckled. "I thought that with your British background, mi-lord," he said with a broad English accent, "you'd wear tails to dinner."

It occurred to me only after hanging up that I had not told him I had been born in England.

*   *   *

The news of Matusow's imminent visit precipitated a minor crisis in the family. I had only myself to blame for my wife's reaction. Over the years Riette had shown a singular resilience, especially for someone who cherished peace and privacy, in coping with the vicissitudes of my literary efforts. There were calmer situations than being married to a writer of my political inclinations which resulted in blacklists, FBI surveillance, and perennial brushes with other government agencies. Riette rarely complained about the inconveniences and intrusions imposed upon her—I had come, in fact, to take for granted a tolerance considerably above and beyond the call of duty. Her patience, however, had its limits; and I strongly suspected I'd exceeded them by inviting Matusow to dinner without first consulting her.

Though it was shortly after lunch when I hung up after talking with Matusow, I decided I'd better head home on the next train and do my best to straighten out matters.

I found Riette in the garden behind the house. She was kneeling by a flower bed, planting bulbs. She was so absorbed in her work that she didn't hear me come out on the terrace. The scene was not unfamiliar but, as so often, I marveled at the dancer's ease and grace she brought to the most casual movement. She had a bright scarf around her head. Caught in the sun, an occasional leaf slipped from the silver birches and drifted down beside her. For a moment I forgot my mission.

I was standing beside her before she sensed my presence and looked up. "Home so soon, darling?" she said. "What a nice surprise!"

I bent down and kissed her. "It was too lovely to work, even in the city," I told her, and brushed a smudge of dirt from her nose.

"Sometimes I think you're actually growing up," she said with a pleased smile, in a way that made me almost feel I had earned the compliment. "I'll stop in a minute and make some tea. I just want to finish this row."

She dug a small hole with her trowel, dropped in a pinch of fertilizer, and sprinkled dirt over it. She set a bulb in the hole and tamped the earth firmly.

I crouched down at her side. "Why do you put the dirt between the fertilizer and the bulb?" I asked.

"So the roots won't be in direct contact with the fertilizer," she explained. She gestured toward the profusion of bulbs lying on the grass—her cheeks were pink with the chill air and her excitement. "Look at all of them! I wasn't extravagant either—they were on special at the market. I just couldn't resist them."

"What are they? Petunias?"

She laughed as she dug another hole. "Of course not! Petunias are annuals. You plant annuals in the spring. They'd winter-kill if you planted them now. These are tulips—all kinds of tulips. Can you imagine what this border will be like? I can't wait until—" She suddenly stopped her work and gazed at me penetratingly. The pleasure had gone from her face. "Why this sudden interest in gardening?" she said.

I knew I had overdone things and mentally cursed my clumsiness. "I was just curious," I said as casually as possible. "It's time I knew something about gardening."

She got up, her gray eyes still holding my face. "What's happened?" she said.

"Nothing's happened. Why?"

"You might as well tell me. There's no sense stalling."

I put my arm around her. "Let's talk over tea. It's nothing important."

She didn't move.

"It's really nothing," I repeated. "I just need your help on something."

"I'm still waiting."

"Well, all right. But it's no great event," I said. "I've invited Matusow for supper tonight."

"You've what!" She drew a long breath. Her slender body grew rigid with anger.

"Jesus Christ—" I began.

"Don't Jesus Christ me," she said. "How could you do such a thing?"

"I don't see any reason for making such a fuss." I did my best to sound indignant. "He doesn't have horns, you know. He won't contaminate our precious hearth."

"Petunias!" she scoffed angrily. "I should have known the moment you opened your mouth you'd done something like this. So you've invited this miserable creature to come here for supper! And without even consulting me! I can't believe it. Yes, I can. It's typical. This is *our* home, you know, not just yours. If you want to hobnob with spies and informers, that's your affair. But I don't have to have them as guests."

I followed her as she strode toward the house. "You know how important his story is. You know what's involved in it. You know it's a special case."

"Of course," she said sarcastically, "every case is a special case."

"You'd think I did this every day. Goddamn it, how many Matusows have I brought home?"

"What about that odious spy for the Ford Motor Company? Ralph Rimar. He practically lived with us for two weeks!"

I was glad she had not picked a more recent example. "That was years ago. It's ancient history."[13]

I adopted a calm, reasonable tone. "Look, sweetheart, I know I should have asked you beforehand. And I apologize. But I didn't invite Matusow just because I wanted him to come for a meal. He's been living in a political underworld. I doubt if he trusts anyone at this point. If he comes here—"

"You don't have to give me your devious motives," she said wearily, washing her hands at the kitchen sink. "I already know them. You're going to say that if you have him into your home, and if he meets the boys and me, he'll feel . . ." She sighed, running her hand through her hair, and said with resentful resignation, "You know I'm going to give in. It seems I always do. But I'll tell you one thing. If it weren't for Clint Jencks, I wouldn't let Matusow in the door." She shook her head. "I suppose you know what you're doing."

She obviously thought I did not.

She paused on her way upstairs and said emphatically: "I want you to know I'm not handling this with the boys. That'll be your job."

The oldest of our three sons, Steven, was thirteen; and Tim and Brian were ten and seven respectively. All of them, despite their youthfulness, understood the meaning of the word "informer." When your friends are going to jail for their principles or political beliefs (and you've a fair chance of joining them), your children need to know about some facts of life not ordinarily taught in the lower grades—like the role of political informers.[14]

The boys knew that Matusow was responsible for my friend Jencks getting a five-year prison sentence. A certain finesse with them would obviously be required in accounting for Matusow's coming to our house for supper.

I found Steven and Brian down the road tossing a football, and Tim up in his room reading *Wind in the Willows*. We assembled for our conference in the living room. Streaming through the windows, the afternoon sun shone on the boys' faces and glinted in Steven's and Tim's red hair. From where I sat I could see outside on the lawn the scattered bulbs and garden tools Riette had left lying in atypical disarray—a mute, unnecessary reminder of my immediate predicament.

I lit my pipe, and the boys waited for me to begin, Steven curiously, Tim beaming with good-nature and Brian stirring with impatience to get back outside.

"We've got to discuss something important," I told them solemnly. "It's something that concerns all of us. You know about Clint Jencks's case and his prison sentence, and I told you I was trying to do something about it." I drew in deeply on my pipe and exhaled a large cloud of smoke to stress the gravity of what I was about to say.

"Look!" said Tim. He pointed dramatically at the smoke.

"What about it?" I asked, resenting the diversion.

"Look at all those little specks! Moving up in the smoke."

"Of course they move up, stupid," said Steven. "Smoke goes up and dust goes with it."

"I don't want to talk about smoke." I spoke sternly, in an effort to restore the right mood. "I want to talk about the Jencks case. There's something you can do to help in it." The words made me feel foolish.

"Something *we* can do?" asked Steven, his freckled face perplexed.

I told them how I'd managed to get Matusow to come to New York and agree to write a book for Angus and me. "And tonight," I concluded in a triumphant voice, "Matusow is coming here for supper."

They looked at me for a moment in silent disbelief. Then they all started speaking at once. Their response was unanimous. Our friend Clint had been sentenced to prison because of lies Matusow had told about him, hadn't he? Then how, they angrily chorused, could such a person be invited to our house?

"Look, guys," I argued in a persuasive man-to-man tone, "I told you Matusow wants to tell the truth now. If he does, Clint will go free."

Steven asked, "Why can't he tell the truth without coming to sup-per?"

His logic won vociferous support from his younger brothers.

"You don't get the picture," I said. "Sure, Matusow has done something very wrong. But he wants to change. Perhaps we can help him. I want to try to make a friend out of him."

The argument went back and forth. Finally, with manifest reluc-tance, Steven and Tim agreed to Matusow's coming.

Brian however, stood up scowling, his fists on his hips, his sturdy little body thrust forward aggressively. "If he comes," he said, "I won't be here. I'll eat somewhere else!"

When Matusow arrived that night, at least a surface calm pre-vailed. Steven and Tim greeted him with studied, awkward polite-ness. Brian (whom I had persuaded to stay home) remained at a distance glowering at Matusow and pointedly refrained from shaking hands with him. Soon after, when I came out of the living room where I had been talking with Matusow, I found Brian standing in the hall like a diminutive sentinel, his arms folded stiffly across his chest. In a fierce whisper, he hissed: "I hope the bastard drops dead!"

While Riette was preparing supper, Matusow wandered into the kitchen and launched into a chattering account of his recent bicycle trip. She seemed to be listening with cordial attentiveness, but I knew how much the effort was costing her. All at once Matusow whipped off his jacket, flexed his biceps, and expanded his barrel–like chest until it seemed about to burst from his sweater. "That trip," he said, "really put me in shape!" He proceeded to do a series of deep knee bends. "Of course, I still need to lose a little weight," he granted.

"Yes," Riette quietly agreed, "I think that would be good for you."

During the meal Matusow so monopolized the conversation that for once the boys were scarcely audible. They were, in fact, perceptibly subdued and responded with embarrassment to his effusive overtures. He seemed oblivious to his effect upon them. I had the impression that, if anything, he felt he was giving a convincing demonstration of his winning ways with children.

As I was helping Riette clear the table before dessert, she took me aside in the kitchen. "If he doesn't stop that marathon babble," she said, "I'll go out of my mind. You'd better get him on the nine-thirty train to New York, or I'll be on it myself."

I kissed her. "Thanks for everything, love," I said. "You've been terrific."

She smiled. "Flattery will get you nowhere."

After supper, Matusow and I went into my study.

"You've got a wonderful family, Al," he told me. "You're a lucky man." He wandered around the room, looking at my books. "I can see you like to read as much as I do," he said. Obviously I was supposed to feel complimented.

"These are my research books," I told him.

He glanced idly at the shelves. "Tell me," he said, "what do you think of Thomas Wolfe?"

"I like him very much."

"He's my favorite modern author," Matusow said. "You know something? He and I have the same birthday— October third."

Abruptly, he changed the subject. "Well, let's get down to business. Have you got the contract?"

The letter I had drafted was lying on my desk. I handed it to Matusow.

"Of course, this is just a preliminary agreement," I told him. "Angus will draw up the formal contract. It won't take long, but right now he's getting a book to press."

Matusow studied the letter for several minutes. Then in a low voice, and as if to himself, he began reading aloud the paragraph containing the statement that much of his testimony as a government witness "was not a true and complete reflection of the actual facts."

I waited for his protest.

But suddenly he reached into his pocket, took out a fountain pen, and with decision signed his name under Angus's and mine.

CHAPTER THREE

THE STORY UNFOLDS

1. *Documentary Evidence*

The apartment Matusow found for himself in New York made me apprehensive the moment I saw it. It was a drably furnished, cold-water flat in a dilapidated section of Greenwich Village. Scant daylight penetrated its two small rooms. To reach it you had to climb three creaking flights of stairs. At night, the block on which the apartment building stood had a desolate and lonely air, accentuated by shadows cast between widely separated streetlights. I couldn't have imagined a less suitable place for Matusow to live while writing his book.

It wasn't of course only in detective stories that key witnesses in criminal cases had the unfortunate habit of mysteriously disappearing or meeting with sudden accidents. Such episodes occurred frequently enough in the daily press. Nor were comparable mishaps uncommon in certain circles of the political underworld. As editor of *The Hour* during the war years, I had worked on several stories in which double agents providing information about Nazi intelligence operations had abruptly vanished and—to the best of my knowledge—not turned up again. Like other intelligence agencies, the FBI had a limited fondness for undercover operatives who divulged Bureau secrets or sought to leave the fold; and while I had no personal knowledge of anyone's being eliminated by the FBI during or after the war (the OSS and CIA were another matter), I had no reason to assume that J. Edgar Hoover had special sensitivities in such matters. I was not counting on trouble but I saw no sense in courting it.

The apartment, however, had an entirely different effect on Matusow. He found enchantment in its every dingy corner. No compulsive housewife ever fussed over her home more zealously. For days on end, as suitcases and cartons arrived with his belongings, he puttered about the place, hanging pictures, setting up displays of knicknacks and souvenirs, stringing up his marionettes, arranging and rearranging his books and government reports. He tacked brightly colored travel posters over spots where plaster was peeling on the walls, repaired plumbing fixtures, scrubbed, painted, cleaned. Whenever I dropped by, he would proudly exhibit the latest renovation.

Periodically he asked when Angus would be coming by. "I'm in no hurry for the final contract," he told me. "I want him to see how I've fixed things up here." Watching Matusow's hectic activities, I came to feel that this shabby, cluttered apartment perhaps had for him a significance of which he was unaware. It was as if, after much wandering, he were trying to find a haven, to sink some roots, to create a home of his own.

Once his files were unpacked, Matusow eagerly offered to show me some of their voluminous contents. "You'll see," he boasted. "I kept everything."

He wasn't exaggerating. He had apparently been unable to bring himself to discard anything mentioning his name; and over the last few years he had accumulated a copious and indiscriminate assortment of letters, memoranda, photographs, newspaper clippings, transcripts of his testimony before congressional committees, copies of his reports to various investigative agencies. Thanks to his inordinate ego, he was superbly equipped to document every sordid detail of his recent life.

Even now, as he sorted out the material, he handled it with affectionate familiarity, savoring each prominent reference to him. "Look at this!" he chortled, picking up an official report of the House Un-American Activities Committee entitled *Communist Activities Among Youth Groups (Based on Testimony of Harvey M. Matusow)*. "That gives you some idea of the play my testimony got," he declared. "The whole thing is devoted to me. I was the authority on Communist penetration of American youth. I figured out that angle myself. If you wanted top billing, you had to offer something special. Just like in show business."

He opened the committee's report. "See, sixty-six pages. Closely printed text too. That's about—" he hesitated momentarily—"let's see, at five hundred words a page, thirty thousand words anyway. About half the length of a regular book. And that was just my *debut* as a witness!"

He leafed through the pages. "Let me show you something." He found what he was looking for and handed me the report. "Read that," he said. "I'm being questioned there by Congressman Clyde Doyle of California."

DOYLE: Are you familiar with the book *A Hundred Things You Should Know About Communism*, as published by this committee?
MATUSOW: I am, sir.
DOYLE: What is your appraisal of it as a matter of whether or not it is instructive and a valuable contribution to the American public in the area which it covers, or not?
MATUSOW: I might answer that, sir, by saying that right now in the State of Ohio, when I contact people in industry and schools in relation to my work with the Ohio Un-American Activities Committee, I recommend that and other publications of this committee, and in many cases I find that those people have already gotten the very publication which you have referred to, and do use it quite frequently.
DOYLE: Then would it be your opinion that the distribution of this sort of an explanation of what Communism is constitutes a valuable contribution to the American public in the fight of the American government against Communism?
MATUSOW: That is right, sir.

I handed the report back to Matusow. I felt he expected some sort of compliment from me, but I could not think of anything appropriate to say. "You see, they were actually asking for my approval of their work," he explained, as if he thought I might have failed to fully appreciate what I'd read. He added: "Now listen to this. Doyle is still questioning me." He intoned the congressman's words: "'Are you familiar with the standing of the present legislation as regards the Communist party? Do you have any suggestion for the benefit of this

committee in our obligation to report to Congress any remedial legislation? Is there anything that you have in mind in addition to, or
different from, what is presently on the statute books?'" He paused
for dramatic effect. "How's that? Asking *me* for my advice on legislation!" He beamed. "And I was only twenty-four and had never gone
to college!"

"Well," I said, "you could have been a child prodigy."

He laughed. "Right. The Mozart of McCarthyism!"

"Did you give them any advice?"

"Of course. I tell them right here we should have laws forbidding
Communists to hold positions in government. Also that Communist
party members shouldn't be allowed to occupy certain positions in
basic industry." As he spoke, he was busying himself with a pile of
folders crammed with newspaper clippings. He held up a sheet. It was
the front page of the *Columbus (Ohio) Citizen*. Splashed across it was
the headline: "Says Reds Used Sex to Lure Members—Ex Communist Tells Senators Weakness of Youth Exploited."

"That's the sort of publicity my testimony got," he said. "Mind
you, that story's a UP dispatch from Washington. It was carried by
newspapers all across the country."

He showed me a copy of the *New York Journal-American* with the
banner headline: "Secret FBI Man Reveals: 3,500 Students Recruited
Here for Red Fifth-Column." The lead story carried the by-line: "Harvey M. Matusow, undercover operative for the FBI in many Communist organizations and youth organizations for the Reds in the city's
public high schools and colleges."

"You covered a lot of territory," I said.

"That was one of a series of five articles I wrote for the *Journal*,"
he told me matter-of-factly. He searched in another folder. "Speaking
of covering territory, take a look at this." He handed me an issue of
the *American Legion Magazine*. It featured an article by Matusow
entitled, "Reds in Khaki—How Communists Operated as Members of
Our Armed Forces."

"So you were an expert on military affairs, too."

"Why not?" he said.

Soon the floor was strewn with clippings concerning Matusow's
appearances at congressional hearings, his statements to the press, his
lectures, his speeches at political rallies for Senator McCarthy. One
clipping from the front page of the *Wisconsin State Journal* featured a

photograph of Matusow chatting amiably with Governor Walter Kohler at a pro-McCarthy rally they were both about to address. "Not bad, huh?" said Matusow. "Me and the governor of Wisconsin!" He added smugly, "You know, the Republican party chartered a special plane for me on part of that speaking tour."

Matusow and I spent almost three days looking over material from his files. Among the items he showed me were his reports to the FBI when he had been operating as an informer in the Communist party; memoranda prepared by Justice Department attorneys for him to study prior to his appearances as a government witness; vouchers of payment to him from a well-known New York advertising firm for compiling lists of radio and TV actors and writers with "Red affiliations"; a copy of Senator McCarthy's book, *McCarthyism—The Fight for America*, with the handwritten inscription: "To Harvey Matusow-A Great American. Thanks, Good Luck & Best Wishes—Joe McCarthy."

One document I found especially intriguing was a letter Matusow had received early in 1952 from the office of the New York City Board of Education. Written by the Superintendent of Schools, William Jansen, the letter began:

> Dear Mr. Matusow:
> I am extremely interested in the material that appeared in the public press and was attributed to you. It may be that you have some information that would be of value to us, concerning New York City teachers who are members of the Communist Party. I would like to speak with you and would appreciate it if you will contact me as soon as you return to New York City. . . .

Additional correspondence revealed that Matusow had subsequently gone to work as a confidential adviser to the Board of Education. "I find," stated a letter from the Board counsel, Saul Moskoff, "that Mr. Harvey M. Matusow is in possession of important information . . . and that he is in a position to perform a public service for the Board."

I asked Matusow: "Didn't it strike you as rather strange that the Board of Education of the nation's largest city should employ you to help decide which teachers were fit to teach its schoolchildren?"

He smiled broadly. "Why, the president of Queens College, Dr. John Theobald, came to see me privately to get my advice. He wanted me to help him track down Communists among the students and faculty members at the college."

"Just a few weeks ago," I said, "there was a series of articles in the *Denver Post* dealing with the use of secret informers against school-teachers and college professors. They showed it's happening today in every part of the country."

He nodded abruptly. "I read the series," he said. "It wasn't bad. But it really only skimmed the surface." He sounded slightly piqued, as if the articles represented a challenge to his own expertise.[15]

Of all the documents Matusow showed me during our initial examination of his files, none aroused my interest more than a letter on the stationery of the United States Department of Justice. The letter was dated February 5, 1954, directly after the trial in El Paso, Texas, at which Clinton Jencks had been convicted of violating the Taft-Hartley Law and sentenced to five years imprisonment.

The letter read:

Dear Harvey,

As I told you before you left El Paso, I am sincerely grateful to you for your fine cooperation in the case of the United States v. Clinton E. Jencks.

As you know, your testimony was absolutely essential to a successful prosecution and you presented it in a fine intelligent manner.

If you are ever in my part of the country, be sure and look me up.

Sincerely,
(Signed)
Charles F. Herring
United States Attorney

U.S. Attorney Herring of the Western District of Texas had been the chief government prosecutor at the Jencks trial. I did not need to be a lawyer to realize that if Matusow were now to admit he had lied at the trial, Herring's characterization of his testimony as "absolutely essential" to Jencks's conviction could be a major factor in securing a retrial and reversal of the sentence.

I had not intended to ask Matusow any questions about the Jencks case at this early stage of our acquaintance. Since Matusow had clearly perjured himself at the trial, I wanted to be on much surer footing with him before discussing the case. But now that he had introduced the subject himself, and in so compelling a manner, I was momentarily tempted to ask him what he'd done to earn such glowing praise from the government prosecutor. Instead, I merely said, "Clint Jencks is a good friend of mine."

"I know he is."

"I think you should also know," I told him, "that Clint and the Mine-Mill Union are aware Angus and I are planning to publish your book."

"I assumed they were," Matusow said.

As if by mutual consent, we let the matter rest there.

Prior to seeing Matusow's files I had thought he probably had a sensational story to tell. I now had some idea of its scope and potential impact. His book, I felt, had the possibility of creating a national scandal.

The trouble was that Matusow wasn't putting anything on paper. As the days went by, he found one reason after another for not writing. At first, he had given the plausible enough excuse that he could not get started on the book until he was comfortably settled and his files had arrived. However, after the apartment was completely redecorated and all his files were unpacked, he found other alibis. He needed, he said, time to organize his research materials. He had to read through all the documents and newspaper clippings. His outline of the book had to be completely revised. He required a secretary to properly catalogue his correspondence and other papers. With every day it became more apparent that consciously or unconsciously, Matusow was avoiding work on the book.

"Maybe," I suggested to Angus, "in spite of all his boasting, he's actually so ashamed of what he's done he just doesn't want to put it down."

"Well," said Angus, "you'll remember I didn't put much stock in the speed with which he said he'd write the book."

I voiced a thought I knew was in back of both of our minds. "It could be, of course, that he really has no intention of writing it."

"Anyway, I wouldn't pressure him."

"Pressure him! Christ almighty, Angus, I've been catering to his every whim: I've been handling him like a newborn babe. But I know what's in his files. What I've told you about them gives a partial picture. You've got to see them for yourself.

"I've got a pretty good idea of what's there."

"The more I think about it," I said, "the less sleep I get. Every time I go to his apartment, I wonder if he's still going to be there, or whether something's happened to him, or if he's just changed his mind and run off."

My misgivings were considerably increased when Matusow informed me one day that he had been visited by two Justice Department agents.

"What did they have to say?" I asked as casually as possible.

"They asked me about my statement to Bishop Oxnam," he said, "and they wanted me to come to Washington for a conference. I said I couldn't go right now."

"Did they say anything about the book?"

He shook his head. "No, and I didn't tell them anything about it."

I wondered, however, just what Matusow had told his visitors, and how soon they would return.

Three weeks after Matusow's arrival in New York, the only piece of writing he had produced was a slightly revised version of the preface he had shown Angus and me at our first meeting at the Delmonico Hotel. It was obvious that if Matusow's book were ever going to be written, there would have to be some drastic change in his approach. A possible solution occurred to me. "I think you've got so much to tell," I told Matusow, "that perhaps you don't know where to start or how to pull it together. And you're so familiar with the material, you know, that possibly you don't realize how goddamn dramatic some of it is. What if I were to go through the stuff in your files and organize it into various categories? Then I could ask you questions about it and we could tape-record your answers. They might provide you with the basis for a major portion of the book."

To my surprise, Matusow responded with enthusiasm to the proposal. "I was thinking of something like that myself," he said. "If there's one thing that's second nature to me, it's working with a mike!"

"All right," I said, "I'll get a tape recorder."

"If you're buying one," said Matusow, "the Japanese make the best for the money." He added with a chuckle, "Forget Pearl Harbor!"

Angus's reaction, when I told him what I had proposed to Matusow, was less favorable.

"I'm not so sure it's such a good idea," he said.

"Why not?"

"For one thing, books don't get written that way." He raised his hand, anticipating my answer. "I'm not talking about what's customary. I'm talking about what *happens*. If a guy's going to write a book, he writes it. That's the way it is. You know it as well as I do. A writer doesn't need someone to ask him questions. I believe there's another reason Matusow isn't writing. And I think that you think so too."

"Well, whatever the reason, he sure as hell isn't writing. And this just might get him going."

Angus looked at me owlishly. "If you're the one asking him the questions, it puts you in sort of a special position, doesn't it?"

"I don't see why."

"Come on, Albert," Angus chided me. "You're the one who's been talking about the chance of the Justice Department interfering. You could play right into their hands, couldn't you? Anyone asking questions can have quite an influence on what goes into a book. It wouldn't be too hard to claim you'd ghosted it."

"Naturally I'm planning to hold on to the tape recordings. They'll show that all the answers are his." I knew that Angus's point was sound and that I was not really answering it.

He shrugged. "Just be damn sure they're in a safe place."

"Sure," I said. "I'll ask J. Edgar to keep them for me."

I bought a tape recorder.

2. *Question and Answer*

The tape-recorded discussions between Matusow and me began in the middle of November and continued, almost daily, for the next four weeks. Each evening I'd take home folders crammed with newspaper clippings, letters, and other material from his files. From this data I prepared a "work sheet" for the following day, summarizing the contents of the folders and listing various questions to ask him about the material. As soon as we finished a reel of tape, I had it transcribed and made a duplicate recording. I stored the duplicate recordings in a safety deposit box and gave copies of the transcriptions to the Mine-Mill attorney, Nat Witt. I wanted to be sure that no matter what happened, there would be a permanent record of our conversations.

I told Matusow of these precautionary measures. Angus and I agreed Matusow should be kept informed of every move we made in connection with the book, no matter how seemingly inconsequential. It was essential, we felt, that he realize we trusted him enough to take him fully into our confidence in such matters and were doing nothing affecting the book without his knowledge.

We had, however, made one exception to this rule. While I had told Matusow of Nat Witt's interest as Jencks's attorney in the book's disclosures, I had deliberately refrained from mentioning the advance order Cameron & Kahn had received from the Mine-Mill union. Conceivably, Matusow might at some future date be accused by government authorities of having been bribed by the Mine-Mill union to write his book. In that contingency, we wanted him to be able to state he had not known of the union's order while he was working on the book.

From the start of our tape-recorded talks, both Matusow and I were impelled by ambivalent motives. Although repeatedly voicing his desire to make amends for the harm he had done, Matusow clearly wanted to avoid incurring any legal risks by his disclosures. While I was on tenterhooks to have him divulge everything about his activities as a government agent, I wanted to steer clear of any questions that might make him think I was trying to inveigle him into incriminating admissions.

I decided, under the circumstances, to restrict my initial questions to the emotions he had experienced as an informer and professional witness. This was one subject, I felt, he could discuss freely without feeling he was running any undue risk; and I hoped that after a while he would reach the point where he himself would be ready to make more significant disclosures about his exploits.

Although a slow and frustrating process (how much so, I didn't realize), it seemed to me the only feasible approach.

Our first tape-recorded discussion began with this interchange.[16]

KAHN: I think one question that would be interesting for you to discuss is the sort of feelings you had when you were on the witness stand. On the one hand, how did you feel, let us say, when you testified before a committee? On the other hand, how did you feel when you were testifying in an actual court case?

MATUSOW: Well, I'm glad you separated it, because the feeling, though in many cases the same, is different. You feel it in your belly, I would say. You don't feel emotion, or I don't. . . . Let's get to the question of the congressional committee and how I felt the first day I walked in the hearing room of the House Un-American Activities Committee. . . . I walked in. My mouth was pretty dry. I didn't know what to expect.

KAHN: Was there a full room at this session?

MATUSOW: It wasn't full when we started, but it didn't take long for it to fill up. . . . Of course, I didn't know it when I got on the witness stand, but King George VI had just died.

He paused with a grin before adding, "That was one of the biggest disillusionments of my entire life. It knocked me right off the front page."

He returned to the subject of his emotions on the witness stand:

MATUSOW: I felt kind of strange. . . . I was afraid to turn around. At first, I didn't want to look at anybody. But I was cocky and sure of myself as an actor is on the stage. Nervous as an actor is. I treated it as a performance.

KAHN: You wanted to put on as good a show as you were capable of?

MATUSOW: Almost everything is a performance. . . . I was very careful to throw in things like "the Communists use intellectual as well as sexual weaknesses to recruit people."

KAHN: Why?

MATUSOW: Knowing that the headline would read: "Communists Use Sex to Snare Youth." I knew the headlines weren't going to say "intellectual weaknesses". . . . The *Daily News* had an editorial about two days later, and they were very complimentary. They said they were thankful to Mr. Harvey Matusow for opening up their eyes to the fact that the Communists use sexual weaknesses to get young people in.

Matusow leafed through a batch of newspaper clippings, and read
from the *News* editorial: " 'The Matusow revelations about Communist use of intellectual and sexual appeals to rope young people into
the party's lower echelons pose a new light on the brutishly immoral
and completely conscienceless strategies of the red traitors. . . .' "

He went on to relate with delight that during his testimony before
the House committee he had charged that the Communist party had
cunningly altered Mother Goose nursery rhymes for the purpose of
inculcating small children with "Moscow propaganda."

"I gave them a couple of examples." He laughed. "One of them
was

> Jack Sprat could eat no fat,
> His wife could eat no lean,
> Because the Congress done them in,
> And picked their pockets clean.

"Another was

> Jack and Jill went up the hill,
> To see their men in action.
> And there they found
> Their men were bound,
> By NAM reaction."

He read the headline of a clipping: " 'Reds Rewrite Mother Goose,
Probe Is Told—Tots Indoctrinated.' " He said smugly, "I think I was
probably the first person to accuse the Communists of subverting the
kindergarten."

We returned to our discussion.

KAHN: In other words, what you're saying is that when you put on a
performance, you not only thought of it in terms of your actual
conduct, your manner on the stand—
MATUSOW: But the lines were important, and the improvising—
KAHN: And you also thought in terms of the actual publicity your
performance would get?
MATUSOW: That's right. . . . I knew I couldn't be a dull witness. I'd
been in show business too long. I appreciate press values.

That Matusow regarded the witness stand as a stage on which he appeared as a star performer was a recurrent theme in our transcribed discussions. His greatest satisfaction in testifying, he stressed, had been the feeling of giving what he called "a successful performance." Like any actor, he said, he had judged the success of his performances not only in terms of their effect upon his immediate audience but also by the reaction of the press. He was thrilled at seeing his name in headlines, his photograph in the newspapers. He had become, as he put it, "an addict of the narcotic of newsprint."

Even now, as he described his appearances at various congressional hearings, he did so with unconcealed relish, savoring what he considered to be his wittiest lines and playing the part again, like an actor reminiscing over former theatrical triumphs.

However, while readily granting he had played a role on the witness stand, he stubbornly avoided admitting he had ever perjured himself. Time and again he drew a distinction between creating a false impression and deliberately telling a lie. In fact, he painstakingly shunned the word "lie." He referred, instead, to "half-truths," or said he had "omitted part of the truth," "distorted the facts," "implied by innuendo."

"I was very careful to weigh what I said," he insisted. "It wasn't a question of telling a lie as we know a lie opposed to the truth, because this is where people who have gone into the subject make their mistake. They deal with it as lies opposed to the truth. It is wrong, because it is a question of the whole truth as opposed to the half-truth."

He cited his testimony to the effect that Communists used sex as a device for recruiting young people. "There is no lie to the answer that at some time or other . . . sex was used by somebody to recruit someone into the Communist party. Nobody could deny this. There are many people who join churches, the Republican party, for the same reason. This I didn't say. I just said it happened to the Communists. I tell something which is a fact but leave out many of the important ingredients, so it has another meaning. But," he emphasized, "it's not a lie."

In a later discussion, as another example of his use of the "half-truth," Matusow mentioned an incident which he said had occurred when he had been a prosecution witness at the trial of Clinton Jencks.

I listened expectantly. It was the first time during our tape-recorded talks that he had referred to the trial:

> MATUSOW: The defense attorney asked me where I lived, and I said, "I'm sorry, I'm not going to give you my address." I knew he knew where I lived, and I made no secret about my address. I was in the phone book. But I was just dramatizing this thing for the jury. And he said, "We would like your address." And I turned to the judge and said, "Your honor, in 1952 my father was beaten up and almost killed, and I just fear for the life of my family." Of course, at that point everything was objected to and stricken from the record. But the jury picked it up. The newspaper headlines the next day said, "Witness' Father Beaten Up. . . ." My father was merely robbed. But I thought I'd use the fact that he was mugged and robbed—ten days before I testified—as an attack on the Communist party, claiming the party did it to intimidate me.
>
> KAHN: Had you used that before? Or was this the first time you used it?
>
> MATUSOW: It's the first time I used it at a trial, but I had used it in testimony. It's very dramatic.
>
> KAHN: In other words, when you talked to the judge like that, you did it thinking of the effect it would have?
>
> MATUSOW: Of course, it had an effect on the jury. . . . It made me a better witness before that jury. Don't forget, my life was in danger because of what I was doing. It made me out to be a hero psychologically. The jury was on my side. I'm the underdog, not the defendant.

Now that he himself had brought up the Jencks trial I hoped he would elaborate on it, but he changed the subject.

In the dimly lit room where we sat talking in Matusow's apartment stood a small table and on it a chess board with the pieces in place. The chess board seemed symbolic. As our discussions progressed, it became increasingly apparent that Matusow and I were playing a game with each other. I was sure that as much as I sensed Matusow's determination to avoid admitting he had ever committed perjury, he was aware of my intention to get him to tell precisely when and how he had. But one of the unspoken rules of our game was that we never acknowledged our mutual recognition of my plan.

In one of our talks I asked Matusow whether his conscience had ever bothered him while he had been testifying.

"If I looked at it from the point of view of conscience," he said, "I couldn't do it. Your conscience is dead. You're playing a part."

It was clear, however, that he had not always been completely at ease on the witness stand. When we were discussing his testimony at a Senate Internal Security Subcommittee hearing in El Paso, Texas, on the "Communist infiltration" of the Mine, Mill and Smelter Workers' Union, this exchange occurred:

MATUSOW: In the hearing room there were a couple of hundred men, all Mine-Mill people, and of course I had to pass them going in.
KAHN: How did you feel when you testified?
MATUSOW: Very belligerent.
KAHN: Why did you feel belligerent?
MATUSOW: The fact that I was outnumbered. I had to walk through the crowd. I heard their talk and I felt their cursing and I felt their pushing. My normal reaction was—well, you son of a bitch, you think you can push me around, I can be just as bastardly as you want to be. Do you want to curse me? I'll curse you. I can do it on the witness stand where it can hurt you more than it can hurt me. . . . It was just a—just a—I guess, normal reaction. The best defense is an offense. . . . It's hard to put into words the intangible feelings of guilt you have. And the more guilty I felt, the more vindictive I got.

He sat in silence for a moment and then added, "You know, it's strange to think of it now. . . . I think back at myself and the hate and bitterness toward people and about things I've lived with, and I find it hard to understand how I was ever in a position where I could act that way."

Nevertheless, Matusow still derived marked satisfaction from describing what a difficult witness he had been to cross-examine and how he had bested defense attorneys who interrogated him in federal court proceedings.

* * *

One afternoon, when we were having a cup of coffee after finishing our recording for the day, I asked Matusow why he had joined the Communist party in the first place.

"Look, I was a kid off a street corner in the Bronx when I went into the army," he said, "and when I got out—I was only nineteen then—I really didn't know what I wanted to do. But one thing I didn't want to do was to go back to that Bronx street corner. While I was in the army I'd traveled in Europe and done things. I'd been part of something, I'd had a sense of belonging. The first Communists I met were in the Army. There were a couple in my outfit, and I met some French Communists, too. They were good guys; I liked their spirit. And don't forget, the Communists—Russia was our ally then. Anyway, after I'd gotten out of service, I went one night to an affair run by the American Youth for Democracy. I liked the kids. They sort of gave me a sense of belonging again. So I became a member of the AYD. The ones who impressed me most were Communists. And after a while I joined the party."

"But you make it sound like joining a college fraternity," I said. "Didn't the political views of the Communists have anything to do with it?"

"Oh, sure. They were against discrimination, they were for peace and things like that. So was I. And the Communists seemed to have an organized way of fighting for the things I believed in. You've got to remember something else. It wasn't hard to be a Communist then—there was a very different attitude toward Communists than now."

"What changed your own attitude?"

"A lot of things. For one, I like to do things efficiently. The party wasn't the disciplined outfit I'd thought it was. It was pretty damn sloppy, in fact. I worked hard as hell getting *Daily Worker* subscriptions and distributing pamphlets and carrying out other assignments like that. The party leaders didn't seem to care or even notice. As a matter of fact, I think they probably suspected anyone who did something efficiently—it was such a rarity they probably thought him a spy. Nobody paid me much attention. I got fed up, disillusioned." He shrugged. "It didn't happen all at once. . . . Then the Cold War came. The Soviet Union wasn't our ally anymore—they were the enemy. No one talked about Stalingrad or praised the Red Army any more. Truman and everyone else were talking about the Red Menace. Communists started getting sent to jail. I was sure war with Russia was coming. And I got scared." He paused. "It was a slow process. Anyway, in the end I got in touch with the FBI."

"It was you who contacted them, not vice versa?"

"I called them on the telephone. Here in New York. It wasn't easy. As a matter of fact, I hung up the first time their office answered. Then I flipped a coin to see if I'd call them again. Heads I would; tails I wouldn't. It was heads."

"But it couldn't have been quite as simple as flipping a coin. Your friends were Communists. You must have had some feelings about informing on them."

"I did. And when I first started turning in reports, I used to leave out certain names. As if that made a difference! But I kidded myself into thinking it did. . . . Sure, I felt guilty at first. But you can rationalize anything if you try hard enough. And don't forget something else. By then informers and ex-Communists—like Philbrick, Bentley, Budenz, Whittaker Chambers—they were regarded as heroes. They weren't only star performers—they were given medals, literally. They didn't just get headlines. They were honored citizens. I got on the bandwagon. It was a way to get ahead. I was somebody."

Matusow frowned. "I guess you could say I was looking for identity when I became a Communist, and when I became a witness too. Sometimes I wonder how many other young guys might not have done the same thing if they'd had the chance, with all the glamour that was attached. . . . Mind you, I'm not trying to excuse myself, because I really knew better."

He walked over to the fireplace and stirred the coals. His face averted, he blurted out: "Tell me, Al, how do you stand talking with me after the things I've done? What do you really think of me, anyway?"

It was not a simple question to answer. "I don't have a conditioned reflex, Harvey," I said. "I think of what you're trying to do now, not what you've done in the past. I respect you for what you're doing."

He returned to his chair. "You know, it's funny," he mused, "when I came east I didn't know whether I'd even be able to talk to you and Angus. I was suspicious too. I thought maybe you were just going to try to get me to sign affidavits that I'd lied in the Flynn trial or the Jencks case, or something like that, and that you really didn't have any intention of publishing a book by me. I know different now."

"Look, Harvey," I said, "I don't have to tell you I'd like to see you set the record straight in those cases. You know Clint's my friend, and I've known several defendants in the Flynn case for years. And it's not just that, of course. I mean, it's not simply a personal matter. They're innocent and they're being railroaded. That's the main issue. Naturally I want to do anything I can to help get them off. But there's more involved in your book than those cases." I paused while refilling my pipe. "I don't think even you realize what a bombshell your book can be. Or the effect it may have nationally. I didn't myself at first, but I'm goddamn sure now. As far as I'm concerned, the main thing is to get your book out as soon as possible. There'll be time afterward for you to write affidavits in those cases, if that's what you decide to do. I happen to believe that will be your decision."

"Anyway," he said, "like I was saying—now I trust you."

3. *Crossing the Rubicon*

Slowly, and at first almost imperceptibly, as our tape-recorded discussions continued day after day, Harvey showed signs of undergoing other changes.

If he was still the showman, and periodically interrupted our talks to act out some impromptu skit with his puppets or pipe cleaners, he boasted less of his performances on the witness stand. And although he continued to display an inordinate fondness for sudden parodies of public figures, he was noticeably more thoughtful when discussing his work for Senator McCarthy. Despite his undiminished exhibitionism, I had the feeling that in the mirror of the facts he was relating, Matusow was seeing a sharper image of himself.

One topic we both avoided, as if by tacit consent, was the "religious experience" he had told Bishop Oxnam had led to his decision to break with his past. In accordance with Mormon doctrine, he had continued since our first meeting at the Delmonico to refrain (somewhat ostentatiously) from smoking. Now he began to smoke. There was another and unmistakable change in him: he had lost considerable weight and grown a full, jet-black beard. The beard was quite becoming—he looked like a cross between a French-Canadian trapper and a jaunty buccaneer. "At any rate," he told me half jokingly, "I won't have to see my face any more the way it was."

Whatever the metamorphosis in Matusow, my family's feeling toward him had changed perceptibly.

After lunching with us in New York one day, Riette told me as we were walking down Madison Avenue, "He's really unbelievable. I've never seen anyone so egotistical! But, you know, there's something behind it." She stopped for a moment. "There's something under all that braggadocio. Part of it's insecurity, of course. But there's something else. I don't quite know what it is. I feel a real struggle in him. A painful struggle, too."

A few days later, she suggested inviting Harvey out for the weekend.

"You're sure?" I said, remembering her reaction to his previous visit.

"Yes, I'm sure." She smiled. "Only this time I'll do the inviting."

From then on Harvey began visiting us almost every weekend. He spent most of the time with the boys—joining in their games and fascinating them with fantastic yarns.

One afternoon, when Brian and he were throwing a ball in the backyard, Harvey had to jump into the air to catch a wild toss.

"Sorry," Brian apologized. "That was a lousy peg."

"It sure was, but did you see my catch!" Harvey gloated. "I'm another Yogi Berra!"

Riette, who had been watching, asked, "Harvey, do you really have to prove you're better than a seven-year-old boy?"

He laughed self-consciously.

That evening he spoke to her about the incident. "Next time I do something like that," he said, "you tell me. I'd appreciate it."

At our meals Harvey introduced a special ritual. When the clamor of the three boys reached a height of cacophony, he would whip out his watch and command with mock sternness, "A minute of silence!" The ensuing sixty seconds of utter silence came as a welcome balm.

On Monday mornings, before taking the train into New York, Harvey and I would drop the boys off at school. His parting words to them, delivered in a robust French accent, invariably were *"Travaille bien!* Do well, boys!"

After leaving them one morning, he asked me, "Have you noticed something, Al?"

"What's that?"

He said proudly, "They like me now."
And the fact was that they did.

There was, however, one vital respect in which Matusow showed
no sign of changing. In our tape-recorded talks he continued to avoid
going into any detail regarding his role in the Jencks and Flynn trials.
When either trial was mentioned, he quickly veered away from the
subject. And he still tenaciously evaded admitting he had ever committed perjury on the witness stand.

Then one evening during the third week of our discussions, while
preparing my list of questions for the next day, I came upon a glaring
discrepancy in his transcribed testimony at two different congressional hearings.

Appearing before the House Un-American Activities Committee in
February 1952, Matusow had charged that Communist party members
in trade unions were secretly pledged to "slowing down production in
arms and ammunition and materials for national defense of the United
States." Asked for a specific example by one of the congressmen, he
had lamely replied: "I can't pin it down to any individual right
now. . . ."

Only a few months later, at a hearing of the Senate Internal Security Subcommittee, Matusow had testified that the Mine-Mill union
official Clinton Jencks had once confided to him the details of a Communist plot to sabotage war production, declaring:

> . . . We discussed the possibility of what can the Communist
> party within the Mine, Mill and Smelter Workers' Union do in
> relation to hindering our efforts in the Korean war. . . . Jencks said
> that they were making efforts, that is, the Communists within the
> union, to see that a strike was called in the copper industry in this
> area, under the guise of wage increases, etc., and better working
> conditions for the guys in the shops; that they would call that strike
> . . . in an effort to cut down production of copper for the Korean
> war effort.

I produced these two contradictory pieces of testimony at my session with Harvey the following morning. "When you testified later at
Jencks's trial," I told him, "you repeated the accusation that Clint had

plotted to sabotage war production. Yet you'd already told the Un-American Activities Committee you couldn't recall any instance of such plottings by Communists. If such an episode had actually occurred between you and Jencks, it's inconceivable that you—an FBI informer when it supposedly happened—wouldn't have reported it to the FBI, or could have forgotten it."

Matusow carefully read his testimony at the two congressional hearings. "I'm surprised Jencks's lawyers didn't catch something that obvious," he mused. "They were usually on their toes." He compressed his lips thoughtfully. "I'll have to use that in the book," he told me. Somewhat sheepishly he added, "Do me a favor, Al, let me take the credit for spotting it."

From then on, Harvey dropped the euphemism "half-truth" in our discussions and began using the word "lie" when referring to false testimony he had given. He was no less conscious of this development than I was. "Have you noticed, Al," he asked proudly, "that it doesn't bother me anymore to say I was a liar?" With an air of delighted discovery he declared: "Now I don't even mind saying I was a stool pigeon!"

On December 14 the last of our tape-recorded talks took place.

When I arrived at Matusow's apartment that morning, he had a newspaper in his hand. Pointing at a story as he thrust the paper toward me, he exclaimed, "Look at this!"

The dispatch concerned the case of Carl Braden, a newspaperman in Louisville, Kentucky, who some months before had helped a black veteran and his family purchase a house in an all-white community.

The veteran's home had been dynamited shortly afterward, and—while no action had been taken against the real culprits—Braden had been indicted on the charge of having bombed the house himself as part of a "Communist conspiracy." At Braden's trial the prosecution witnesses had included several well-known government informers, none of whom knew Braden personally but all of whom told hair-raising tales about the subversive practices of Communists.

According to the present news dispatch, Braden had now been found guilty of sedition and sentenced to fifteen years in prison, with bail set at $40,000.

"What do you think of that!" said Matusow heatedly. "And they call this a democracy!"

The indignant tone was too much to ignore. "You know, Harvey," I said, "that's exactly the sort of thing you yourself made possible. Sure, Braden's been framed because he stood up for the rights of a black man. Well, Jencks was framed because he stood up for union rights. Your testimony got him a five-year jail sentence. You say you like children. Jencks has two kids—they won't be seeing him for a while if he goes to jail. Maybe it's not pleasant to talk about, but you're going to have to face facts like that in your book."

Matusow's face had grown pale. For several moments he sat motionless. Then he got up abruptly, took a few steps, turned, and said in a strained voice, "Let me try to tell some of the things I feel about that right now." He switched on the tape recorder and began talking rapidly into the microphone: "During the period when I was a witness and reporting on people, I had a guilt complex. When I'd walk down the street in New York and run into a party member I'd known— somebody I'd mentioned in testimony—I'd kind of want to slink away. That's the way I felt. . . . But yesterday I was on the street, and I passed somebody I'd mentioned in testimony. For the first time in this whole period I didn't feel like slinking away. . . . I knew that part of my life is past." He went on, "Because this man Braden purchased a home for a Negro, he was accused of seditious acts, of being a Communist. I look at this and I think of myself down in El Paso."

There was a subtle but unmistakable change in his manner. He continued speaking without a pause, but once again he had gone on guard. Instead of discussing his testimony at Jencks's trial in El Paso, he started to recount how he used to steal across the Mexican border at night to give performances as a comedian in a nightclub in Juarez.

This time, however, I was determined to make him face the issue. I interrupted him. "At Jencks's trial," I said, "you testified you knew Jencks was a Communist party member when he signed a non-Communist affidavit."

Matusow was visibly agitated. "I knew that Jencks was a party member and I said so," he declared defensively. "I can't say here that Jencks wasn't a party member after he signed the affidavit because I know he was. But I shouldn't have testified. That's the important thing."

"Why do you say he was?" I asked.

He stammered. "I said I knew he was—I mean in this way—men like Ben Gold who have been indicted on the same charge. He officially resigned from the Communist party. Or he could have. But in—to my mind then—in my thinking, it made him no less a Communist because he put a piece of paper down and said, 'I'm no longer a member.' As far as I was concerned, Jencks was still under Communist party discipline. He legally might not have been a party member. Jencks didn't change his thinking because he issued that scrap of paper."

Matusow noticed the reel was almost at an end and switched off the tape recorder.

The time had come for a showdown.

"Look, Harvey," I said, "there's no sense in our playing games any longer. We've reached the point where we can talk frankly. Both of us know damn well that whenever we start to discuss certain aspects of your testimony, you change the subject or get evasive. Why?"

There was a discernible note of relief in his answer. "I know it's been obvious. And it isn't because I don't trust you, Al. Believe me, it isn't."

"Then why is it, Harvey?"

The words came in a rush. "I'll tell you what's bothering me. I know the transcripts of these recordings are safe in your hands, but you've told me you're giving copies to Nat Witt. How can we be sure what will happen to them? Don't forget, he's counsel for Mine-Mill. What if the union started to publish some of these transcripts in their paper? Suppose I told everything about my testimony at Jencks's trial, and they took the matter to court before I even had a chance to write the book. That would really foul things up, wouldn't it?"

He started pacing up and down. "Look, Al, I intend to straighten things out in the Jencks case. I'm going to give an affidavit saying I lied against him. I plan to do it in the Flynn case, too, or any other case where it's necessary. But if I do it now—well, I'm just not willing to take the chance of screwing up the book, that's all."

"What if Witt were to promise you not to use any of your material without your okay?"

"That would be fine," said Matusow eagerly. "I know his reputation. I know he'd keep his word."

"Would you like to get together with him?"

"Absolutely!"

I phoned Witt immediately. I made an appointment for us to meet with him at his office that afternoon.

The last time Matusow and Witt had seen one another had been the previous January at Jencks's trial, when Matusow had been the chief prosecution witness and Witt had been Clint's attorney. One might have expected their present encounter to reflect in some way that past relationship. The reunion, however, had entirely different overtones.

As Harvey and I entered Witt's office, he came from behind his desk, a smile lighting his lean, saturnine face.

"It's good to see you!" said Witt, warmly shaking hands with Harvey as if greeting an old friend. "How are you anyway? You look in good shape."

"I'm training for the 1956 Olympics in Melbourne," Harvey retorted. "I'll be wrestling koala bears. Albert's coaching me. He's got me on a diet of eucalyptus leaves."

Witt laughed. Pointing at Harvey's beard, he said, "You didn't have that in El Paso."

Matusow grinned. "It's my Australian bush."

These amenities concluded, Witt asked us to be seated. I told Witt why we'd come to see him. He listened attentively, giving an occasional nod, his hands folded on the desk. When I was through, he turned to Matusow. "Is that the whole picture?" he inquired. "Your concern about part of the book becoming public prematurely?"

"That's it," said Harvey.

"I can give you my word," Witt told him soberly, "that without your specific permission no use whatsoever will be made by me or by the union of anything you say or write in connection with the book." His words sounded like a phrase from a legal document. "Naturally, I'm interested in what's in the book because I represent the Mine-Mill union, and I'm especially concerned with whatever affects my client, Jencks. But I've ample time for filing a retrial motion in his case. If there happens to be anything in your book I may want to use in that motion, we can discuss that later."

"Well," said Harvey, "the way I plan to handle the case in the book—"

Witt held up his hand. "No, I don't want to hear anything about that. That's entirely up to you. If we were to discuss that now, it might later be claimed I'd tried as Jencks's attorney to influence you in some way."

"I'd like to ask a question," said Harvey.

"Sure."

"In a perjury trial, what sort of evidence does there have to be? I mean, to get a conviction."

"Are you speaking about a federal case?"

Harvey nodded.

"The federal law," said Witt, "stipulates there needs to be two witnesses in order to prosecute a perjury case, or conclusive documentary evidence. Does that answer your question?"

"Yes," Harvey said thoughtfully. "Yes, it does."

I would have reason later to remember Harvey's question and Witt's answer.

When we left, Harvey was jubilant. He stopped outside the office building, oblivious to the light snow powdering his bare head and beard. "I feel wonderful, Al!" he said. "It's a hell of a weight off my mind to know nothing will break until the book's done!"

"Enough of a weight," I asked, "for you to get it done?"

"You'll see. I'll start tomorrow." He linked his arm in mine and swept me down the sidewalk, which was crowded with Christmas shoppers. "Your worries, Al, are over!"

On the corner a Salvation Army Santa Claus stood ringing a bell beside a small imitation chimney. Harvey strode over to the man and dropped a coin into the chimney. With his black beard thrust toward the Santa Claus's white one, Harvey sang in a deep baritone in the man's startled face, "'Tis the season to be jolly, tra-la-la-la-la, la-la-la-la!"

CHAPTER FOUR

BIRTH OF A BOOK

1. *False Witness*

It seemed inevitable in our dealings with Matusow that the moment one problem was solved, another arose immediately.

Two days after proclaiming his readiness to start writing, Harvey complained of a new obstacle. "I simply can't type the book," he flatly declared. "I've got to dictate it to someone."

"You typed those two sample chapters, didn't you?" I said.

"You know as well as I do, Al, that they weren't right. And that's not like doing a whole book, anyway."

"But you haven't even really tried typing this," I protested. "What can two days prove?"

"Listen, it's no good. The typewriter hangs me up. It gets between me and what I want to say. It's too mechanical."

"Don't you think you should wait a bit before deciding?" I said. "I can tell you that dictating a book just doesn't work. Not a book like yours, anyway."

He shook his head stubbornly. "I've got to talk it out. I need an audience. You know how easily I express myself when I'm talking."

I knew only too well. But I was not convinced that Harvey would, or could, dictate a book. Of one thing I was sure—he couldn't dictate a book worth publishing. Angus gloomily agreed. "It would be a sheer waste of time and money," he said. "We'd be wrong to humor him on this. Besides, it's not the typewriter that's bothering him. He's still avoiding the book."

Harvey, however, remained adamant. "Get me a stenographer and I'll show you," he told me. "If it doesn't work, what's lost? I can always go back to the typewriter."

We had no choice.

Now, another question had to be addressed. Whoever took Matusow's dictation would require a variety of qualifications—the least important of which was stenographic skills. The person had to be willing to accept Harvey's unsavory background; be able to adjust to his idiosyncracies; and (such were the exigencies of the time) be prepared to face possible government harassment for being involved in the book—even in a technical capacity. While likely candidates for such a job weren't plentiful, I had one in mind. Her name was Ruth Sommers.

An expert stenographer in her early thirties, Ruth had held various positions in public relations, radio, and trade union work. She had a quiet, thoroughgoing competence which contrasted oddly with the impression she gave—perhaps not unintentionally—of being a femme fatale. Her avocation was writing poetry—as nonconformist as her politics. Her cosmopolitan outlook derived in part from several years of residence in Paris. Ruth already knew about Matusow's book; she had transcribed some of our tape-recorded discussions. But it was one thing to type Harvey's words at an impersonal distance and quite another to work in daily contact with him.

All she asked, however, was: "Am I likely to get involved in an investigation?"

I said it was quite possible.

"Well, I'd certainly prefer not to," she said laconically, then shrugged. "Never mind," she said. "*Que sera*—"

The day after Ruth started working with Harvey, I visited his apartment.

He greeted me at the door with a triumphant air. He waved a sheaf of papers in my face. "So you thought I couldn't do it, eh?" he gloated. "Well, there's fifteen pages! Did ten of them yesterday and," he looked at his watch, "well, we started work at nine-thirty this morning, it's now twenty to twelve and I've already dictated five more." He studied my reaction, his teeth gleaming in his beard.

"Mind you, I haven't even hit my stride. I'm just getting warmed up. Fabulous, eh?" He tossed the pages on the kitchen table and, hooking his thumbs in his belt, stood rocking back and forth on the balls of his feet. "Read it!" he said.

Ruth, seated at the typewriter sipping coffee, looked on with a cryptic smile.

I picked up the manuscript with considerable skepticism. The first few pages changed my attitude. I forgot my annoyance about Harvey's hovering at my shoulder as I read on with growing surprise. Harvey had begun by describing his appearance, in the fall of 1952, at the Senate Internal Security Subcommittee hearing in Salt Lake City on the Mine-Mill union. He had touched on this hearing briefly in our taped talks. But now there was a striking difference. His present account brought the whole scene alive: the public fanfare surrounding the hearing; the tense atmosphere in the hearing room, crowded with union members; the personalities of the senators and their scurrying aides; Matusow's mixed emotions on the witness stand and the cold deliberation with which he had lied to make headlines. Curiously enough, the writing showed none of Harvey's usual verbosity. If it wasn't finished copy, it was remarkably close to it.

One thing impressed me in particular—there was no sign of equivocation in what Harvey had dictated. The manuscript read in part:

> The Internal Security Subcommittee of the United States picked the International Mine, Mill and Smelter Workers' Union for more than one reason. Holding hearings on that union, Senator McCarran had said, would help conservative candidates in the whole Rocky Mountain area. In Utah it was to the advantage of Senator Watkins, not only in vote-getting but also in obtaining the financial support of the Kennecott Copper Corporation.
>
> This was big league stuff. . . . I thought, "I have to make this good. I've got to hit the headlines."
>
> I also had made up my mind that I would place in the record a statement of "the number of Communists working for the *New York Times* and *Time* magazine." I had previously discussed this with Senator McCarthy and it had his approval. Once the "facts" were in the record McCarthy knew he could accuse the *Times* and *Time* of being pro-Communist. And we would both make headlines.[17]

Harvey's account continued:

I also gave thought to the nature of my testimony relating to the Mine-Mill union, claiming that the union had plotted to cut off copper production for the Korean War. . . . I knew that the union leaders would probably invoke the Fifth Amendment. I also realized that with the hysteria that the hearings had created no one would believe a "Fifth Amendment Communist."

I had deliberately avoided testifying about the "plot to cut off copper production" in the past. Not merely because it was untrue but because I wanted its full publicity value. I had concocted the idea of a "plot" when . . . I had first read about a week-long copper strike, and then built my story knowing that the strike would make it difficult for the union to deny my charges.

Recounting that he had already told the Senate committee in a closed session that Clinton Jencks had "divulged this plot" to him, Matusow went on with his description of the public hearing:

It was here that I had my first face-to-face encounter with Clinton Jencks, who was once a friend, and whom I later helped convict in a federal court. . . . Jencks was brought in for interrogation. The committee confronted him with my charges.

I was then called back to the hearing room, and there faced him. I was . . . asked to repeat my charges. . . .

My story of the "copper plot" had become so ingrained in me and was so much a part of me that I began to hate Jencks for it. If I hadn't built up this hatred for him, my story would not have been convincing. As an actor I knew that I had first to convince myself if I were going to convince anyone else. Jencks was the fall guy that enabled me to have a "perfect" story.

When I finished reading the material, I no longer had any doubt that Matusow could dictate the book.

"I never thought it possible you could handle it this way," I told him. "But you've got me convinced. It's really good, Harvey, damn good."

He strutted about the kitchen, swollen like a pouter pigeon. "That's nothing. I'll be averaging twenty pages a day before I'm through." He turned to Ruth. "Tell Al how it goes."

She shrugged. "It goes," she said noncommittally.

"But, Ruth," he pleaded, "tell *how* I do it."

"What am I supposed to say? You keep talking and I keep typing." Relenting, she added. "It's all I can do to keep up with him."

Matusow rubbed his hands together with satisfaction.

Before I left his apartment that day, Matusow asked me to get from Witt the transcript of his testimony at the Jencks trial. "I want to be able to quote directly from it when I get to that part of the book," he said.

I brought the transcript to him the next day.

The manuscript of Matusow's book grew at a remarkable rate. Each time I visited his apartment he announced gleefully how many pages he had written since the previous day.

"Fourteen and a half pages so far today, Al," he would say, trying to thrust them into my hand before I could get out of my overcoat. "Not bad, eh? That makes a total of—let's see—seventy-six pages. If I keep this up, I'll be finishing a couple of weeks ahead of the original deadline. Isn't that a fabulous way to write a book?"

I admitted it was.

Occasionally the routine varied slightly.

On my arrival one afternoon, Matusow was slumped dejectedly in a chair, his chin resting on his fist, his eyes staring at the floor. He did not look up when I came in. "Hello, Al," he muttered disconsolately.

"What's the matter?" I asked.

"Ah, the damn book. Just couldn't get going. Couldn't do a lousy paragraph."

"Don't let it get you down, for God's sake," I consoled him. "Every writer has off days."

He sprang from the chair and whipped into view a stack of typed sheets. "Maybe every *other* writer has off days. Not yours truly. There's sixteen more pages!"

He showed considerably more concern about the quantity than the quality of his work. "Maybe it needs a little polishing," he said as if quite unconvinced it did. "But that'll be easy to do later."

I myself was by no means preoccupied mainly with matters of style. I still feared that Matusow might somehow be prevented from finishing the book. Despite the delays and difficulties, I could not help feeling that things in general had gone far more smoothly than we had any right to expect. For me, one consideration dominated every other—getting all the facts on paper, in any form, as quickly as possible.

My impatience was heightened by the tale unfolding in Matusow's manuscript. With every day it became clearer that his story represented far more than the sordid chronicle of a single ex-informer and paid perjurer. What was taking form was a microcosm of the political underworld of McCarthyism.

There was, it seemed, scarcely a corner of that underworld Matusow had not explored.

He had not only turned in scores of names of Communist party members and "sympathizers" as an FBI informer. He had also—as a special investigator for the Ohio State Un-American Activities Commission—catalogued "subversives" from lists of Communist party petition signers dating back twelve years; acted as an agent provocateur by "collecting signatures on peace petitions" and then added these names to the commission's files; compiled dossiers on students at Antioch College and members of the National Negro Labor Council; and, working in collaboration with "police department antisubversive squads," helped stage a widely publicized commission investigation "to prove that trade unions were 'Communist-dominated' in the key industrial cities of Ohio." He had not only repeatedly perjured himself as an expert witness for the Justice Department and congressional committees. He had also—while campaigning for Senator McCarthy in Wisconsin and for McCarthy-endorsed senatorial candidates in four other states—made widely publicized, lying charges of "Commie connections" against anti-McCarthy candidates; lectured high school students with "gory tales about Communism" which "brought it down to a teenage level"; and had his "bankroll fattened" for such campaign services by "fees and expenses" he received from the offices of Senators McCarthy, Arthur Watkins, Zales Ecton, and Harry Cain.

Not only had he been a "paid consultant" who furnished lists of "Communist-inclined teachers" to the New York City Board of Education: he had also worked for a state commission investigating "Communism in the trade unions in Texas"; undertaken an assignment from Senator Pat McCarran "to pin the Communist label" on Hank Greenspun, anti-McCarthy editor of the *Las Vegas Sun*; and been employed as a "research specialist" preparing "blacklists of subversives, pro-communists and liberals" for motion picture companies, television networks and advertising agencies.

On finishing the first half-dozen chapters, I wrote in my journal:

> I'm beginning to doubt if there's a person in the whole country better qualified to write a firsthand account of the inner workings of McCarthyism—or, for that matter, of the whole ersatz crusade against the Red Menace. It's as if, by some perverse intent, Matusow had been deliberately initiated into every phase of the witch-hunt so he'd be ideally equipped for the ultimate job of exposing all of it. I'm starting to feel as if he were some zany latter-day Virgil conducting me, a dubious substitute for Dante, 'from round to lower round' on a Cook's tour of our contemporary political underworld!

Harvey's manuscript, as was to be expected, was not without defects. His presentation of the facts sometimes tended to be superficial and glib. While showing no reluctance to reveal what he had done, he revealed a good deal less about why he had done it. His reasons for becoming an informer, the causes of his subsequent decision to recant, and the relationship between his own personal conduct and the political climate of the time were handled in a cursory and almost casual fashion. It was not, I felt, that Harvey was consciously deleting portions of his story, but rather that he was telling it with too much speed and too little thought. Then, too, of course, there was the question of the extent to which Harvey was yet capable of such introspection.

None of these shortcomings escaped Angus when I gave him the first hundred or so pages of copy to read. Knowing his discerning eye and exacting standards, I had hesitated to put the manuscript in his hands until a fairly sizable portion had accumulated. One thing I wanted to avoid at all costs was to have Harvey's spirits dampened in any way or his productivity decreased by too critical an assessment of his work.

"It's a hell of a lot better than those two sample chapters he showed us," Angus granted after reading the material. "He knows how to tell a story—no doubt about that. It's got pace, all right." He hefted the manuscript. "In fact, it's got too much pace, hasn't it, Albert? You know what I mean. It's like having a race horse and not realizing how much weight that horse can carry. A lot more can go into this book without slowing the story. You remember what I said in the beginning about Harvey's having to tell more about himself. About his motivations and emotions, and his feelings about other people."

"Of course, you're right about what's missing," I admitted.

"Well, that has to be included if the book is going to be multi-dimensional. He's dealing with major changes that have taken place in himself and in his attitude toward the world around him, right? He can't make those changes seem real without going into them in some depth. There's no shortcut."

"I agree."

He looked at me suspiciously. "Well, have you talked about this with Harvey?"

"No, not yet."

"Don't you think you should?"

"It's less than two weeks, Angus, since he started dictating the thing. I wanted to wait until he hit his stride."

"I'd say he's already hit his stride, wouldn't you?"

I couldn't deny that he had.

"The sooner you discuss it with him, the better," said Angus. "You can handle it without inhibiting him in any way, and it will help him with his future material. There's no reason for his rewriting anything so far. That can be done when he's finished his first draft of the book."

I reported to Harvey that Angus felt portions of the material he had seen needed more development. I stressed, however, that Angus and I agreed he should postpone any rewriting until the first draft of the book was completed.

"I think," said Harvey, "that's a sensible decision."

It was also a fortunate one.

For reasons none of us foresaw, Matusow was to have little opportunity to rewrite any of his manuscript.

2. *Crisis*

It was toward the end of December that Matusow asked me to get him a transcript of the trial of the thirteen Communist leaders imprisoned on charges of violating the Smith Act in the Flynn case. He was, he said, about to dictate a chapter on his role as a government witness against them and he wanted—as he had with the Jencks case—to be able to refer to his actual testimony.

I had no reason to anticipate this simple request would precipitate a major crisis with Matusow's book.

I went to see the attorney, Harry Sacher, one of the members of the Flynn defense team. The defense lawyers, I knew, had been advised by Natt Witt some weeks before that Angus and I had arranged to publish Matusow's book. Even so, I expected Sacher would be more than a little surprised to learn of some of its contents. It was I who was in for the surprise.

Having known Sacher for some time, I found nothing unusual in the fact that he listened to me with an impatient air, tapping a pencil on his desk as I described the progress on the book. The diminutive high-strung attorney, whose brilliance as a trial lawyer was matched by few in his profession, often appeared impatient when someone else was talking. I saved for the end of my story the fact that Matusow had now reached that point in the book where he was about to reveal the part he had played in the Flynn case. He wanted, I said, to have available a transcript of the trial in writing this chapter.

I sat back awaiting Sacher's reaction, and struck a match to light my pipe.

Sacher said abruptly, "I assume you know we've a deadline to meet on any motion we make for a retrial in the case?"

"Deadline?"

He gave a curt nod. "The law stipulates that such a motion must be filed in court within two years after conviction," he said in a rapid businesslike monotone. "No new evidence can be introduced after that. Two years will have elapsed on February third since the conviction in this case."

"You mean," I asked incredulously, "that any retrial motion based on an admission of perjury by Matusow would have to be made within the next five weeks?"

"Exactly. Matusow's affidavit of recantation has to be submitted in court by February third—with a retrial motion, of course—if it's going to be of any use in getting a new trial."

I was dumbfounded. It was the first I had heard of any such deadline.

My pipe had gone out—it remained unlit in my hand. I said, "And what makes you think Matusow is prepared to give an affidavit at this point?"

"You say he wants to tell the truth," Sacher remarked drily. His dark eyes challenged me. "Here's his chance."

"There's a hell of a difference between telling the truth in a book and telling a judge you've committed perjury!"

"So?"

I contained my irritation. "Look, Harry," I said as evenly as possible, relighting my pipe, "Matusow suspected at first that Angus and I really didn't intend to publish his book. He thought we might only be trying to trick him into admitting he'd lied in the Flynn and Jencks cases. He's told me so himself. I've assured him there's no need to write any affidavits before the book is published. What's he going to think if I now tell him he has to write an affidavit in the next couple of weeks? Supposing he decides we've been fooling him all along? He's not such a stable person, you know."

Sacher showed no sign of being impressed. "That's the deadline," he said tersely.

Sacher was perhaps the best known of that diminishing breed of lawyers who'd been willing since the start of the witch-hunt to risk their professional careers (and not infrequently their freedom) by representing those accused of being Communist and charged with various forms of sedition. To most left wingers he was the Clarence Darrow of the day, totally committed to the defense of leading heretics; I admired and respected him for his fiery courage and iron integrity. Right now he struck me as arbitrary, pigheaded and pontifical.

"Damn it," I told him, "you guys in this case have known for weeks Matusow was writing this book for Angus and me! Witt told me when he let you know. How come none of you told us about the deadline? At least we could have planned ahead. Supposing I hadn't come today to get the transcript? How the hell would I have found out?"

Sacher shrugged. "I don't know the details. I entered the case only recently. Maybe you're right, but it doesn't change the picture."

"Well, I doubt Matusow will want to write an affidavit now. What's more, I strongly question the advisability of trying to persuade him to. He's liable to give up the whole goddamn shooting match."

"Perhaps you don't understand," said Sacher acidly, "that people are in jail because of his lies."

"That's one damn good reason I'm not willing to jeopardize his ever telling the truth. As far as I'm concerned, the most important thing right now is to get him to finish the book. It's not simply a question of keeping our word. I happen to know what's in the book and what it can accomplish."

"I appreciate the book's importance," Sacher said without persuading me that he did, "but I fail to see any choice in the matter."

The more we argued, the more each convinced himself of the validity of his own viewpoint.

As I was leaving I told him, "I can't promise you anything. I'll have to talk with Angus." I closed the door without waiting for an answer.

It was a Thursday afternoon, and Angus was planning a long weekend at home with his family in the Adirondacks. He was catching the 5:30 upstate train. It was almost four o'clock when I reached him by phone at the office.

I told him that something urgent had come up. "We've got to talk right away," I said. "I'm uptown. How about meeting at Grand Central in half an hour? That'll give us enough time before your train leaves."

"Is it really urgent, Albert?" His tone reflected his usual distaste at being hurried or having to make any sudden change in his plans.

"Yes, damn it, it's urgent."

"All right." His nasal twang seemed especially pronounced. "I'll meet you at the information desk."

When I entered Grand Central from Vanderbilt Avenue and looked

down from the top of the marble stairs into the cavernous station, I
spotted Angus's Stetson bobbing like a cork among the sea of com-
muters pouring in from Fifth Avenue. (My own Stetson never seemed
to acquire the natural, weatherbeaten look of his; and only he periodically wore a string tie to complete the Western effect.)

We reached the information desk almost simultaneously.

"Well, what's it all about?" He grunted as he set down his battered
briefcase, bulging as always with manuscripts and unanswered correspondence. It must have weighed a good twenty pounds.

"That thing will give you a heart attack one day," I said.

"I need the exercise." He patted his stomach and hitched up his
belt, causing his trouser cuffs to rise several inches above his shoes.

"Let's have a drink while we're talking," I said.

Angus glanced at the station clock and took out his heavy pocket
watch. "Damn watch is still running slow," he muttered. "Do you
know the only watches that really keep time?"

I shook my head.

"Railroad watches," he told me with satisfaction. "I've got two at
home."

We went down to the lower level of the station.

"Let's not drink at the bar," I said. "The restaurant's more comfort-
able."

The old-fashioned restaurant was pleasantly quiet and calm, as if
FBI informers and their confessions belonged to another world—
there were only a scattering of diners in the spacious room.

"You'd better order a double," I said. "You'll need it."

Angus told the waiter, "A double scotch. Glenlivet. With water."
He added: "And no ice. The last time I was here they put in ice."

"It wasn't me," said the waiter.

"Well, I don't care who it was," said Angus truculently.

"I'll have a scotch and soda, please," I said. "One shot."

Angus raised his eyebrows. "Not sherry? This really must be serious."

By the time our drinks arrived, I had briefly summarized the
Sacher meeting.

Angus's outraged expression showed the bare facts needed no dra-
matizing. "Why in hell," he snapped, "didn't they let us know about
the deadline before!"

"That's precisely what I asked."

"And what did Sacher say?"

"He hadn't any answer."

"What the hell makes them think Harvey's ready to give them an affidavit?"

"I asked that too. I said Harvey might decide we'd been stringing him along and walk out on us."

"You're damn right he might!"

"So what do you suggest?"

Angus took out a package of cigarettes and struck a match angrily. "We gave Harvey our word we'd publish the book. That's how it's going to be."

"What about the affidavit?"

He scowled, his thin lips pursed. "What an insufferable mess!" He summoned the waiter and ordered another double scotch. "How could anyone be so stupid—or just plain negligent?" he asked me. "You know what it is, don't you? It's not just the lawyers. The party leaders are calling the shots. Those boobs couldn't stand the idea of someone even talking with Matusow. They're like virtuous dowagers who cross the street to avoid meeting a reformed prostitute."

"The fact remains that the defendants will stay in jail if Harvey doesn't give the affidavit before February third. There'll be no chance of a retrial."

Angus absently stirred his drink with his finger. "Do you think he'd consider giving one now? You know his frame of mind better than I do."

"I'm no psychoanalyst."

"Thank God for that," he muttered.

"Sure, Harvey's changed. But I don't need to tell you how mixed up he is. We'd be crazy to pressure him, I know that."

"There's another problem," Angus said. "I'm hesitant to raise it—it seems selfish and commercial. But if Harvey gives the affidavit before the book is published, there's no question that it will cut back on the news value of the book. Our sales will depend on the publicity it will generate when it comes out. We've got no resources for advertising, and there's nothing as stale as yesterday's news. The book has a broader purpose than helping Jencks and others—it's the chance to break the informer racket once and for all. We don't want to jeopardize that possibility."

"I hadn't thought about the question of publicity," I said. "It presents a tough problem." In the end we agreed that we could not let that stand in the way of Harvey's giving an affidavit if he wanted to.

As we walked down the platform beside the train, Angus said, "One thing's clear. Harvey has to be told about the deadline. The problem is how to tell him without making him think we're pushing him on the affidavit."

"We've only one choice, as far as I can see," I said. "Tell him the whole story and leave the decision entirely to him."

"That's going to be one hell of a decision," said Angus.

Waiting outside the railroad car for the conductor to call all aboard, I told Angus, "I sure as hell wish I were spending the weekend with you—instead of breaking the news to Matusow. We could settle a few world problems and snare some snowshoe rabbits."

"They're hares, you know," he said. "The snowshoe or varying hare. *Lepus americanus*."

"Of course, if I'm not with you," I needled him, "you'll have time to draw up the final contract on the book. Seriously though, it's two months since we told Harvey you'd get it to him. It's not just that he's been asking for it. We may very well be needing it soon."

"Listen, I've had other things to—" Angus began in an annoyed tone. Then he smiled. "Don't worry. I'll get it done."

I broached the matter of the Flynn case with Harvey the following afternoon. He had finished his dictation for the day, and we were alone in his apartment. He was fussing around the fireplace, chattering cheerfully about his literary talents, when I said that something very important had come up. My tone must have indicated how important I thought it was because he promptly stopped what he was doing, looked at me searchingly and sat down.

He listened intently, without any visible reaction, as I told him what I had learned on my visit to Sacher's office about the February 3 deadline in the Flynn case and the need of his affidavit before that date. I had told Sacher, I said, that Angus and I were committed to publishing Matusow's book before he gave affidavits recanting his testimony in any court cases. "Of course," I said, "I didn't know anything about this damn deadline when I assured you there'd be no need for any affidavits before the book came out." I made no attempt to belittle the problems if he filed an affidavit within the designated time. "You'd have to finish writing the book in a month—you might not get the chance afterward. We'd have to rush it to press, because your affidavit would stir up all hell. In fact, there'd be no guarantee we could get the book out at all. The Justice Department may try to stop it altogether."

He waited for me to continue. "On the other hand, if you put off writing the affidavit until the book's published, your recantation will be worthless as far as getting a new trial for any of the defendants. That's the situation in a nutshell, Harvey. It's up to you to decide what to do. Angus and I will go along with whatever you decide."

Harvey heard me out in silence. He lit a cigarette and inhaled deeply. When he spoke, it was quietly, without any trace of his usual bravado. "Why did I say I wanted to write the book anyway, Al?" he asked. "I said I wanted to write it to undo the harm I'd done. Well, I obviously can't undo the harm in this case unless I give an affidavit before the deadline. It's that simple, isn't it? So I have to do it before that date, that's all."

He had put it plainly enough, but I understood how crucial a decision it was for him. For all he knew, he was at this point possibly sacrificing the book and everything it had come to mean to him. Perhaps all he had to look forward to now was a jail sentence for perjury. But he had made the choice; he had made it of his own volition and without hesitation.

As if reading my thoughts, he said: "There's just one favor, Al, I'd like to ask of you. If I do have to go to jail, will you—and maybe Riette—see my folks and explain why I'm going? You know, they really don't understand what I've done in the past or what I'm doing now. They don't think politically. They're just simple people."

"Of course I'll see them, Harvey. I'll be glad to," I said.

Late that night, as I drove homeward along the deserted highway under a chill, dark sky, I wondered why I was so moved by Matusow's decision. He had, after all, been an informer. He had betrayed his friends, lied for money, sent innocent individuals to jail, and

wronged countless others. There were enough suffering people in the
world who really deserved one's sympathy. Why did I feel compas-
sion for him?

I was still pondering the question when I got home. In the quiet of
my study before going to bed, I wrote in my journal: "Perhaps it's
because the inner torment of any human being—even one who has
done such harm—is painful to see. Perhaps it's because I've gradually, or all at once, become truly aware of the hidden turmoil in him,
of the wretched warping of his life, and of his lonely groping effort to
regain self-respect and human decency."

3. *Mr. and Mrs. Matusow*

In his book Harvey had made scant mention of his parents. "There
were only four of us in my family—my mother, father, my older
brother, Danny, and myself," he had written in the opening chapter.
"We lived in a middle-class section of the Bronx. Although I grew up
in the depression of the early 1930s, it didn't scar or hurt me as it did
others. We always had a clean, warm apartment, and I was unfamiliar
with the reality of slums and cold-water tenements. My father was a
merchant. He had a cigar store in downtown New York."

Harvey made few other references to his mother or father in the
book—almost as if they hadn't existed during his adolescent years or
when he had operated as an informer in the Communist party and
later made national news as a professional witness and aide to Senator
McCarthy. It was as though, consciously or unconsciously, he had
orphaned himself.

Only one passage dealt at any length with his parents or gave any
inkling to his relationship with them. It described an episode which
had occurred just prior to his first appearance before the House
Un-American Activities Committee, when the *New York Journal-
American* was about to serialize his "revelations" of his activities as a "youth organizer for the Reds." The passage read:

Howard Rushmore[18] [a *Journal-American* reporter] and I . . .
went to my parent's home in the Bronx, where we were met by a
photographer for the paper. A number of pictures were taken, but
the one that was used showed me planting a farewell kiss on my

mother's cheek as I held my black briefcase, supposedly containing my report on Communism.

This was the first indication my parents had that I was going to testify and that I would become a controversial national figure. They had never sympathized with my views on Communism but they tolerated them ... Their attitude was one of—well, let him have his head.

I thought it perhaps would please my parents to know I was no longer a Communist. But here again their attitude remained one of passive disagreement. They did not measure success by the number of newspaper headlines.

As I left my parents' home I could see the look of bewilderment on their faces. They didn't know what was going on. My sudden appearance, the popping of flashbulbs and then my hurried exit with the remark, "I don't have time to tell you about it now. Read about it in tomorrow's *Journal*."

During the time Harvey and I had been working together, I had come to feel he was still moving in and out of his parents' lives like a stranger. He seldom mentioned them; and when he did, though he voiced fondness and concern for them, he did so with an odd detachment. When they occasionally phoned, no matter how brief the conversation, he showed impatience to bring it to an end. He went infrequently to their home in the Bronx, or to the cigar stand they now operated in Manhattan (his father, he had told me, had lost his former shop as a result of financial reverses); and he seemed to regard each visit to his parents as an onerous duty which he postponed as long as possible and concluded with relief.

A few days after his decision to write the affidavit in the Flynn case, Harvey again brought up the subject of my going to see his parents.

"Like you say," he told me, "things may move pretty fast once the affidavit is filed in court. I've told my folks that I'm writing it. But it's hard for me to explain these things to them. And they're worried. I think it would help if you talked to them now."

"Whenever you say, Harvey. What about this afternoon?"

Harvey phoned and said we would be dropping by.

The afternoon was cold and gray. It had snowed the night before and the streets were awash with dirty slush. It made a slapping sound under the Sixth Avenue bus as we rode uptown from Greenwich Village. For once, in contrast to his usual garrulousness, Harvey was completely silent; and I couldn't help thinking—somewhat perversely—that perhaps we should visit his parents more often.

We got off at 34th Street and walked west. We stopped in front of an antiquated office building near Seventh Avenue.

Harvey turned to me. "My folks aren't young anymore," he said. He spoke hesitantly, and the dark rings under his eyes seemed accentuated. "They're here every morning at seven o'clock and they don't close up until seven at night. It's not easy on them."

"I understand," I told him. "I'll do the best I can."

He pushed his way through the revolving doors.

The fact that life had not dealt gently with Mr. and Mrs. Matusow was written indelibly on their faces. They came from behind the cigar stand—a small plump woman and a fragile man—and welcomed Harvey with an anxious tenderness. He returned his mother's kiss perfunctorily and, as she brushed something from his coat collar, helped himself to a package of cigarettes from the counter.

They were very pleased to meet me, they told me. Harvey had talked a lot about me. And how were my wife and three sons? Harvey had said what a lovely family I had. As they talked, their eyes kept darting toward Harvey. I felt there were questions they wanted to ask him but would probably have hesitated to even if I hadn't been there.

After a few minutes Harvey said abruptly to them, "I'm sorry, but I have to go. I've got an appointment I can't miss." He hadn't previously mentioned it to me. "Why don't you stay awhile, Al?"

Mrs. Matusow smiled tremulously. "You'll be coming to the house soon, Harvey?"

"As soon as I can, Mom, but you know how much work I've got to do on the book."

She nodded silently.

They watched him as he walked through the revolving doors and out to the street. A gust of cold air swept into the lobby.

Mrs. Matusow sighed. "You know, Mr. Kahn," she said softly, looking at me with dark, sorrowful eyes, "I lost two sons in the war. My oldest boy, Danny, was killed. He never came home. And when Harvey came back, I knew I'd lost him too. He'd changed that much. He was a different person." She shook her head, and her lips quivered. "He was a sweet child, a good boy. He never wanted to hurt anybody. I used to take him and his friends to the zoo on Sundays. He always wanted his friends to have a good time." She paused and sighed again. "I don't know what happened to him, Mr. Kahn. He was so strange after the war. He didn't want to talk to his father or me. He'd lock himself in his bedroom and hang a sign on the door—'Don't disturb.' The war did something to him, Mr. Kahn. When he went into the army he promised he'd find his brother—he was missing then. 'I'll find Danny, Mom,' he told me. And he did. He found where Danny was buried in Germany." She took my hand between her small plump ones. "You think that doesn't change a boy? To find the body of his brother and to see other boys killed. . . ."

In her quiet grieving voice she talked on about her second-born, her youngest and now only child—about how bright he'd been as a small boy, and what hopes they'd had for him, and how hard, how terribly hard, it all was to understand.

Her husband stood staring at the floor, nodding occasionally at something she said, weary resignation on his deeply lined face. Fluttering his bony hands, he murmured, "Who knows why these things happen? Who knows?"

From time to time customers approached the cigar stand, and Mrs. Matusow waited on them with a forced smile and some attempted sprightly phrase. At last, hesitantly, she asked me, "Is Harvey going to be in great trouble, Mr. Kahn?"

I wanted to console them. They had already had more than their share of grief. Yet nothing, I knew, would be more cruel than to arouse false hopes in them. "Harvey's made some serious mistakes," I said, feeling the sorry ineptness of my words. They nodded in a childlike way. "It's true that he's hurt others," I went on, "but the important thing is that now he's trying to remedy what he's done. And that's what you'd want him to do, isn't it?"

They waited for me to continue, their eyes never leaving my face.

"There's a young man whose name is Clinton Jencks," I said. "He's a friend of mine. He's married and he has two children. He was sentenced to five years in prison because of testimony Harvey gave against him. The testimony wasn't true." Mrs. Matusow shook her head sorrowfully. "Harvey's trying to keep Jencks from going to jail by telling the truth now," I said. "He's doing the same thing with other people he lied against. It's not easy to stand up and tell the whole world, 'I lied against these people.' That takes real courage. I know it sounds strange, but you've got reason to be proud of what Harvey's doing."

"Tell me, Mr. Kahn," asked Mrs. Matusow, "will Harvey go to jail?"

CHAPTER FIVE

BEFORE THE STORM

1. *Team Work*

Sufficient work attends the publishing of any book. Once the author's manuscript has been edited and copyedited, the format of the book must be styled, galleys proofread, jacket designed, pages printed and bound: arrangements must be made for sales, promotion and distribution. All of this takes time. And time was something of which we now had precious little.

Prior to learning the imminent deadline for a retrial motion in the Flynn case, Angus and I had considered early May the earliest feasible publication date for *False Witness* (the title chosen for Harvey's book)—and that was rushing things. Clearly, this date would no longer do. We now planned to announce Matusow's forthcoming book when his affidavits of recantation were filed in court the first week in February. The combination of these events, we were sure, would create a furor and the book would be in immediate demand.

Advancing the publication date of the book would involve major problems. But we had no choice. We decided to bring the book out in March. Since our firm's facilities were extremely limited, both in terms of office space and personnel (the latter consisted of Angus, a secretary and me), we set up a separate office to expedite publishing the book. Our office "annex" consisted of a two-room suite in the Chelsea Hotel, that old-fashioned edifice with its dark brick facade and wrought-iron balconies which was once the haunt of literary celebrities. Our rooms overlooking 23rd Street were well-suited to our purposes: one, spacious and high-ceilinged provided ample work space for several persons; the other, a smaller adjoining one, was secluded enough for Harvey to finish his work on the book and for general editorial purposes.

Harvey at first objected to working in the Chelsea. "I used to have appointments here," he explained embarrassedly, "with other government witnesses and FBI agents in the old days." Before long, however, as he set about putting the final touches on his manuscript, his attitude altered markedly. "You know, of course, Albert," he said to me one day, "that this is where Thomas Wolfe lived and work for quite a while. I told you, didn't I, that we both have the same birthday?" With his book nearing the printing stage, he was already discussing the possibility of writing a novel; and, perhaps stirred by this vision of a future career as a man of letters, he derived growing satisfaction from the literary traditions of his surroundings.

Ruth Sommers had agreed to manage affairs at the new office. She and I made our headquarters in the larger room, which, with characteristic efficiency, she quickly outfitted with typewriters, office supplies and extra telephones.

In a few days we were moving ahead on all fronts.

Having set for ourselves a production schedule of about a third the time normally required, we had recruited a team of volunteers to help us meet the deadline. All its members shared one goal—to see that Matusow's disclosures reached the public as soon as possible.

A former member of the Teachers' Union, whose professional career had been abruptly ended by the "loyalty" purge in the schools, began checking the accuracy of names, dates, and other factual data in Matusow's manuscript. A veteran newspaper proofreader, whose proficiency at his craft was matched by his anti-McCarthy sentiments, was going over the finished chapters in the early morning hours after leaving his regular job. A professional book designer set about styling the format. A talented commercial artist volunteered to design the jacket.

Arthur Kahn, no relation but a close friend, who had helped with the research on my book *High Treason,* joined the team. Himself an author, and a brilliant if somewhat pedantic scholar, he was copyediting the manuscript, preparing an index for the book, and supervising a variety of production matters with his usual energy and competence.

(Arthur's varied experience included service in the OSS during World War II, afterward becoming chief editor of the Intelligence Information Division of the U.S. military government in Germany.)

In addition to his many skills, Arthur brought to the undertaking a sardonic sense of humor which—as the going became increasingly hectic and tempers strained—had the virtue of making us see ourselves in clearer perspective. "You have to look at things *sub specie aeternitatis,*" he told me one day after I had had a tense argument with Harvey. "Rome *did* have its decline and fall—Julius Caesar is dust. And you'll soon be dust too, you know." The one problem with Arthur was that, being a perfectionist in matters of syntax, he found in almost every paragraph of the manuscript some phrase or use of punctuation that caused him to assert sternly: "I'm sorry—this is just not English."

"For God's sake," I told Angus (who was still holding the fort at the Cameron & Kahn office), "we'd better get the book out of Arthur's hands before he persuades Harvey to write a new one!"

Soon, throughout the day and well into the night, two stenographers were pounding away at typewriters, making stencils of the entire manuscript, so that when the manuscript went to the typesetter we would have mimeographed copies available for editorial and promotional purposes, or for any special contingency that might arise.

The task force had come to include one other member—with duties not ordinarily associated with book publishing. His function was to act as our author's bodyguard.

I had become increasingly concerned about Harvey's safety, and I managed to communicate at least some of my anxiety to Angus (though later he told me he was never fully convinced of how serious I was). If Matusow had suffered no mishap to date, I felt, it was perhaps due more to luck than to circumspection. It seemed high time to afford him proper protection against possible inconvenience from those who might want to forestall his revelations. I had learned, moreover, that FBI agents had rented an apartment in a building across the street from the Chelsea; several members of our staff were being followed frequently.

At my suggestion, Harvey stopped sleeping at his Greenwich Village apartment and came home with me every night (an arrangement that soon had Riette and me longing for a little privacy); during the daytime Harvey was left alone as little as possible. But I was far from satisfied with these makeshift precautions. I decided he should have a bodyguard day and night.

The first person I thought of for the job was a friend, Charles Allen, a resourceful young journalist and former associate editor of *The Nation,* who had been a professional athlete and paratrooper. However, while Allen knew how to take care of himself, the idea of taking care of Matusow did not appeal to him. "Guard that stool pigeon!" he snorted. "Why, I'd probably drop him down a stairwell, myself!" With such inclinations—and standing six feet and weighing 200 pounds—he clearly was not suited for the job.

Next I approached Herb Tank, a former merchant seaman who at thirty-two was already well known in leftwing circles as a playwright and drama critic. Like Chuck Allen, Herb's talents were not limited to the realm of literature: he had at one time been a boxer. If I saw in Herb the means of guarding Matusow against dramatic misadventures, Herb saw in him dramatic material for a new play. Our interests merged—Herb became Harvey's bodyguard.

Actually, Herb preferred the title of "companion" to that of "bodyguard"—something in the latter characterization perhaps offended his literary sensibilities. But he applied himself to the job with such zeal and wariness, never letting Harvey out of his sight and periodically spiriting him out of everyone else's, that I sometimes felt he either found the role of bodyguard more engrossing than he would admit or was, in real life, rehearsing the bodyguard's part for his contemplated play.

A welcome bonus resulted from Herb's presence: Harvey and I now saw less of each other. We had been together almost constantly for more than two months, and our increasing squabbles over picayune matters indicated I was getting on his nerves as much as he was on mine.

With work pressures mounting and affairs becoming increasingly hectic, tempers in general were getting strained. As Ruth put it, surveying our crowded quarters, "It's a crisis of overpopulation."

2. *The Affidavits*

In the midst of the feverish preparations to get his book to press, Harvey had started to draft affidavits admitting he had lied at the Flynn and Jencks trials. "If I'm going to write the Flynn one now," he said, "I might as well get the other out of the way too. In fact, I'll do the Jencks one first."

Poker-faced, he added: "You don't suppose Witt will have any objection to getting it, do you?" He asked that Witt indicate the correct legal terminology for the opening and closing paragraphs of his affidavits. "He doesn't need to tell me about anything else. I think I know more about this sort of thing than most lawyers. Anyway, I want it in my own words."

As soon as he had completed the draft of the Jencks affidavit, Harvey showed it to me. "See what you think of it," he said with studied casualness.

Addressed to the federal court in El Paso, Texas, it opened with these words:

> I make this affidavit in support of the motion of the defendant for a new trial, and to do what I can to remedy the harm I have done to Clinton E. Jencks and to the administration of justice.
>
> I appeared as a witness for the Government against the defendant in the course of the trial in this Court in January, 1954, on an indictment charging Mr. Jencks with having filed a false non-Communist affidavit with the National Labor Relations Board....
>
> The matters I testified to were either false or not entirely true, and were known to me to be false or not entirely true, at the time I so testified.

The affidavit recapitulated Harvey's testimony that in the summer of 1950 he had held conversations with Jencks in which the latter revealed himself to be a party member. Harvey went on to state that these charges were completely untrue. "There was no basis for my stating that Clinton E. Jencks was a member of the Communist party at the time I so stated in court."

The affidavit concluded: "I am willing to appear and testify to the truth of the above matters at any time."

Harvey hadn't taken his eyes off me as I read. When I looked up from the page, he said, "What do you think?"

I didn't know how to answer him. I put my hand on his shoulder. "Those few sheets of paper will probably save Clint five years in prison."

A few days later, Harvey's draft of his affidavit in the Flynn case was also ready. It recounted how at this Smith Act trial of thirteen Communist leaders in the summer of 1952 he had testified that several of the defendants had discussed with him plans "to forcibly overthrow" the U.S. government and to sabotage production "in the event of any war with the Soviet Union." All of his testimony to this effect, the affidavit declared, was false.

His perjurious testimony against one of the defendants, continued the affidavit, had been induced by Assistant U.S. Attorney Roy Cohn[19] (later chief counsel on the McCarthy subcommittee), who had helped prepare Harvey as a government witness.

Harvey related that at the trial he had testified that one of the defendants, the Communist publisher Alexander Trachtenberg, had urged him to promote the sale of Andrei Vyshinskii's book, *The Law of the Soviet State,* asserting it contained directives for the overthrow of capitalism. Cohn, said Harvey's affidavit, had first broached the subject of the book in the presence of several other Justice Department officials:

> A subsequent conversation concerning the book occurred in Roy Cohn's office. Cohn pointed to a passage in the book and told me that the passage was important in proving the government's case. He then asked me if I had discussed anything with Trachtenberg which would tie him with this passage, and I said, "No," I had not. Nevertheless, thereafter, in several sessions with Cohn, we developed the answer which I gave in my testimony, tying Trachtenberg to that passage. We both knew that Trachtenberg had never made the statements I attributed to him in my testimony.

Like Harvey's affidavit in the Jencks case, this one concluded with the statement that he was willing to appear in court and testify about the truth of its contents.

I phoned Harry Sacher and Nat Witt and told them I was sending them, by messenger, copies of Harvey's affidavits in their respective cases.

Nat called me back shortly after he'd received the affidavit of Harvey's testimony regarding Jencks. "Tell Harvey the affidavit's terrific. I've been in touch with Mine-Mill headquarters in Denver. We'd like to file a retrial motion at the end of this month. Is that okay with Harvey?"

Harvey said it was fine with him.

3. *Washington Interlude*

On January 18 I received a phone call from Abe Fortas of the Washington law firm of Arnold, Fortas & Porter.[20] Its name was well known to me. During the postwar witch-hunt, this firm—unlike most prominent law firms—had repeatedly handled controversial cases involving the defense of constitutional rights.

Fortas told me he had learned we were planning to publish Matusow's book. He and his colleagues, he said, had reason to be interested. They were acting counsel for Owen Lattimore. Early in 1952, at a Senate hearing, Matusow had charged the noted authority on Far Eastern affairs with having Communist ties. Other government witnesses repeated the accusation. When Lattimore denied the charge, the Justice Department brought perjury proceedings against him. "Possibly," said Fortas, "Matusow's book contains some material of importance to the Lattimore case. We were wondering if we might be able to see the manuscript."

It happened that Matusow had included in the manuscript a detailed account of his testimony against Lattimore, revealing he had deliberately lied in charging that Lattimore's books were "official Communist party guides on Asia."

I told Fortas I'd be glad to bring a copy of the manuscript to Washington.

* * *

I was curious to see what Fortas and his partners thought about Matusow's book. Besides being eminently able attorneys, they'd had considerable experience in political affairs: Thurman Arnold, author of several books on law and politics, formerly had been a federal judge and Assistant U.S. Attorney General; Abe Fortas had been Under-Secretary of the Interior during the days of the New Deal; Paul Porter had held government posts under Roosevelt. Whatever else, their reaction to Harvey's manuscript would not be that of unsophisticates.

The offices of Arnold, Fortas & Porter occupied a handsome Georgian house in a quiet residential district in Washington. I was received by Abe Fortas. He was a brisk, slender man who gave the impression of being fully aware of his own capabilities, accustomed to making decisions not only for himself but for others as well. His manner was politely reserved.

Judge Arnold was out to lunch but expected back soon, said Fortas. He led the way to the judge's office. It was a spacious room, furnished with restrained elegance, overlooking a small courtyard and garden. While awaiting Judge Arnold I described to Fortas the circumstances under which I had met Matusow, and some of the complexities of our subsequent dealings with him. Periodically Fortas interposed questions that reflected his growing interest and a perceptive curiosity about Matusow's character and motivations. We had been talking about half an hour when a large, slow-moving man with graying hair and grizzled mustache entered the room. With his ruddy look and slightly rumpled tweeds, you might have taken him for a well-to-do English squire. Actually, Judge Arnold hailed from Laramie, Wyoming.

I had brought along a copy of my book, *High Treason,* to give to Judge Arnold. It contained a section, I told him, dealing with his work as assistant attorney general in exposing the collusion between American monopolies and Nazi cartels. He thanked me warmly for the book.

"Mr. Kahn has been telling me an extremely interesting story," said Fortas.

"Is that so?" said Judge Arnold, peering at me from under bushy eyebrows as he leaned back in the chair behind his desk.

Fortas had me repeat the whole story.

Every so often Judge Arnold snorted with surprise or gruffly ejaculated, "Remarkable!"

After a while he said, "Where's Porter? What's he doing? He ought to hear this!" He reached for the telephone. "Ask Mr. Porter to come down as soon as he's free."

At one point when I was describing Matusow's role in the Flynn case, Judge Arnold cocked his head to one side and inquired affably: "Tell me, Mr. Kahn, have you ever been called a Red?"

"God, yes! So have you, of course. Though probably with less reason."

He chuckled. "Is that so?" He picked up his copy of *High Treason* and looked at the quotations on the jacket from reviews of my previous books.

"Those reviews," I told him, "are pre-McCarthy vintage."

Judge Arnold passed the book to Fortas. "Take a look at this, Abe," he said solemnly, pointing to the quote. "Here's what the critics said about Mr. Kahn in the days before McCarthy."

It sounded a little like an obituary.

We were joined by a tall, loose-limbed man, who sat down heavily on the arm of the leather couch. Judge Arnold addressed him. "Paul, you must hear Mr. Kahn's story about Matusow. You've never heard anything quite like it."

As the afternoon wore on, I related for the third time how the book project, *False Witness,* had come into being.

I read from the manuscript the section dealing with Harvey's testimony against Lattimore. He had told this "complete falsehood," Harvey related, to make news by "deliberately dropping big names." The passage continued: "The results of my testimony were most gratifying to me when I saw the newspaper headlines: 'MATUSOW SAYS HE BELIEVES LATTIMORE RED', 'LATTIMORE BOOK HAS OFFICIAL RED OK, WITNESS SAYS'. . . . I made the front pages across the United States, thanks to Lattimore."

The three lawyers exchanged glances.

"There ought to be a thorough investigation of this whole damned professional witness business," drawled Judge Arnold.

Before leaving Washington that day, I met with Stewart Alsop. The syndicated column he wrote with his brother would, I felt, be a good means of breaking the news of Matusow's forthcoming book. The Alsops not only commanded national attention but had written some trenchant columns on the Justice Department's use of paid professional witnesses. Despite their ultra-conservative views on foreign affairs, they had repeatedly spoken out against McCarthyite encroachments on constitutional rights at home.

Stewart Alsop's reaction to my story was quite unlike that of Judge Arnold and his associates. He listened with cold detachment, his slender, handsome face expressionless, his aloof mien suggesting not so much hauteur as an aristocrat's calm acceptance of his high station. From his dry queries, I gathered he considered extreme skepticism the hallmark of the journalistic profession.

"If I were to write something about Matusow," Alsop reflected after I had told him Harvey's affidavit in the Jencks case was to be filed in court within ten days, "I'm not so sure how soon I could run it." It all depended, he said, on what material his brother, Joseph, sent from the Far East. "We're expecting a major incident over the weekend." He implied that some international crisis, possibly the outbreak of open hostilities between the major powers, might occur at any minute. "In that event," he said soberly, "we'll have to postpone the column on Matusow."

I could not deny that the start of a third world war would be more newsworthy than Matusow's recantation.

Other possible contingencies troubled Alsop.

"How do we know that Matusow won't go back on these admissions and claim the Communists put him up to all of this?"

I said there was no guarantee but I was convinced of Matusow's sincerity. "Then, too, we have documents to substantiate what he says, and there are his affidavits."

"It is a pity, you know," he mused, "that some other publisher isn't bringing out Matusow's book. It would have been better if it had been published by one of the old established firms."

Apparently to make sure I wouldn't get the wrong impression from his interest in the Matusow case, Alsop stressed that he and his brother had been in the forefront of the fight against Communism. "We helped expose the Communists' efforts to seize control of the CIO, you know. And I don't doubt that this fellow Jencks is a Communist. Or that if he isn't now, he was until recently. He has taken the Fifth Amendment, hasn't he?"

It was my understanding, I said, that the exercise of this constitutional privilege wasn't intended to connote guilt of anything. My patience was wearing thin, and I was beginning to doubt he would use the story at all.

Then pensively he said: "Of course, that isn't the point—I mean, whether or not he used the Fifth. The point is that if Matusow lied against Jencks, and if Jencks was unjustly sentenced on this account, the sentence should be reversed."

His words took me by surprise. I realized his patrician manner had led me to underestimate him.

Alsop went on: "Could I have a copy of Matusow's manuscript? I think I may do a column or two on it."

4. *Meeting in Denver*

On January 26, two days before Matusow's affidavit in the Jencks case was due to be filed in court, I flew to Denver to attend an executive board meeting of the Mine-Mill union. I had been invited to discuss the distribution and promotion of Matusow's book in the union.

With events moving swiftly toward a climax, Angus and I had a special interest in the Mine-Mill meeting. We had sent mimeographed copies of Harvey's manuscript to the union's officers and wanted to find out the total Mine-Mill order now that they had read the book. Much depended on the size of the union's order. Our firm's financial resources were, as usual, virtually nonexistent; our credit was strained to the breaking point; and, what with the myriad tasks of rushing Harvey's book to press, we'd had little opportunity to get advance orders other than the initial Mine-Mill one for 2,000 copies. We had a manuscript with the potential of becoming a best seller—and we didn't have enough money in the bank to pay for the printing.

As my plane headed west, I thought about other aspects of the Mine-Mill meeting. No American trade union was more bitterly familiar with the role of informers. Years of grim labor struggles in mining camps and company towns of the west had bred in the union's members a fierce hatred of labor spies, stool pigeons and secret police operatives. In recent years, as one of the most militant unions in the country, Mine-Mill had been the frequent target of congressional investigations and federal court actions based largely on the perjurious testimony of informer-witnesses. For these trade unionists the role of the informer was no academic question of constitutional law, but one affecting their ability to earn a living and feed their families.

Matusow had probably spread more slander against the Mine-Mill union than had any other professional witness, and his lying testimony had already resulted in a five-year prison term for one of their officials. Others of their leaders were also now facing prison sentences on similar charges. What would be the attitude of the Mine-Mill members toward Harvey now that he had recanted his testimony?

There was a charged atmosphere at Mine-Mill headquarters. The whole office staff obviously knew about Matusow's affidavit of recantation in the Jencks case. Stenographers were busily collating mimeographed press releases to be distributed to newspapers, wire services and radio-TV newscasters as soon as the affidavit was presented in court. The forthcoming issue of the union's weekly organ was devoted largely to excerpts from Matusow's affidavit and manuscript, and the paper's front page featured reproductions of past newspaper headlines that had heralded Harvey's lurid charges against Jencks and the union.

I was ushered into a large conference room where the executive board meeting was already under way. Some forty Mine-Mill officials were seated around two long tables. Among them were several friends and acquaintances of mine: Maurice Travis, secretary-treasurer of the union, massive and somber-looking, wearing a black patch over the eye he had lost when attacked by strikebreakers (known as one of the most militant trade unionists in the country, he at present faced three jail sentences on political charges); Vice-President Asbury Howard, a balding, rugged black man; Vice-President Orville Larson, a ruddy-faced giant with a shock of graying hair; district organizer Al Pezzati, dark, slender, scholarly in appearance. Chairing the meeting was the union president, John Clark. A short, compact, bespectacled man who had gone to work in the mines as a boy in the early 1900s, he looked more like a Baptist minister than a labor leader.

While Clark was introducing me before I addressed the meeting, Travis leaned over toward me. "Keep it brief," he told me tersely. "We've got a hell of an agenda." I did my best to follow Travis's advice. I related a few facts about my dealings with Matusow, summarized the content of his book, mentioned the publication date we now hoped to meet, and sat down.

Immediately, board members began bombarding me with questions, whose nature and profusion indicated far less concern than Travis's with the crowded state of the agenda. Most of them were unrelated to the union's concern with the case. How sincere did I think Matusow was? Why had he gotten divorced from his millionairess wife? Had he really joined the Mormon church? (A sizable portion of the union's membership in Utah were Mormons.) How could one be sure Matusow wouldn't revert to his former role? While some board members voiced doubts as to the extent of the change in Matusow, few evidenced hostility toward him. Much to my surprise, a number of the speakers seemed actually sorry for him.

Only a couple of passing references were made to what I had expected would be the main topic of discussion—the sale of Matusow's book in the union.

After the meeting Travis took me aside. "You sure messed things up!" he growled. "You were supposed to ask for an extra order."

"I thought the meeting would settle that," I said lamely.

"When you want something, ask for it."

The next morning I met with the union's top officers. They agreed the union would increase its initial order by 5,000 copies.

"It's a queer thing," Clark told me before I left Denver, "that we've been talking like we have about a man who was a stool pigeon. Perhaps you've heard about the way informers were treated in the mines in the old days. They weren't shown much mercy." The Mine-Mill president puffed reflectively on his pipe. "But when a man wants to mend his ways, you know, he should be given the chance. And if you're right in what you feel about this guy, he deserves to be helped."

Clark added with a thin smile that there had even been some talk of inviting Matusow to the approaching annual convention of the union. "Of course, that's out of the question. Some of the boys don't forget too easily. Matusow might get hurt."

CHAPTER SIX

MAJOR EXPLOSIONS

1. *The Story Breaks*

On Friday, January 28, 1955, the news of Harvey Matusow's recantation became known to millions of Americans. That day, Stewart Alsop devoted his nationally syndicated column to an article entitled "Legal Lying." It began:

> The youthful former Communist, former professional witness and former aide to Sen. Joseph R. McCarthy is currently writing a remarkable political confession which may cause major explosions. For the author of this confession, Harvey Matusow, calmly explains how he made a business of bearing false witness and how the American government made his business a profitable one, courtesy of the American taxpayer.

After citing examples of the book's revelations, Alsop commented:

> ... He has documentation for much of his amazing story. And the story is also inherently credible, simply because Matusow himself is the chief object of his own accusations.
> At any rate, Matusow's revelation simply cannot be ignored, either by Congress or by the Justice Department.

The column concluded:

Matusow's confession is likely to initiate a serious investigation
of this new postwar profession of the informer, and this could have
good results for the political health of the United States.[21]

Alsop's prediction that Matusow's admission might cause "major ex-
plosions" was to be swiftly confirmed. On the very day Alsop's column appeared, Matusow's affidavit in the Jencks case was being filed
in federal court in El Paso, Texas, with a motion for a new trial. The
magistrate who had presided at the original trial, Judge E.R. Thomason, set March 7 for a hearing on the motion.

Though we had anticipated that these events would cause something of a stir, we were hardly prepared for the storm that followed.
Few radio or TV newscasters that Friday night failed to mention
Matusow's recantation. Next day every wire service carried the story.
The weekend papers were full of it. Monday morning, Matusow's
affidavit stating he had lied in the Flynn case and been persuaded to
do so by Assistant U.S. Attorney Roy Cohn, was filed in federal
court in New York City. Judge Edward Dimock, who had presided at
the original trial, set March 10 for a hearing on the retrial motion.

The second affidavit made front-page news from coast to coast.
The faces of the dark, youthful ex-informer, Matusow, and the dark,
youthful ex-inquisitor, Cohn, peered forth from newspapers and TV
screens in every city and town. Millions of words about Matusow
began pouring into print and over the air as columnists, feature-story
writers, and radio-TV commentators recounted the details of his career and speculated on the political consequences of his disclosures.

The manager of our press clipping service, who was aware of the
limited resources of Cameron & Kahn, telephoned our office. "How
many clips do you want on this Matusow story?" he asked me ner-
vously. "I mean, you could run up quite a bill. The way things look
now, there could be several thousand before the end of the week."

The estimate was unquestionably accurate. No current event was
more widely featured in the news.

Overnight, the affair of Harvey Matusow had become a national
scandal.

It was hard to believe that only a few days before, a bare handful
of individuals had known the details of the Matusow story.

* * *

"What's happening," Angus observed when we met to discuss developments, "isn't just another political scandal. It's more significant
than that. Now everybody's going to have his say. You'll see, this is
only the beginning. The dam's broken."

The newspaper editorials that were piling up seemed to bear out
Angus's prediction. The comment of *The New York Times* was typical:

> The shabby business of the paid professional informer, which
> has received new dimensions under governmental encouragement
> during the past few years, has been given a blow by one of the
> well-known practitioners of the art who now says he has been lying
> all along. . . .
>
> It is essential in the interests of elementary fairness that the ef-
> fects of Matusow's worthless testimony be erased from every case
> in which he was seriously involved.

Other papers called for a thorough investigation of the Matusow case
and upbraided the Justice Department for its wholesale use of informer-witnesses.

"How many Americans have been unjustly convicted on the basis
of Matusow's testimony?" demanded the *Washington Post and Times
Herald,* which had been consistently critical of the professional witness system. "How many others have been sent to prison or condemned before congressional investigating committees by other
former Communist perjurers who, like Matusow, decide to make witnessing a lucrative career?"

In one of the most trenchant editorials, the *Milwaukee Journal*
stated:

> A shocking thing increasingly stands out. . . . Lying has been
> made easy by the Government, the gullible, and the self-appointed
> saviors of the country.
>
> There has been in this nation a willingness and even an eager-
> ness to suspect anyone and everyone. . . . That fervor for witch-
> hunting has invited irresponsible, pathological or sinister
> individuals like Matusow to smear, falsify and fictionalize. . . .
>
> The manner in which Matusow was used and encouraged by men
> like Senator McCarthy and Roy Cohn is a matter of record. How
> could they have helped knowing that some of the things he said
> were lies?. . . . The same can be said for the Justice Department.

As was to be expected, there were some newspapers whose indignation was directed not against the government for using liars like Matusow as expert witnesses, but against Matusow for revealing how he had been used. One such paper, the *Knoxville Journal,* said:

> We suspect that not many citizens will be much concerned by the revelation that Matusow is an admitted perjurer. The "confession" of perjury, however, serves as a reminder . . . that lying and deception are the accepted tools of Communism and Communists. . . .
>
> Most of us will feel that the ends of justice will be well served if Matusow . . . is now sent to the penitentiary for a term of years and preferably given a cell in close proximity to some of those other traitors in whose trials he testified.

One couldn't deny the ingenuity of the logic in holding Matusow's victims responsible for his crimes against them and urging—in the name of justice—that he be jailed not for committing but for confessing those crimes. Hardly less ingenious was the theory advanced to the press by Representative Francis E. Walters for Matusow's apostasy. According to the congressman, Harvey had obviously been planted by the Communist party as an FBI informer and government witness "to discredit congressional investigations." The doubtful likelihood of the party's assigning Harvey to help imprison its own leaders didn't deter Walters from urging that the Justice Department indict him for his part in "this sinister conspiracy." (The congressman's judgment in the matter was possibly influenced by the fact that he himself was chairman of the House Un-American Activities Committee when this body had introduced Matusow to the American public as an expert witness.)

In Washington, Justice Department officials were besieged by reporters demanding some comment on Matusow's recantation. The officials promised that the matter would be investigated. "An aide to Attorney General Brownell," wryly noted the *New York Post,* "made it clear that the government does not intend to employ Matusow's services as an 'expert' pending its inquiry."

From his New York law office, Roy Cohn, who had recently relinquished his job as Senator McCarthy's counsel, hurried into print with an indignant denial that he had encouraged Matusow to lie in the Flynn case. "I left for Europe," he declared, "before I even knew he was to be a witness." He discreetly refrained from mentioning that prior to his departure he had—as assistant U.S. attorney—spent days with Matusow grooming him for his trial testimony. "Matusow's accusation," Cohn added, "is just another Communist maneuver."

"Maybe so," commented the *Washington Post*, "but it would have been better if Mr. Cohn had been equally skeptical when Matusow pointed his finger at other Americans."

Perhaps more noteworthy than Cohn's protestation of purity was the reaction of some of those "other Americans" to Matusow's public admission that he had given false testimony against them. In his column in the Mine-Mill paper, the union's president, John Clark, wrote:

> In this case, we see a man willingly facing the charge of perjury and a possible jail sentence—in a sweeping denial of the evidence he had sworn to—in order "to do what I can to remedy the harm I have done...."
> It doesn't take a man to inform against his fellow workers. Mr. Matusow must have the core of a real human being to take the drastic step he has taken....

And in a letter to Harvey, Clint Jencks wrote: "I admire your courage in doing what you're doing.... I'm aware that a hard road still lies ahead of you and many of us who have been your victims.... Thank you for what you are doing, and for what you have yet to do."

2. *On the Air*

Up until January 1955, the existence of the publishing firm of Cameron & Kahn had been little known outside liberal and left-wing circles and the dossiers of certain federal agencies. Now this comparative obscurity abruptly ended. All at once our modest publishing enterprise became the focus of national attention. So many things began happening simultaneously, and one development so swiftly followed another, that the days had a blurred, kaleidoscopic quality. Our office functioned around the clock. We ate with a sandwich in one hand and a telephone in the other, and we took it for granted that on leaving the Chelsea Hotel for a breath of air, we would find parked outside an automobile whose two occupants, sitting like unsmiling twins, had the unmistakable stamp of the FBI.

Throughout the day and late into the night we were bombarded with phone calls. A Wisconsin newspaper phoned for details on Matusow's 1952 campaign activities on behalf of Senator McCarthy; a newspaper in Salt Lake City wanted material on Matusow's testimony at a Senate committee hearing in the Utah capital; *Life* magazine requested photographs of Matusow as an infant, teenager and soldier in army uniform, but all I could offer was a photo of Harvey with his beard.

The chief of the Washington bureau of CBS called to inquire if Matusow was "hiding out." Justice Department officials, he told me, had indicated he was, but I advised him that Harvey was in the adjoining room making final corrections in the manuscript of his book.

Matusow meanwhile was also becoming an international celebrity.

A British publisher called by transatlantic phone and, through crackling static, asked about acquiring the rights to *False Witness* for "the Empire."

The newspaper *France-Soir* cabled from Paris asking for galleys of Matusow's book for possible serialization.

An Italian magazine solicited a photograph of Matusow "at work on his book—or, preferably, with a girlfriend."

Peter Freuchen, the Danish explorer who was acting as United Nations correspondent for the Copenhagen newspaper, *Politken,* invited me to his office to discuss his newspaper's serializing the book. He thumbed through the manuscript, frowning; with his massive head and unruly beard he looked like Thor himself. "I do not think my paper would want to print it," he rumbled. "The subject is too degrading for Danish readers."

With requests to interview Matusow mounting hourly, we decided to call a press conference at which Matusow would appear and answer all questions. We announced that the conference would take place on the afternoon of February 3 at the Biltmore Hotel.

We immediately received calls from the TV networks saying they wanted to conduct their own interviews with Matusow. To avoid any conflict with the press conference, they proposed filming their interviews beforehand and telecasting them afterwards. Interviews by

CBS, ABC, and United Press Movietone News were scheduled for the day before the Biltmore conference.

Up to this point Harvey had been in a high state of excitement over the furor he was causing. "It's fabulous, simply fabulous!" he exclaimed, shaking his head in wonder. "Did you ever see so much publicity? We've got an international smash hit. You'd have to start a war to beat it!" Whenever he left the hotel—still under the alert guardianship of Herb Tank—he returned with his arms laden with newspapers. Seated on the floor, he methodically scissored all items dealing with his case, read them aloud whether anyone was listening or not, and added them to an already mountainous pile of clippings. With a certain embarrassment he told me, "It's different now, Al, from what it used to be. Then I just wanted headlines for their own sake. But now I've got reason to be proud of these stories."

As the time for his TV interviews approached, however, Harvey began to show signs of nervousness. He had shaved off his beard that same morning. He speculated about the attitude of the interviewers and the questions they would ask. How antagonistic were the interviewers likely to be? Would their questions be slanted? Did I think he would get the chance to say what he really wanted to? If I was not entirely successful in allaying his anxiety, it was perhaps because of my own. This would, after all, be his first public appearance since his recantation.

The first TV interview took place at the UP Movietone News studio.

It became clear almost immediately that, at least in this instance, our apprehensions were unwarranted. The questions put to Harvey were impartial and to the point. How had Harvey happened to become an FBI informer in the first place? What were some of the lies he had told as a government witness? Why had he now decided to recant?

If Harvey was still nervous, he showed no sign of it. Seated behind a desk in the office of one of the studio executives, and looking himself like a young executive in his dark suit and bow tie, he seemed completely at ease as he gazed unblinkingly into the klieg lights and answered the interviewer's questions. "I sacrificed the reputations of others to satisfy my own ends," he said with a strangely detached air. "I didn't care what happened to Owen Lattimore and the others. I only cared what happened to me. I was paid to lie, and that's what I did. . . . Well, I finally decided to quit the racket, and that's what I've done. Now I'm trying to set things straight."

When we left the studio, Harvey was in high spirits. "Those questions were really fair," he exulted as we hurried across town for the CBS interview. "He just wanted to get at the truth. And I think I really spelled it out!"

The questions at CBS were much the same. The newscaster conducting the interview had the air of a harried impresario as he ordered the cameraman about. Prematurely bald, with a pink, unlined face, he seemed chiefly preoccupied with the angle from which his own profile was filmed.

While Harvey was recounting some of his exploits as a professional witness, one of the TV technicians told me in a low voice, "We had a stool pigeon in our union who testified at one of those congressional hearings. Said the union was run by Reds and all that sort of shit. Several guys got fired from their jobs." At the end of the interview, he handed me a slip of paper on which the TV crew had written their names and addresses. When Matusow's book was published, he asked, could I send them copies?

Our first direct confrontation with the government was to take place, incongruously enough, at the ABC interview. As Harvey and I were approaching the building where the interview was scheduled, we both noticed two men following us down the street. They were youthful, neatly groomed and wore gray fedoras. In the lobby of the building lounged several of their brethren, conspicuously trying to look inconspicuous. Two of them stepped into the elevator with us. They got off when we did.

"I recognized one of those guys in the elevator," said Harvey in a low voice as we walked down the hall. "He's an FBI agent I used to report to."

"I think I'll ask them if they're lost," I told Harvey. "Or suggest they get lost."

"Let it go, Al," he said. "It won't do any good."

I was beginning to feel annoyed. I had long since been aware that various government agencies kept detailed files on my writings, lectures and other activities, and I had grown accustomed to having my phone tapped and mail opened.[22] But such forms of surveillance were usually accompanied by a certain discretion. And there was something about being so openly trailed by these public servants—whose salaries my taxes helped pay—that I found insolent. I wondered whether Nat Witt would be in his office in case his legal services were required.

In a room cluttered with television equipment Harvey and I were received by the ABC news commentator, a handsome, grayhaired man with a friendly manner. "Why don't we first talk the program over, Harvey?" he suggested. "Maybe you've some idea how you'd like it handled. It's not the ordinary sort of interview. I mean, you must have some pretty personal feelings about what you've been through."

They sat down and began an animated conversation.

There was a knock on the door. A member of the TV crew opened it. The two FBI agents stepped into the room. One of them walked in a leisurely manner over to Harvey. "I've got something for you, Matusow," he said.

The room had become suddenly quiet.

The FBI agent handed Harvey a piece of paper and started to walk away.

"Hey, wait a minute," said Harvey aggressively. "Wait until I've read it."

The agent stopped and turned around, running the brim of his hat through his fingers.

Harvey took what seemed a long time to read the document. Then he said, "Okay, you can go now."

As the door closed, Harvey flourished the document with a forced smile. "It's a subpoena," he announced. "I've got to appear before a federal grand jury tomorrow."

The Justice Department had made its first move.

While the interview was being filmed, I went into an adjoining room and called Nat Witt. I told him what had happened. He didn't sound surprised. "It's obvious what they're up to," he said. "The

Justice Department wants to get Harvey behind closed doors in a grand jury room before he gets the chance to testify in open court on either of the retrial motions. That way, they figure, they can put the pressure on him. Maybe shut him up—get him to recant his recantation. Okay, we'll have to move fast. I'll call the lawyers in the Flynn case. They can try to get Judge Dimock to postpone Harvey's appearance before the grand jury."

"One question," I said.

"Shoot."

"Can you recommend a lawyer for Harvey? He'll be needing one now. Angus and me, too, for that matter."

"Sure," he said. "Give Stan Faulkner a ring. You know who he is, don't you? You couldn't have a better guy on a case like this."

"One other thing," I said. "Is it customary for FBI agents to serve subpoenas?"

"Hell, no," he said. "That was for effect. Maybe to put the heat on Harvey and you. Maybe to make the TV guys wonder about going ahead with their show."

"That's what I thought," I said.

"Well, let's not waste time. There's work to be done."[23]

That same afternoon, attorneys for the Flynn case defendants appeared before Judge Dimock and asked that he postpone or quash Matusow's grand jury subpoena. The Justice Department, they contended, had acted "not in good faith but solely for the purpose of eliciting before the grand jury all the evidence that the defendants might want to present at the retrial hearing." They also made the point that the grand jury proceedings could be used to intimidate Matusow before he had testified in public.

We were not optimistic about the prospective ruling. The courts, like all institutions of government, were under intense pressure. Many judges felt compelled to respond to the "Communist menace" by ignoring fundamental civil liberties and constitutional guarantees. Others, however, held their ground. For us, the difference was not academic. Where did Judge Dimock stand?

The judge quickly made that clear: "There is no better way to determine what the facts are than in open court," he stated. Over the strenuous objections of government counsel, the judge ruled that Matusow's grand jury appearance should be deferred until after he had testified at the retrial hearing.

We had won our first legal skirmish with the Justice Department. And, as a result of Judge Dimock's ruling, Harvey would now be able to keep his appointment with the press.

3. *Gentlemen of the Press*

I am inclined to doubt whether there was ever another press conference quite like the one at the Biltmore Hotel on the afternoon of February 3, 1955.

Various obvious ingredients made it unique. If Matusow was a former key government witness who now admitted he'd been lying all along, most of the papers interviewing him had given prodigious—and usually unquestioning—circulation to his lies. Moreover, Matusow's interrogators would include reporters from extreme right-wing periodicals, but also some newsmen who at one time had actually collaborated with him in writing feature articles on his exposés of "Communist plots."

Under such circumstances, we might have been better prepared for what was to come. Perhaps we had been lulled by the temperate tone of Harvey's TV interviews and the general tenor of the editorials we had read.

The press conference took place in one of the hotel's large meeting rooms. Rows of chairs, flanked by potted palms, had been set up facing a table at one end. By two o'clock some fifty newsmen had crowded into the room. Among them were representatives from major metropolitan papers, national magazines, wire services, and the foreign press. I recognized several members of the Mine-Mill union seated inconspicuously in the back of the room and briefly wondered about their presence.

Flashbulbs popped on all sides as Harvey, Angus and I sat down at the table. The photographers, perched on chairs, crouching gnomelike on the floor and importuning one another to get out of the way, kept up a barrage of instructions to Matusow: "Stand up, Harvey"—"Look over here and point"—"Hold that paper like you're reading from it."

Harvey complied with the unruffled expertise of a veteran performer.

Angus rapped on the table to get attention and the room quieted down.

"I want to state at the outset," Angus told the reporters, "that if it hadn't been for Judge Dimock's ruling postponing Matusow's grand jury appearance, the Justice Department would have prevented him from being at this press conference. As the publishers of Matusow's book, we think it's pertinent to note that while other informer-witnesses have been proven to have lied under oath, the Justice Department has taken no legal action against them. But when a man tries to publish the truth about his former false testimony, the Department goes all out against him." Angus paused. "Anyway, Mr. Matusow is here now and ready to answer your questions."

Harvey got up and started to read a short statement he had prepared. Immediately a reporter called out, "How can we be sure you're telling the truth now?"[24]

Angus raised his hand. "I think that Mr. Matusow should be given the chance to read his statement. After that, he'll answer questions."

Harvey began reading again. "Before answering your questions I'd like to say one thing. I welcome an investigation of the disclosures I'm making about my past activities. But I believe that this investigation should be conducted by some government body more impartial than the Department of Justice, which is implicated in some of my charges."

The same reporter shouted, "How about answering my question? How do we know you're telling the truth now?"

Harvey looked at him calmly. "There's no way you can be absolutely sure," he said, "but I've documents proving much of what I'm saying. Affidavits of mine are now in the courts, and I'm ready to stand behind them."

Another reporter spoke up. "Congressman Walters says you were planted by the Communists to work in federal agencies. Do you have anything to say about this?"

"I haven't been a Communist party member since January 19, 1951, the date of my expulsion as an FBI informer."

All at once a chorus of questions began to pour from various parts of the room. They came from a small but highly vocal group:

"Are Cameron and Kahn members of the Communist party?"

"How do you feel about the Nazi-Soviet Pact, Mr. Matusow?"

"How about the slave camps in Russia?"

"Would you give us a few sentences, Mr. Matusow, on your views on Soviet dictatorship, Red aggression, and the Korean war prisoners?"

I recognized several of the questioners. One was an ex-radical who had become a featured Hearst columnist; another was an ardent exponent of Senator McCarthy; a third was the editor of a well-known blacklisting periodical. The questions came with such rapidity that Harvey couldn't complete an answer or in most cases even start one—a fact which, considering the nature of the questions, represented no great loss to anybody's understanding of anything.

Angus arose. After several efforts, he managed to make himself heard above the din. "Perhaps," he said in a tone clearly intended to be reasonable and persuasive, "questions could be asked one at a time so that—"

Angry cries drowned him out.

A bespectacled young man demanded righteously, "Is Mr. Matusow here to answer questions or isn't he? Who do you think he is, Mr. Cameron—the president?"

Angus looked startled and resumed his seat. Things, I reflected, had probably never been quite this way at editorial meetings at Little, Brown.

"Mr. Matusow," a stout, ruddy-faced man asked with an air of earnest curiosity, "would you mind telling us if you think there's a dictatorship in the Soviet Union? If you don't, doesn't that discredit you? What possible credence can we give to what you're telling us now?"

For the first time Harvey showed annoyance. "You're putting words in my mouth. I'm ready to criticize the Soviet Union—"

"And what about taking up arms against Russia?"

"I served in the U.S. armed forces in World War II," asserted Harvey. "I'd serve again. But not in the same way. My brother died in Germany. I don't like war. And when the question is asked if I'll support my country by killing, I will say categorically no!"

The clique of hecklers were momentarily silenced; and some of the other newsmen took advantage of the lull to ask questions of their own.

"Did anybody help you write your book, Mr. Matusow?"

"I wrote it myself."

"Why did you write the book?"

"Because I hurt a lot of people, and I want to put things straight now. I want to live with myself."

The hecklers started in again.

"Are you being blackmailed, Mr. Matusow?"

"No."

"Are you preparing to skip the country?"

"I am staying in the United States."

The Hearst columnist asked, "Why did you lie in the first place?"

"I don't mean to discuss you personally," Harvey replied. "But writers like you helped make me lie. I mean, the sort of things you wrote in your column. I thought—this is a good racket. I was looking for identity. I wanted to see my name in print. I wanted the glamour professional ex-Communists have today." Harvey leaned forward toward his questioner. "Maybe you remember how often you and I talked together, and how much of my material you used. I'm not trying to embarrass you."

Pandemonium broke out once more. There was now no chance of Harvey's being heard at all. He stood in silence.

Amid the uproar Angus got resignedly to his feet again, started to say something, shrugged his shoulders, and sat down. I felt he was giving up too easily. Obviously, a firm hand was needed. I stood up and declared in an authorative tone that if questions were to be answered, there would have to be some order. I was promptly shouted down.

Up until now the Mine-Mill members in the back of the room had remained silent. While these miners were ordinarily not bashful about expressing their views, this was, after all, supposed to be a press conference. However, they could no longer restrain themselves. They began calling out: "Give Matusow a chance!"—"Quit interrupting!" —"Let him speak!"

Suddenly, a furious voice cut through the din. It came from "Izzie" Stone, editor of the Washington newsletter, *Weekly*. He was standing in the front row, facing the gathering. A small, usually mild-looking man, he glowered at the hecklers through thick glasses. "What the hell's the matter with you bastards!" he shouted. "Why don't you want him to be heard? You call yourselves newspapermen! You make me sick! I've never seen such a shameful exhibition!"

For several moments there was complete silence in the room.

The few questions that followed were noticeably restrained. No one again interrupted Harvey's answers.

At the end of the conference, a few of the reporters stopped at our table. "That was some business," said one with a rueful smile. "I've never seen half those guys who were making all the row. I feel like apologizing."

The following morning, the *New York Post* columnist, Murray Kempton, commented:

> Matusow was asked again and again yesterday how anyone could believe that he is telling the truth now if he lied so long. What is relevant about Matusow is not whether he lied then or is a liar now. . . . What is undisputed fact is that he was either a liar then or is a liar now.
>
> You and I didn't offer him as a trustworthy man; the United States government did. . . .
>
> If the government cannot send a man to jail except on the testimony of a perjurer, then we are all safer if that man is freed. It doesn't make too much difference if Matusow has stopped playing dirty pool. The important question is whether the government is going to stop.

It was soon to become amply clear that the government did not intend to stop.

CHAPTER SEVEN

FIRST ENCOUNTER

1. *Theory and Practice*

The government's reaction to Matusow's sensational disclosures verged on the traumatic.

"The developments," reported Murray Marder of the *Washington Post and Times Herald*, "have caused consternation behind the scenes in the Justice Department and on Capitol Hill."

It wasn't hard to understand. A decade of arduous labor had gone into building the government's apparatus of paid informers and professional witnesses. Now, all at once, the whole elaborate structure was being shaken by the revelations of a single defector. One could appreciate the dismay in the Justice Department, the FBI, and other investigative government agencies.

Only recently Attorney General Brownell had issued a public statement exhorting Communists and their cohorts to "rejoin decent society" by becoming government informers. In a similar plea, FBI Director Hoover had proclaimed: "All great religions teach that the sinner can always redeem himself. Who, then, shall sit in judgment on the ex-Communist? Who dare deny him the promise held out to those who repent of the evil they have done and who try to make amends?" But the idea of perjurious informer-witnesses repenting and rejoining decent society was, of course, an unexpected variation of the redemption Brownell and Hoover had contemplated. How were they to slam shut the lid on the Pandora's box that Matusow had opened?

Attorney General Brownell ventured his first public utterance on the affair in the form of a statement to the press. Matusow's recantation, he warned gravely, had become "the subject of worldwide Communist propaganda." He did not identify the individuals responsible for this international crisis but his implication was clear enough: the real culprits were the Reds.

The Justice Department, announced Brownell, was launching an intensive investigation into the Matusow case. It would be "continued vigorously until all the facts were ascertained." Assistant Attorney General William F. Tompkins had been placed in charge of the probe and dispatched to New York to supervise matters for the government at the federal grand jury inquiry. Tompkins headed the Justice Department's recently formed Internal Security Division, which was responsible for "the prosecution of all crimes relating to subversion."

At a Washington press conference Brownell was asked if he believed there had been "any dereliction" on the part of the Justice Department in its former dealings with Matusow. "Why do you think I ordered the investigation?" the attorney general retorted.

That answer seemed to make excellent sense—since Matusow had not only admitted lying repeatedly as a government witness but had charged complicity on the part of the Justice Department. And what seemed more appropriate than that an investigation into the Department's possible dereliction be conducted by a grand jury? A traditional function of grand juries was inquiry into corruption and malfeasance among public officials.

Still, one wondered if the New York grand jury was ideally qualified to conduct an impartial probe. Theoretically, the panel was an independent body of unbiased citizens, whose sole concern would be uncovering the truth. Actually, however, the grand jury had an intimate association with the Justice Department. Its investigation had been initiated at the behest of the Department; and its deliberations would be dependent on Department attorneys for guidance and advice for most of the examination of witnesses, and for the general presentation of the facts in the case. And just how disinterested could a grand jury be if its proceedings were supervised by the very government agency that was most deeply implicated in the matter under investigation? Moreover, the fact was that in one political case after another during recent years, grand juries functioning under Justice Department supervision had handed down indictments based on spurious charges, false testimony, and fraudulent evidence. Under such circumstances, instead of fulfilling their original purpose of protecting citizens against tyrannical acts of the state, grand juries had themselves become powerful instruments of governmental repression.[25]

Before long the attorney general himself defined the exact tactic the Justice Department intended to pursue through its grand jury inquiry. Brownell proclaimed that Matusow had told the truth when he testified as a government witness, and that his recantation was the "focal point" of an ambitious "Communist plot" to discredit the Justice Department's "campaign against subversion" and "to destroy the informant system of the Federal Bureau of Investigation."

Obviously, if there were such a plot, Matusow's publishers were deeply involved in it.

2. *Battle Joined*

On Monday, February 7, Angus's secretary telephoned me at the Chelsea Hotel in the mid-afternoon. She was calling from the Cameron & Kahn office. Her usually dulcet southern accent had a strained quality.

"There's a process server here from the Justice Department." She managed to convey the impression he was looming at her side. "He's got grand jury subpoenas for you and Angus."

"When's Angus due back?" I asked. He had gone to spend the weekend with his family at his home in the Adirondacks. With Angus such a weekend could easily turn into a week, especially if the trout were rising.

"I think he's coming in on the train this evening."

I told her to send the process server over to the Chelsea Hotel.

All day a biting wind had been whipping snow flurries through the city, and it occurred to me that anyone serving subpoenas in such weather would appreciate some warming refreshment.

"Let's put some coffee on, Ruth," I suggested. "We're expecting a guest—with a subpoena."

"Here we go," she said.

There soon arrived a middle-aged, plainly dressed man with a doleful countenance. He looked chilled to the bone. He had the diffident manner of a man whose occupation compelled him continually to meet people who regarded him as an enemy. Apologetically he told me, "I've got a subpoena for you, Mr. Kahn."

"How about a cup of coffee?" I said.

A smile crept over his woeful face. "Say, that would really hit the spot."

Ruth poured three cups.

"You know," the process server confided as he sipped his coffee with noisy relish, "lots of people don't understand that serving subpoenas is just a job. They think there's something personal in it."

I told him he had no reason to apologize.

"And where is Mr. Cameron?" he asked.

I explained Angus had gone upstate for the weekend. "Cameron isn't a city man," I told him. With the vicarious pleasure I always derived from these attributes of Angus's, I related what an expert hunter and fisherman he was, and how his trophies included most species of North American big game.

The process server sighed. "That must be the life," he said.

"Anyway, he's due back tonight. You can probably reach him later in the evening."

He nodded lugubriously. "See the sort of hours we have to keep?"

As he was about to leave, he paused. "Mind if I make a suggestion, Mr. Kahn?" he said earnestly. "Your subpoena tells you to bring a lot of stuff with you tomorrow. Maybe it'll be hard for you to get it all together. If it is, just tell them you need more time."

The subpoena I had received summoned me, in archaic terminology, to "appear and attend before the GRAND INQUEST of the body of the people of the United States of America . . . at Room 513 in the United States Courthouse, Foley Square . . . on the 8th day of February 1955, at 11:00 o'clock in the forenoon to testify and give evidence . . . and not to depart the Court without leave thereof."

I was instructed to bring with me this conglomeration of material:

The original or true copies of all correspondence, records, memoranda, receipts, cancelled checks, book accounts, contracts, memoranda of contracts and other documents and writings, and ALL manuscripts and drafts thereof and galley proofs, prepared by or in any manner relating to a proposed book or other writing written by one HARVEY M. MATUSOW, which is being considered by you, or in the publication of which you may have any interest.

And for failure to attend and produce the said documents, you will be deemed guilty of contempt of court and liable to penalties of the law.

Affixed to the document were the names of United States Attorney J. Edward Lumbard and Assistant United States Attorney George H. Bailey. I telephoned our newly acquired lawyer, Stanley Faulkner, and told him about the subpoena.

He said he had an appointment in the morning but would get to the courthouse in time for my grand jury appearance.

He added, "At grand jury proceedings, you know, you can't have your lawyer with you in the jury room. But they'll let you leave the room when you want to consult me."

My legal education was under way.

When Angus arrived early that evening at Grand Central Station, I was waiting for him.

He showed more irritation than surprise at the news. "Well, they'll have to bring my subpoena to me," he said curtly. "I'm sure as hell not going to chase after it!"

"They'll probably serve yours tonight."

"Suits me fine," he growled.

When I suggested supper at Luchow's, one of his favorite restaurants, he brightened up. "The hasenpfeffer for me," he said.

Over the meal, we discussed the significance of our being summoned before the grand jury at this state of events.

One thing was clear. The jury was to begin its inquiry by investigating Matusow's publishers rather than the validity of his admissions. And while neither of us regarded the Justice Department as a model of restraint, we were struck by the brazenness of the order we surrender the data listed in the subpoena. If we complied, we would have nothing left to publish. The demand for all manuscripts, drafts and galley proofs of Matusow's book was nothing less than an overt attempt to seize it before publication. To the best of our knowledge, such an action by the U.S. government was without precedent. Nor were we disposed to assist the government in this pioneering effort.

"Here," said Angus, fishing into his inside coat pocket, "let me show you something."

He produced a batch of papers, singled out one and handed it to me. It was a manifesto entitled *The Freedom to Read*, recently issued by the American Library Association:

> The freedom to read is essential to our democracy. It is under attack. Private groups and public authorities in various parts of the country are working to remove books from sale, to censor textbooks, to label "controversial" books, to distribute lists of "objectionable" books or authors and to purge libraries.
>
> These actions apparently rise from a view that our national tradition of free expression is no longer valid; that censorship and suppression are needed to avoid the subversion of politics and the corruption of morals. . . .
>
> Suppression is never more dangerous than in such a time of social tension. . . . The freedom to read is guaranteed by the Constitution. Those with faith in free men will stand firm on these Constitutional guarantees of essential rights and will exercise the responsibilities that accompany these rights.

Angus peered over his glasses at me when I finished reading. "That pretty well sums up the reasons we announced in the first place for setting up Cameron & Kahn, right?"

I raised my glass. "Here's to standing firm, to quote the librarians."

He added, "And to hell with the censors."

We drank the toast.

"You know, Angus," I told him, "you look too respectable to go to jail wearing that vest and all. But me, what chance do I have?"

"You can always *talk* the guards into letting you out," he said with a laugh.

Though jail was not such a remote possibility, we did not discuss the personal aspects of the risks and the added hardships for our families. These were understood. Since neither of us relished the prospect of imprisonment, we discussed our strategy—particularly the use of the Fifth Amendment[26] in refusing to answer certain questions before the grand jury. It was a difficult matter to decide. The right not to testify against oneself was a vital Constitutional guarantee, protecting the innocent as well as the guilty against government abuses. It had been exercised for decades as a safeguard against persecution for political and religious heresy. Yet we had to admit that, given the temper of the times, those who used the Fifth were widely regarded as subversives. If we invoked the Fifth Amendment in refusing to surrender the material ordered in our subpoenas, we could create the impression that we had something to hide. We agreed, therefore, to cite the First Amendment, covering freedom of the press, as our grounds for not cooperating with the demand. We knew, of course, that the government would do all in its power to shift that focus.

Angus looked up from his dessert. "Let's deal with the standard question, 'Are you now or have you ever been a member of the Communist party?' We agree, of course, that any questions about political beliefs infringe on the right of free speech and free association. It's none of their damn business. We won't answer them."

"Right. But we know that the courts have held that the First Amendment can't be cited as grounds for refusal to answer that question. So that leaves us with the Fifth."

"Well," Angus said, "unfortunately you can't explain you're using the Fifth on the grounds that if you deny party membership, the government may produce their paid informers to testify that you're lying, and claim perjury. If you attempt to explain on those grounds, you are disqualified from using the Fifth. In a recent case that's exactly what happened." He chuckled. "I remember when I was before the Jenner committee in '52 his game was to say, 'You mean that if you testify truthfully to this question instead of evading it by taking the Fifth, you would incriminate yourself?' I told him, 'Don't put words in my mouth. The Constitution says nothing about incrimination—it doesn't use the word at all. Don't try to rewrite the Fifth Amendment!' "

We decided to invoke the Fifth Amendment as seldom as possible and to conduct an aggressive campaign through our answers to the grand jury.

Of decisive importance in the contest ahead was the question of public opinion. Marshalled against us were the elaborate resources of the Justice Department. But on our side were potential allies of greater power—the growing number of people opposed to McCarthyism and that sizable portion of the press now speaking out against the informer-witness system. If we were to have a motto in the coming days, it perhaps should be Arnold Bennett's maxim: "The price of justice is eternal publicity."

After dinner Angus and I drafted a press release. It read in part:

We regard the service upon us of these subpoenas as a flagrant
attempt to subvert the freedom of the press, a right . . . guaranteed
in the First Amendment to the Constitution. One of the manifest
purposes of the First Amendment is to permit the American people
to judge for themselves the truth of such facts as are contained in
Matusow's forthcoming book. In hauling us before a federal grand
jury, the Justice Department is continuing its attempt to keep from
the public the book's disclosures, some of which implicate the Department itself.

Therefore we do not intend to comply with the brazen dictates of
the subpoenas. We will not submit to the Justice Department for its
scrutiny or would-be censorship the text of Matusow's book prior to
its publication. We will not permit the seizure of it. Nor will we
allow ourselves to be intimidated into not publishing the book. The
book will shortly be available to the public as a whole, and at that
time to the Justice Department as well.

3. *Arm of the Law*

The United States Courthouse in New York City is a massive structure of darkening gray stone and granite. The architect, apparently in
some indecision, superimposed a thirty-story office building on a
three-story replica of a Greek temple. Whatever the structure's es-
thetics, it conveys an impression of solidity and power generally considered appropriate for houses of government. Reporters and
photographers were clustered in front of the courthouse when Angus
and I, accompanied by Riette, arrived to keep our grand jury appointment. They swarmed around us as we got out of our taxi. We talked
briefly with the newsmen, handed out copies of our press statement,
headed up the courthouse steps past ponderous stone columns and into
a mausoleum-like marble hall. On the fifth floor we were directed to a
waiting room for grand jury witnesses. Large and sparsely furnished,
it had the disinfected atmosphere of a hospital and was suited to make
its occupants feel like patients awaiting an operation.

Angus went to a window that faced on bleak inner walls. "Nice
homey place," he said, abstractedly fingering a loose button on his

overcoat. Riette told him, "Stop fiddling with that button, Angus, or it'll come off. I'll fix it for you later."

"What about these?" He smiled and showed her his frayed shirt-cuffs.

"You both look pretty seedy," she said. "Maybe David only wore a loincloth when he fought Goliath, but there's no need to follow his example."

A neatly dressed young man stepped into the room. His precise features had a freshly scrubbed look. He introduced himself as Assistant U.S. Attorney George Bailey. "The grand jury is ready," he said. "Will you come in first, Mr. Kahn?" It was more an order than a request.

I explained our subpoenas had been served late the previous day and we had had to make last-minute arrangements for counsel. "Our attorney, Mr. Faulkner, had another engagement. We want to wait until he gets here."

Bailey frowned. He glanced sternly at his watch. "We'll allow Mr. Faulkner another ten minutes."

He left the room with his head cocked slightly forward, as if on the alert for crucial tidings.

"That," I said, "is what Shakespeare meant by the insolence of office."

In precisely ten minutes, Bailey returned.

"All right, Mr. Kahn," he said. "Will you come in now?"

I said Faulkner had not arrived yet.

"We can't wait any longer," he said.

"Well, I don't intend going into the grand jury room before my attorney gets here," I told him.

His shocked expression implied that through his person I was flouting the majesty and authority of government itself. "You mean you *refuse* to go in?" he asked incredulously.

"You can put it that way if you want."

Bailey turned to Angus. "What about you, Mr. Cameron?"

Angus stretched and settled back in his chair. "Me, too," he grunted.

Wheeling toward the door, Bailey called, "Marshal! Marshal!"

Angus and I had long shared an intense enthusiasm for the Old West and doted on its legends and lore. Familiar as we were with the deeds of famed U.S. marshals of old, we both dared to hope—as we later acknowledged to each other—that Bailey's urgent summons might bring the tall, sinewy figure of a man with a Stetson hat and Colt revolvers hanging at his sides.

Instead, a stooped, mild-looking man in a rumpled gray suit ambled into the room. In a high-pitched voice he inquired of Bailey. "Yup?"

"Marshal, come over here," commanded Bailey.

"Now, Mr. Kahn," said Bailey, "will you repeat in the presence of the marshal what you just told me?"

"I told you that I refuse to go into the grand jury room until my attorney gets here."

"Did you hear that, marshal?" demanded Bailey.

The marshal, whose expression had not altered, nodded sleepily. "Yup," he said.

Bailey hurried from the room. The marshal plodded after him.

Soon, Bailey was back again. He had a crestfallen air. "All right," he said, "we'll wait for Mr. Faulkner."

Faulkner arrived shortly afterward. Sober and quiet-spoken, he came directly to the business at hand. "You know as well as I do," he told us, "the Justice Department is running this show and they're out to get an indictment against you. Whatever you tell the grand jury, the Justice Department is going to try to use it against you. So the less talking you do, the better."

Logical as was his advice, we said we wanted to pursue a different course. We recognized the influence the Justice Department might wield over the grand jury, and the fact that the major issues would not be settled here. But despite the risks he indicated, we felt they had to be taken. We felt we should do everything we could to acquaint the grand jury with the actual facts of the case.

"We're publishing the book to get the facts to as many people as possible," said Angus. "So why not tell them to the grand jury?"

"Maybe," I said, "we can persuade the jury to investigate the Justice Department instead of Cameron & Kahn."

Faulkner did not smile. He studied us owlishly through his horn-rimmed glasses and shrugged. "All right. I don't agree with you. But you're the ones who have to decide."

When Bailey returned, I said I was ready to testify. He led the way down the corridor, and knocked on a door marked "Grand Jury Room."

A voice called, "Come in."

If the room I had left made one feel like a patient awaiting surgery, the room I now entered completed the illusion—it resembled a hospital operating theatre. In tiers of seats along one wall, like so many medical students, were grouped a score of jurors. I'd forgotten a grand jury has twenty-three members and was momentarily surprised by their number. In the middle of the room—precisely where the operating table should be—was a long conference table. At it were seated three men and a woman.

One of the men at the table introduced himself as the jury foreman. He had a ruddy face and a nervous manner. He presented the two persons between whom he was seated: the assistant jury foreman, a lean-faced, alert-looking man; and the jury secretary, an erect, stylishly dressed black woman. The third man at the table, a court stenographer with a stenotyping machine, waited with a bored expression for the amenities to be over and his work to commence.[27]

In a corner of the room sat three men who were obviously not jurors. I recognized one of them from newspaper photos I had recently seen of him. He was Assistant U.S. Attorney General William Tompkins, whom Brownell had appointed to supervise the Matusow investigation.

The foreman swore me in, and I was asked to be seated at the table.

Bailey drew himself erect and grasped the lapels of his coat. He proceeded directly to the matter of Harvey Matusow.

How, he wanted to know, had I first met Matusow? And what had been the nature of my subsequent dealings with him?

I assumed the jurors had already been advised of the Justice Department's thesis that Matusow's publishers were involved in a conspiracy to hamstring the government's anti-Communist campaign. I also assumed that most of the jurors were approaching this inquiry with certain preconceptions. Like other Americans, they had been subjected in recent years to a massive barrage of propaganda on the "Red Menace." There was no reason to suppose they were less prejudiced on the subject than most citizens. The very factors which had made it possible for countless Americans to believe Matusow was telling the truth when he lied, could lead these jurors to believe he was lying when he told the truth.

How, then, to penetrate the barrier of their prejudices? How to get the real truth across to them?

The key to getting them to understand the meaning of the case of Harvey Matusow lay, I felt, in those aspects of his story which were of universal human interest.

Addressing myself directly to the jurors, I began by recounting how I had happened to get in touch with Matusow and how the manuscript for the book *False Witness* had come into being. I stressed the complications of working with Harvey, the problems of winning the confidence of someone with his record, the complexities of his character, the struggle in which he was still engaged to rehabilitate himself. When I had first looked at the jury, I had seen only a blurred cluster of faces. As I talked, the faces gradually came into individual focus, with distinctive features and varying responses. A sensitive-looking woman listened with a frown of intent curiosity. A large, bull-necked man maintained a look of stolid skepticism. A dapper young man eyed me with hostility and mistrust. From time to time, a gray-haired woman nodded understandingly. An occasional smile flitted across the face of a square-shouldered man with dark eyes—once or twice I even thought he winked.

Periodically, Bailey interrupted my narrative with some question. The questions from the jurors were few—few enough to indicate most of them regarded the inquiry as one being conducted by the Justice Department rather than themselves. Even so, I sensed a growing interest in the facts I was relating.

Perhaps Bailey noticed the same thing. He interrupted to say there was a matter he wished to discuss in private with the jurors. "Will you step out of the room, Mr. Kahn," he said peremptorily.

"No," I said.

He looked nonplussed.

"If you want me to leave the room," I said, "you'll have to ask the jury foreman to request me to. You don't represent any authority to me. The jury is running these proceedings."

I wasn't just being cantankerous. True, I felt that as a public employee Bailey should learn to treat his employers, citizens like me, with more respect. But I thought it more important that the jurors realize the limits of the authority of this young man who bore the impressive title of Assistant U.S. Attorney. Perhaps then they would be more inclined to question the infallibility of the government itself.

Bailey's face reddened. He turned to the foreman. "Will you direct Mr. Kahn to leave the room?"

The first question Bailey asked me when I was summoned back was whether I had with me at the courthouse the material requested in my subpoena.

I said I had not.

"When can you produce it?" he asked.

"I don't intend to. Mr. Cameron and I regard the request for that material as interference with the freedom of the press. It amounts, in fact, to an attempt to seize the book. If we were to surrender all the material listed, we'd have literally nothing left to publish."

"I'm afraid you haven't read the subpoena carefully, Mr. Kahn," said Bailey condescendingly. "It doesn't request the originals of the material. It requests only copies."

"Look at it again. You'll see the subpoena calls for copies of certain office records. But it specifically demands *all* manuscripts, drafts, and galley proofs of Matusow's book, without mentioning the word 'copies.' Why don't you read that paragraph to the jurors and let them decide its meaning."

Bailey studied the subpoena. "It's possible," he granted reluctantly, "there could be two interpretations."

"I suggest you eliminate one."

After a brief delay, Bailey handed me a revised list of items to be produced. It stipulated "copies" in all instances.

"I'll have to think that over," I said, "and discuss it with Mr. Cameron."

I was instructed to return the following morning.

CHAPTER EIGHT

SCALES OF JUSTICE

1. *Contempt of Court*

When I arrived for my second appointment with the grand jury, it was not my intention to get sentenced to jail before the day ended. My plans were actually quite different. Since the previous day I had become increasingly angry that Angus and I were being investigated like a couple of gangsters for exposing Matusow's crimes, whereas the officials who had encouraged his crimes were conducting our investigation. I felt it was time to convince the jury that the Justice Department should be answering—not asking—questions.

As soon as I had taken my place in the grand jury room, I told the foreman I would like to inquire about certain grand jury procedures.

He agreed.

"It is my understanding," I said, "that the grand jury has considerable powers, and that they include the authority to investigate not only private citizens but the government itself."

The foreman looked at Bailey. The latter nodded solemnly. "The jury is thus empowered," he said.

"In that event," I told him, "I appear before this body as an equal of the government, which is implicated in the charges under investigation. These, then, are my questions.

"One: do I, as an equal of the government, have the right to interrogate the government attorney as he's interrogating me? Two: do I have the right to ask that the government be instructed to produce confidential documents from their files as they have instructed me to produce personal documents from mine? And three: do I have the right to request that you instruct the government attorney to leave the room whenever I wish to address the jury in private?"

The foreman consulted with Bailey in a low voice. Bailey—who appeared no more knowledgeable in these matters than the foreman —held a whispered conference with the Justice Department officials seated behind him. He confided something to the foreman.

Clearing his throat, the foreman said, "Yes, Mr. Kahn, you do have those rights."

While it was gratifying to know these rights were at least theoretically mine, I was to have little opportunity to use them.

The proceedings were promptly brought back to the business of investigating Matusow's publishers. Bailey asked if I had with me the material I'd been instructed to bring.

I said I had not.

From the rear of the jury the bull-necked juror called out angrily, "You broke your word! You promised to bring it!"

"No, he didn't," said a second juror.

Other jurors joined in the altercation.

The assistant foreman raised a quieting hand. "Mr. Kahn did not promise to bring the material," he stated. "He said he would think the matter over."

Bailey read aloud the list of the material I had been told to produce.

The following exchange then took place between us.[28]

BAILEY: Are those documents and items presently in the custody of Cameron & Kahn? I want to know, for example, where is the tape recording at this time?
KAHN: I will tell you where part of it is. Part of it is in my personal possession.
BAILEY: And where is that? Do you have it with you at this time?
KAHN: No, I don't.
BAILEY: Where is it?
KAHN: I believe that is a personal matter, and I do not intend to tell you, Mr. Bailey.
BAILEY: So you decline to state where the tape recording is, is that correct?
KAHN: I believe that would be the meaning of my remarks.
BAILEY: And what is your ground for declining so to state?

KAHN: Because I believe you have no right to ask.

BAILEY: Do you believe the answer might tend to incriminate you?

KAHN: I didn't say that. Don't try to give me my answer. I already gave it.

BAILEY: I am now asking you, Mr. Kahn.

KAHN: No, I don't think it would tend to incriminate me at all to tell you where it is. I am just declining to tell you.

BAILEY: With respect to the original contract made by Cameron & Kahn, Incorporated, with Matusow, will you tell the grand jury where that contract is?

KAHN: That contract is in the possession of the firm, in our office, and Mr. Matusow, as is customary with an author, himself has a copy of the contract.

BAILEY: Are you prepared to comply with the instruction previously given by the foreman of the grand jury to produce that contract?

KAHN: No.

BAILEY: On what ground?

KAHN: Well, since this question is going to be asked repeatedly, I'd like at this point to state that I am not prepared to produce here ... the contract with Matusow, the first chapter and outline that Matusow gave us, the galley proofs we have, the tape recordings of the original conversations, the transcriptions of the tape recordings, the draft of the manuscript and the data Mr. Matusow dictated from the tape recordings. . . .

I believe the request for this material represents an infringement upon the First Amendment to the Constitution of the United States. This amendment states very specifically that freedom of the press shall be protected—and it is pertinent here to note that the protection is against the Government. . . . The Amendment specifically states that the Congress of the United States shall pass no measures, no laws, which infringe upon this right of the people. . . . [29]

At Bailey's request, the foreman instructed me to leave the jury room.

When I was summoned back, Bailey gravely informed me the jury had voted to take me before a federal judge and request him to order me to produce the documents I had declined to surrender.

The entire jury trooped out of the jury room and headed down the corridor, with Bailey bustling in advance.

I apprised Angus and Stan Faulkner, who were in the waiting room, of the latest developments. The three of us followed in the rear of the procession, which halted outside the courtroom of Judge John

W. Clancy. The courtroom having been cleared, our band was ushered in.

Judge Clancy was a pale-faced man with short-cropped gray hair. He listened with chill impassivity as the grand jury stenographer read the final portion of my testimony before the grand jury.

"On the basis of the grand jury record, and on behalf of the grand jury," Bailey said, "I request Your Honor to instruct the witness to produce the documents called for and to answer the questions asked him as to the exact whereabouts of these documents and items."[30]

"Does his attorney wish to address me?" asked Judge Clancy.

Faulkner stood up. "Your Honor, we feel that the production of these records would be in direct violation of the freedom of the press. It is not necessarily the ultimate result of a printing press that has to be protected, but all those incidentals which go toward making up a publication such as a book, that should be protected by the court."

"Is that the substance of your remarks?" inquired the judge. From his indifferent monotone, one would not have suspected Faulkner's words concerned a right for which men for centuries had fought and died to achieve.

"We further feel," said Faulkner, "that the production of these records is irrelevant to the issues before the grand jury."

"Is that all?"

"That is all."

"Your objection is overruled," said Judge Clancy curtly. Regarding the requested documents, he added, "I instruct the witness to recover them rapidly and produce them."

Our procession trooped back to the grand jury room.

"Are you prepared to comply with the court's direction?" Bailey asked me.

"No, I am not."

Back we all paraded to Judge Clancy's court.

Bailey advised the judge of my recalcitrance. "I think," said Bailey, "there is a clear case of contempt."

"No doubt about it," Judge Clancy snapped. "I will find him guilty of contempt. I won't do anything further until he goes up and completes his examination."

*   *   *

On our return to the grand jury room, it was no longer Bailey who continued my examination. To my surprise, that function was now taken over by Brownell's aide, Assistant Attorney General William Tompkins.

It was, in a way, a pleasant change.

A lean, sharp-featured man in his mid-forties, Tompkins had a relaxed, urbane manner. Although I gathered he would have few qualms about shipping me off to jail, I felt he would do it with a certain graciousness.

With a quiet amicability, as if we were chatting over cocktails, Tompkins proceeded to name various anti-facist and civil rights organizations and to ask if I had ever been a member of them. Each time I answered affirmatively, he politely inquired if I knew that the organization was on the attorney general's "subversive list." I said I assumed they all were, since they were doing work for democracy and peace.

Tompkins laughed good-naturedly.

Since I had belonged to a fairly sizable number of proscribed organizations, this interchange was lengthy. Finally I interrupted it. "If you're trying to prove I have radical inclinations," I suggested, "you're really going to too much trouble. Most of my public activities over the years make that clear. My views are as radical as those of Jack London or Tom Paine."

"I see," Tompkins smiled.

"But now that we've established that fact," I said, "why don't we proceed to the matter supposedly under investigation? That is—did Matusow commit perjury as a government witness, and, if he did, was the Justice Department implicated in his false testimony?"

Tompkins indicated he had no more questions for the time being.

I was instructed to return to Judge Clancy's court.

As I followed the jurors down the hall, I found Tompkins at my side.

"Tell me," he asked with genuine interest, "was Bill Morton playing football at Dartmouth when you were there?"

"He certainly was. He was perhaps the best quarterback we ever had." I added in a confidential tone: "Speaking of Dartmouth, there's a serious matter I think you should take up in Washington. It concerns this case."

"What's that?"

"Well, I myself ran on the Dartmouth track team. In fact, I was picked to run in the Olympic tryouts—"

"Really!"

"Yes. And the point is that no Dartmouth man will ever believe a member of our team could be involved in a Communist conspiracy. They used to call me 'Red Kahn' because of the color of my hair— they'll think you've made a frightful mistake. You'll mobilize the whole Dartmouth alumni body against the Justice Department."

"Say, that is serious, all right!" He shook his head in mock alarm. "I'm grateful you warned me. I'll take it up with Washington right away."

"On the subject of teams," I said, "doesn't the Justice Department find it embarrassing when so many members on its team of professional witnesses—like Matusow, Paul Crouch, Manning Johnson, and all the rest—are proven to be liars?"

He looked at me earnestly. "I want you to know, Mr. Kahn, that I had nothing to do with any of those witnesses. They were brought into the picture before my time. I was only recently appointed, you know."

Back in Judge Clancy's courtroom, Bailey addressed the magistrate.

"May it please the court," he intoned, "Albert Kahn now stands before you for sentence by virtue of the contempt committed of the Court this morning. . . . "

Judge Clancy asked Faulkner if he had any comment to make.

Faulkner replied that, as he had previously indicated, my rights under the First Amendment had been infringed upon, and that he believed the Court should provide a hearing on this question before any sentence was imposed on me.

"Is that all?" asked Judge Clancy.

"Yes, sir."

"I sentence Albert Kahn to six months," Judge Clancy said. "I will allow him until four o'clock this afternoon to either get a stay or arrange his affairs so that he can start this afternoon."

I couldn't fail to be impressed by the efficiency and smoothness of it all. Without any delay on such minutiae as a hearing to determine the merits of the case, I had been deprived of my freedom for half a year. So swiftly, in fact, had Judge Clancy acted that I felt almost as if nothing had happened, though it crossed my mind that the sentence seemed a bit lengthy and that three months would have been preferable.

On the other hand, it was likely my sentence would prove more distressing to the Justice Department than to me. To imprison the publisher of a book containing serious charges against the government was not very sound public relations—especially with nationwide attention focused on the book. Bailey, I felt, had simply been too enterprising. Carried away by youthful zeal, he had committed what seemed to me a major blunder.

As we left the courtroom Faulkner said, "I'm going to the Appeals Court to try for a stay of sentence. I'm sure Clancy can't get away with this. I think we'll be granted bail and the right to an appeal." Brisk and businesslike, he headed down the hall.

It was already past one o'clock. In less than three hours, unless a stay of sentence were granted, I would be in jail.

I telephoned home. There was no answer—Riette was apparently out, and the boys were still in school. I called a close friend who lived nearby and asked her to get word to Riette of the latest development. Would she also make sure someone met the boys when they got out of school? I didn't want them first hearing the news of my sentence over the radio. She said she'd take care of everything. Her calm voice was as comforting as a warm handclasp.

It was of major importance to get the facts about the contempt sentence publicized as widely as possible. Angus and I went straight to the courthouse press room. Smoke-filled, noisy and hectic, it had an atmosphere that contrasted pleasantly with the rest of the building. Seated at desks littered with crumpled paper were a number of reporters, typing or phoning. They crowded around us, asking about Judge Clancy's ruling. Amid the hubbub an elderly man wandered about taking orders for lunch. One of the reporters called to Angus and me. "How about something to eat?" Our order for coffee and sandwiches was added to the list.

Before long a television reporter hurried into the room. Could we step out into the street? He had his equipment set up there. As Angus and I emerged from the courthouse, cameras whirred. The TV man approached us with his microphone.

"How do you interpret this contempt sentence?" he asked.

"We interpret it as another attempt on the part of the government to interfere with the publication of Matusow's book."

"Do you plan to go ahead with its publication?"

"Of course. We think the American people comprise the most important jury and that they've the right to judge the facts for themselves."

"If I may ask without being facetious, Mr. Kahn—how does it feel to be going to jail?"

"I'll let you know when I get there."

Back in the courthouse, Faulkner was waiting for us. His usually sober countenance was lit by a broad smile.

"We're getting a temporary stay of sentence," Faulkner told us. "The Court of Appeals wants to hear the facts in the case. There's a hearing scheduled for tomorrow morning on an application for bail."

For the fourth time that day I appeared before Judge Clancy.

Faulkner informed the judge that the Appellate Court had requested that Clancy grant a stay of sentence pending the outcome of its hearing on the case.

"I grant it out of deference to the Court of Appeals," growled Judge Clancy. He appeared irritated at the amount of time he was having to spend on my case.

And who could blame him?

2. *No Place Like Home*

Not until I crossed our threshold did I realize how good it was to have at least one more night at home. Bulwer Lytton once said that at sixty a man learns how to value his home; but I can personally attest there's nothing like a jail sentence to expedite that appreciation. From the welcome I received, you might have thought I was returning from a long absence rather than possibly about to begin one. The boys greeted me with a shout.

Steven, his freckles seeming to multiply from excitement, made himself heard first. "They've been talking about you on the radio! On the news, every channel!" He brandished a school book. "Take a look at this, Dad. Know what I'm going to do in school tomorrow? Give a report on Peter Zenger in my history class. This book says he's 'the father of the freedom of the press'!" He added, grinning, "I've told Mom not to worry if they send you to jail. You'll get a story for a new book."

Brian complained, "But then we'll have to put off moving west. I'll miss some good fishing." (Though only seven he was already an ardent protégé of Angus in these skills.)

"All you can think about is fishing!" reprimanded Tim. He was standing to one side, his face revealing his effort to share his brothers' gaiety.

Riette kissed me with the mock-solemn greeting: "This is an unexpected pleasure. From your message I thought you might be eating out, or rather in—as a guest of the government."

At supper I reported to the family the events of the day.

Riette said, "Let me tell you a couple of things that happened here. There was a car parked across the road all afternoon with two men watching the house—obviously FBI. I got so angry I went out and stood in front of the car and copied down their license. They pretended not to notice. I know I didn't accomplish anything, but it made me feel better."

The other incident had been more pleasant. "When I went to the village for groceries," she related, "Jack and Morris took me behind the counter. They were really upset. They'd heard about the sentence on the radio. They said they didn't know how we were fixed for money right now, but I wasn't to worry—we'd have credit at the store as long as we needed." She smiled across the table. "Wasn't that something?"

As a matter of special dispensation, commensurate with the unique occasion, Steven won permission to have his supper in front of the TV. Periodically during the meal there came—punctuated by the click of his switching channels—his boisterous announcement: "Dad, you're on again!"

Tim scarcely touched his food. All at once his face crumpled. He blurted out, "I don't want to have my birthday party." (His eleventh birthday was just a week away.) "How can I have a party if Daddy's in jail?" He put his head on his arms and wept.

Riette stroked his head. "Timmy, I told you it's not certain. And if

Daddy goes, it's because he's doing something right—something you'll be proud of."

"I know," he said, wiping his tears. "I didn't mean to cry."

After supper he slipped away to his room. When we looked in on him he was busily painting a picture of a huge Bunyanesque boy— whose cherubic face markedly resembled his own—towering over mountains and tiny men, and holding a great white dove.

Tim smiled. "This is for you, Daddy." He gave me the picture and went to join his brothers at the TV set.

"You see," said Riette, "you don't have to worry about them. They're solid citizens."

I kissed her. "They take after their mother."

All evening, friends came and went. They offered to raise funds for legal fees, give a hand with the children, or help in any other way they could.

The telephone rang incessantly.

My old friend Rockwell Kent called from his farm in the Adirondacks. "God, I wish I was there!" he boomed with a vigor creating the illusion he actually was. "Whatever I can do, let me know. And tell Matusow for me I think he's done a splendid thing."[31]

There was a telegram from a well-known book publisher and his wife. We were but casually acquainted. It read: *"Courage, mon brave! Butez en avant!"* Their own courage was reflected in the message. They doubtless assumed—with good reason—that all communications to me were being recorded by the FBI and their own names would henceforth be included in J. Edgar's files.

It was almost three in the morning when I awoke. An idea had banished sleep. I had never before telephoned Angus at that hour—he wasn't the sort to relish such calls. But this time I didn't hesitate.

"Angus—listen to this. What would you say to our making public —whether I go to jail or not—all the material we've refused to turn over to the grand jury? The manuscript of the book, the transcripts of my talks with Harvey, everything. We could do it tomorrow. Give it all to the press and send it to the Senate Judiciary Committee with the suggestion that they investigate the Matusow case. Then it will be perfectly clear that we're not trying to hide anything, but that we're not willing to hand the stuff over to a closed proceeding of the Justice Department."

"That's a hell of an idea, Albert! I'm all for it."

3. *Change of Tide*

Next morning when I arrived at the federal courthouse, Faulkner was waiting in the lobby. His sober face wore a puzzled frown. "Something's up," he said. "Bailey says Judge Clancy wants to see us again before we go to the Appeals Court."

"What for?"

"You've got me. He's already sentenced you. Anyway, he'll let us know soon enough."

It was the fifth time in two days that I had faced Judge Clancy. He seemed no less surprised to have me back in his court than I was to be there. "Well, what is it now?" he asked Bailey impatiently.

Bailey looked thoroughly uncomfortable. "Your Honor, it occurred to me," he said, "that the witness, Albert Kahn, having had the opportunity yesterday afternoon and last evening to consider the matter, might reconsider his position. With this thought in mind, I have made arrangements for the witness and his counsel to appear here, and request of the court to inquire of the witness whether he is now prepared to comply with this court's order to produce the documents and items before the grand jury and to testify as to their whereabouts. Will Your Honor so inquire?"[32]

So that was it! Not my position, but the Justice Department's was under reconsideration. Having apparently recognized the blunder of getting me sentenced to jail at this stage of the game, they were now trying to prevent me from going!

Judge Clancy glared at Bailey with ill-concealed disgust. "Are you ready, Mr. Kahn?" he asked.

Faulkner was on his feet. "This comes as a complete surprise to us. I was told by Mr. Bailey it was Your Honor's request. I would like to have about five minutes to consult with my client."

"All right," sighed Judge Clancy wearily.

Outside the courtroom I informed Faulkner of Angus's and my decision. "Tell Clancy our firm is making all the material public today through the press. Since the jurors are also members of the public, it will become available to them too—after it becomes public property. We won't turn it over to them in private, but once it's in the public domain they'll have access to it like everyone else."

Faulkner conveyed the message to Judge Clancy.

Bailey spoke up hastily. "This is an entirely satisfactory disposition to the government."

"Is the question now resolved?" Judge Clancy demanded in an exasperated tone.

"It is," said Faulkner.

All afternoon reporters streamed in and out of our Chelsea Hotel office, while TV commentators with their crews and equipment somehow managed to squeeze into the scant remaining space. To each reporter we showed the manuscript of *False Witness* and the transcript of the tape-recorded talks between Harvey and me. While they copied excerpts, Angus and I were televised reading aloud passages from the book.

During this hurly-burly Angus and I managed to get off into a corner and compose a telegram to the chairman of the Senate Judiciary Committee, Senator Harley Kilgore, urging that his committee publicly investigate the Matusow case and offering to submit all pertinent data in our possession.

Neither of us anticipated the response that telegram would generate.

Following the Clancy interlude, I spent two more days before the grand jury.

When I first reappeared, I was surprised at the cordial reception by most of the jurors. From their cheery greetings of "Good morning, Mr. Kahn," you would never have guessed that only forty-eight hours before they had assisted in my being sentenced to six months in jail. It occurred to me that they themselves had perhaps been somewhat startled at the severity of the sentence, and were now, like myself, pleased I had not gone to jail after all. Nothing, of course, had happened to change the attitude of Assistant Attorney General Tompkins. He sought with undiminished zeal to convince the jurors that in publishing Matusow's manuscript, I had been involved in a sinister Communist campaign to sabotage the government's security program and discredit the Justice Department.

I stressed that the only campaign to discredit the Justice Department of which I knew was the one the Department was conducting against itself through the use of lying professional witnesses and corrupt paid informers.

At one point I left the jury room to consult Faulkner on several questions I did not want to answer without legal advice. However, he was not in the waiting room; and after several minutes Tompkins came in to ask about the delay. I explained I had not been able to locate Faulkner.

"Isn't there some other lawyer you could telephone for advice?" asked Tompkins.

I showed him in my notebook those questions of his to which I had temporarily withheld answers. One of them was that traditional query —was I or had I ever been a member of the Communist party?

"You're a lawyer," I told him. "Why don't you advise me?"

"I might be prejudiced," he said with a thin smile.

"I'd like your advice anyway."

He glanced at the questions, shrugged, and said, "I think I'd take the Fifth Amendment on those."

"That suits me."

Back in the jury room, I followed Tompkins's advice. My interrogation by Tompkins concluded on an interesting note.

"Just a few more questions and we'll be through, Mr. Kahn. Tell me, has there been any attempt on the part of this grand jury to censor Matusow's book?"

"Yes," I said, "there has."

Cries of protest came from the jurors. One called out, "Why, we haven't even read the book yet!"

I pointed out that Tompkins's question had referred to an "attempt" at censorship, and this had occurred when Cameron and I had first been ordered to surrender the manuscript and galleys of the book.

"Has the grand jury treated you courteously, Mr. Kahn?" asked Tompkins.

"Yes, the grand jury members have been courteous to me."

"And has the Department of Justice treated you courteously?"

"No, the Justice Department has treated me with extreme discourtesy."

"Has the grand jury made any attempt to intimidate you?"

"No, it has not."

"And the Department of Justice?"

"Yes, it has. And I suggest that you stop having FBI agents trail me around and annoy my family."

Obviously intending to relieve the mounting tension, the assistant foreman smilingly interjected, "Mr. Kahn, speaking of courtesies extended by the grand jury, I hope you recall that I loaned you my fountain pen." He added: "And you haven't returned it yet."

Amid general laughter, I handed him his pen.

"I'd like to say just one other thing," I told the foreman.

He nodded his assent.

I had been waiting for this moment.

Early that morning I had written a memorandum addressed to the grand jury indicating the sort of investigation I thought it should really be conducting.

I read the memorandum aloud:

I respectfully suggest to the grand jury that, to facilitate the investigation of the Matusow case, the Justice Department be directed to produce to the jury the following data:

1) All records of negotiations with Matusow while he was in the employ of the Justice Department as a paid witness, including stenographic notes of conversations with him, memoranda regarding any matters relating to him, et cetera.

2) All records of meetings and negotiations between Roy Cohn and Matusow, giving time, place, purpose and substance of meetings and negotiations.

3) All records of payments made to Matusow by Justice Department officials.

4) All records of any instructions given to Matusow by Roy Cohn or any other Justice Department official during or prior to his appearance on the witness stand as a prosecution witness for the Department—question-and-answer sheets, et cetera.

5) All records of reports, oral and/or written, made by Matusow to the Justice Department while he was working for them as a paid government witness and also while he was operating as an FBI agent.

I handed the memorandum to the foreman. "I'd like to have that included in the record."

"Did you write that yourself, Mr. Kahn?" asked Tompkins. His urbanity had deserted him, and for once he did not smile.

I replied that I had.

The assistant foreman said earnestly, "Mr. Kahn, you have our assurance that all the persons to whom you refer in that statement will be sitting right where you are."

I didn't doubt he meant every word he said. Unfortunately, the confidential files of the Justice Department were not in his possession. Nor was there much reason to believe that Attorney General Brownell and FBI Director J. Edgar Hoover would readily make available to the grand jury, or anybody else, the evidence of their own malpractices.

CHAPTER NINE

FACT AND FICTION

1. *Retrial Hearing*

While the grand jury and I had been getting acquainted on the fifth floor of the federal courthouse, another phase of the Matusow affair was evolving two floors above us. In a packed courtroom the hearing on the request for a new trial in the Flynn case had started before Judge Edward J. Dimock.

A slight, graying man with delicately chiseled features and slender, expressive hands which he used in sparing gestures, Judge Dimock had the reputation of being a "judge's judge," and the careful dispassion and juridical learning with which he approached the administration of the law were readily apparent. Of course, justice and the law are by no means always synonymous. With rare exceptions during recent years, even the most able American magistrates had administered most iniquitous laws. Judge Dimock was not one of the exceptions. He had sentenced thirteen defendants in the Flynn case to prison terms under the Smith Act, although, possibly because of some inner conflict over what was legal and what was just, he had imposed comparatively lenient sentences and directed the acquittal of two defendants.

Representing the government at the retrial hearing was U.S. Attorney J. Edward Lumbard. Some years before he had been appointed a New York Supreme Court Justice by Governor Dewey; and although he had been voted out of office after a few months, he still favored the title of "Judge Lumbard." A stolid, neatly dressed man in his early fifties, he was assisted in his present duties by a corps of eager young government attorneys, who whispered diverse pieces of intelligence to him and trundled to and from the courtroom mobile stands piled high with various exhibits and other documents. Despite these facilities, Lumbard gave the impression of having some difficulty in grasping exactly what was happening at the proceedings.[33]

The contrast between Lumbard and Harry Sacher, who was acting as counsel for the Flynn case defendants, could not have been more striking. Swift and incisive, rarely wasting a word or motion, the spruce little attorney had at his instant command not only every detail of the case but every aspect of the law relating to it. With the exception of a large yellow pad on which he occasionally jotted notes, the table in front of him was completely bare; but more than once when the team of government lawyers was rummaging in its files for some document under discussion, Sacher advised them on the correct category under which it could be found. The drama of Sacher's performance was heightened by the fact that, after a decade of harassment by the authorities for defending Communists and other political dissenters, the tables were turned. Sacher was now cast in the role of virtually prosecuting the government itself.

Matusow was the first witness to testify. During the preceding days, we had seen little of each other because of my protracted sessions with the grand jury; and although I had not had a great deal of time to think about it, there was some question in my mind as to how he would face the ordeal of testifying in court. Perhaps Harvey sensed this concern on my part. At any rate, on the day I received my contempt sentence, he told me: "I want you to know, Al, that if you're ready to go to jail for publishing my book, I'm ready to go to jail for telling the truth."

His conduct on the stand seemed to bear out that statement. He affirmed the contents of his affidavit of recantation, as the *New York Herald Tribune* reporter put it, "with the air of a man who is never more at home than on the witness stand testifying about himself." And if I found something a little disconcerting about the cool deliberation with which he admitted his past lies, I had to marvel at the metamorphosis in him since that time, not many weeks before, when in our tape-recorded talks he had so stubbornly avoided using the word "lie" in connection with himself.

Under Sacher's interrogation, Harvey related how he had been selected and "prepared" as a witness in the Flynn case. The question of his being a witness had been first discussed with him in December 1951, when he'd been taken by an FBI agent to meet Assistant U.S. Attorney Roy Cohn and two other government lawyers. At this meeting, he said, Cohn had indicated that the prosecution intended to prove the defendants had advocated the overthrow of the government "by force and violence"; and, in this connection, Cohn had mentioned that the government wanted to introduce Andrei Vyshinskii's book, *The Law of the Soviet State*, as one of the pieces of evidence. During the ensuing months the details of Matusow's testimony had been worked out, and "question-and-answer sheets" drafted, in a series of conferences at the U.S. Attorney's office with Cohn and several other government lawyers. Shortly before the trial itself Cohn had sailed for Europe.

"Did you testify falsely at the Flynn trial?" asked Sacher.

"Yes," Matusow replied.[34]

Reading from the Flynn transcript, Sacher questioned Matusow regarding the specific accusations he had made against the defendants. In each instance Matusow admitted he had lied.

Step by step, Sacher built up supplementary evidence to substantiate the fact that Matusow's testimony at the trial had been false, and to prove he had made a habit of lying as a government witness. As part of this evidence, Sacher placed in the record affidavits Matusow had given the *New York Times* and *Time* magazine retracting allegations that the staffs of these publications were overrun by Communists and stating that these allegations had been made "at the behest of McCarthy."

The fact that Matusow had signed the *New York Times* affidavit on September 23, 1953, and the *Time* affidavit on March 24, 1954, hardly supported the Justice Department's present claim that it had had no reason to doubt Matusow's reliability when he was a government witness. Not until the midsummer of 1954 had the Justice Department ceased using Matusow as a witness, and then only at Matusow's own insistence.

Equally interesting was the fact that the well-known New York law firm of Lord, Day & Lord had represented the *New York Times* in connection with obtaining Matusow's affidavit. Herbert Brownell, Jr., had been a member of this law firm until the time of his appointment as U.S. Attorney General. But despite the fact that Lord, Day & Lord possessed conclusive evidence of Matusow's having lied under oath on the witness stand, the Attorney General had seen no reason to question the propriety of the Justice Department's repeatedly using Matusow as an "expert witness." Moreover, Brownell still claimed there had never been any grounds for doubting Matusow's veracity.[35]

Sacher told Judge Dimock there was an effective way of checking the validity of Matusow's assertion that he had lied at the Flynn trial. An examination of the reports Matusow had made to the FBI while a Communist party member would reveal whether or not they included his subsequent charges in court against the Flynn defendants. If these charges were missing from the reports, it would certainly tend to substantiate Matusow's claim that he had later fabricated the accusations. Therefore, said Sacher, he was requesting that the government make available all of Matusow's FBI reports.

A crucial point in the hearing had now been reached. It was not the first time in recent years that an attorney in a political case had requested that the FBI reports be produced in court on grounds that they were essential to the defense. Some judges had previously instructed the Justice Department to make such reports available; but most judges, under the pressure of cold-war tensions, had refused to do so, supporting the Justice Department's claim that it would endanger national security "to violate the secrecy of the FBI files." As of this time, the U.S. Supreme Court had handed down no decision on this matter.

Sacher's request was clearly not to Lumbard's liking. Addressing Judge Dimock, he said, "I think these reports have no reference— those that I looked at, at least—to any of the people in the Flynn case. . . . It seems to me that we would be getting into something that has no relevancy here. . . ." He would therefore prefer not to produce the reports.

Judge Dimock voiced his disagreement with Lumbard. He told the U.S. Attorney he would like to see Matusow's FBI reports.

When the reports were submitted to Matusow for identification, he said he recalled some additional ones.

Would Lumbard, asked Sacher, be good enough to produce the missing reports?

The U.S. Attorney replied that he knew of no other reports Matusow had made to the FBI.

Not until some time later would we learn that among the FBI reports by Matusow that Lumbard failed to produce were several dealing with Clinton Jencks, which would have indicated the falseness of Matusow's testimony at Jencks's trial. We would also subsequently discover that this was not the only significant documentary evidence concerning Matusow which the U.S. Attorney refrained from making available to Judge Dimock.

Matusow's cross-examination by Lumbard lasted five days. Its length was by far the most impressive thing about it. In contrast to Sacher's mode of interrogation, Lumbard's questions limped along painfully, burdened by frequent reiterations and prolonged pauses.

With the obvious aim of proving Matusow had been bribed to recant, Lumbard began by questioning him exhaustively about the money he had thus far received from Cameron & Kahn. All Lumbard succeeded in establishing, however, was that Matusow, like most authors under contract with publishers, had been paid an advance royalty.

As Harvey's cross-examination continued it became apparent that the government's staff was engaging in maneuvers of questionable legality. Although grand jury testimony is supposedly secret and not to be divulged without a court order, Lumbard's aides were constantly scurrying back and forth between the grand jury room and Judge Dimock's court, bringing with them fresh information to aid the U.S. Attorney in his questioning of Matusow. This conveyer-belt system did not escape the alert Sacher, and he soon interrupted the cross-examination to ask Judge Dimock if he would ascertain the source of certain documents Lumbard was seeking to introduce as evidence. If these documents were grand jury exhibits, said Sacher, the presentation of them in court without the judge's permission was in violation of the statute prohibiting "disclosures of matter which is adduced before the grand jury."

Questioned by Judge Dimock, Lumbard admitted the documents had come from the grand jury room.

And was the U.S. Attorney, the judge quietly inquired, now requesting permission to make them public?

With marked chagrin, Lumbard said he was.

* * *

By far the most prolonged phase of Harvey's cross-examination concerned his bicycle trip of the previous fall through Texas and New Mexico. Hour after hour Lumbard questioned him about every minute of his journey in the hope of establishing that, somewhere amid the canyons, deserts and mountains of the Southwest, Communist agents had covertly offered Harvey a small fortune to recant.

"My God, what a trip," exclaimed a newsman at the conclusion of one court session. "And we're not even out of Texas yet!"

During his five days of questioning Harvey, Lumbard undeniably made one telling point. It concerned Matusow's final contract with Cameron & Kahn. Having established that Harvey's initial agreement with us had consisted of a letter written on October 26, 1954, Lumbard brought out the fact that the final contract had not been signed until the following February 1. Wasn't this, Lumbard demanded of Harvey, just one day after he had signed his affidavit of recantation in the Flynn case? And did not the final contract provide more favorable terms for him than the original letter-agreement?

There was little use in Harvey's pointing out that the overall terms of the final contract were not more favorable than those of the first agreement, or that the fourteen weeks lapse of time between the two agreements was simply due to Angus's not having gotten around to drafting the second, more detailed one. Nor was much accomplished by my mentally berating Angus for his procrastination. The damage was done. The government had managed to create the impression that we had dangled the final contract before Harvey as bait in exchange for his affidavit. As the *New York Herald Tribune* headlined the news: "MATUSOW'S ADMISSION IN COURT—Book Contract Followed Affidavit of Perjury."

It was certainly the most effective blow the Justice Department had struck thus far in its campaign to convince the public that we had bribed Matusow, and there was no predicting how this development would affect the outcome of the retrial hearings.

On the whole, Lumbard's interrogation of Matusow constituted an object lesson in the risks of maladroit cross-examination. Time and again he elicited proof of the very facts the government was seeking to disprove. A prime example occurred when he challenged Matusow's assertion that prior to meeting Angus and me he had told various people about the habit of bearing false witness. Perhaps, said Lumbard with a taunting air, Matusow would care to name some of these individuals? Harvey readily obliged. Besides his admissions to Bishop Oxnam, during or before the summer of 1954, he had apologized to the following persons for false accusations made against them: newspaper columnists Drew Pearson and Marquis Childs; radio commentator Elmer Davis; James Wechsler, editor of the *New York Post*; and Senators Henry Jackson, Mike Mansfield, James Murray, Hubert Humphrey, and Herbert Lehman. . . .

Doubtless to the Justice Department's discomfort, corroboration of Matusow's claim was promptly forthcoming from two of the persons he had named.

In his column Drew Pearson related:

> About a year ago a young man named Harvey Matusow came to see me and told me that he had lied about a lot of innocent people and that he felt sorry about it. He said he had lied about people whom he said were Communists when they were not. I told him he should straighten himself out and tell the truth. That's what he's doing now. . . .
>
> The tragedy is that the Government waited so long to act on Mr. Matusow's confession. Over a year ago I wrote that Mr. Matusow then wanted to tell the truth.

And columnist Marquis Childs wrote that in the summer of 1954 Matusow had come to see him "to apologize for lies that he had told about me," and that Matusow had spoken about "all the lying he had done before congressional committees, in the federal courts, and when he had campaigned in 1952 at the instigation, so he said, of Senator McCarthy." Childs added:

> And . . . this was the individual whom the Department of Justice and the FBI used as a witness and who spent days testifying before the Senate Internal Security Subcommittee and the House Un-American Activities Committee.

At the conclusion of Matusow's cross-examination, Lumbard called to the witness stand two former assistant U.S. Attorneys who had been members of the Justice Department's legal staff in the Flynn case. The two lawyers virtuously chorused that Matusow had given every indication of being "truthful" and "sincere," and that no information had ever come to their attention which caused them "to doubt the reliability of Mr. Matusow as a witness for the government." Both attorneys, who had been present when Matusow had been first interviewed as a potential witness by Roy Cohn, stated that the latter had made no mention of Vyshinskii's book, *Law of the Soviet State*, during that interview, as Matusow now claimed.

The next witness was Roy Cohn.

It had been generally expected that the testimony of the youthful, precocious lawyer who had won international notoriety as Senator McCarthy's aide, would constitute one of the dramatic highlights of the hearing. His appearance, however, had a definite anticlimactic quality. Only a few months had elapsed since Cohn had left McCarthy's staff and taken up private law practice, but he already seemed like a political anachronism. He was now less of a celebrity than a curiosity.

Under questioning by Lumbard, the sleek, dark-haired lawyer briskly snapped his replies and seemed to remember the smallest details of all his dealings with Matusow.

"Did you ever have any reason to believe, Mr. Cohn," asked Lumbard, "that Matusow had not stated the truth to you in anything he said to you?"

"No, Judge," said Cohn with an air of intense earnestness. "We made a very careful check on what he said. . . . Every check showed it was true. . . . If there had been any doubt in my mind or in anyone else's mind on the staff, he would never have been used as a witness."

"Did you ever suggest that he say anything which was not completely true?"

"That statement by him is completely untrue."

What drama there was to Cohn's testimony was not of his own making. It came when the erstwhile inquisitor faced interrogation by one of those same heretics whose persecution he had so zealously promoted.

The first exchange between Cohn and Sacher set the tone of the entire cross-examination.

"You say," Sacher began, "you checked everything that Matusow told you against documentation and—"

Cohn broke in. "To the best of our ability we did, Mr. Sacher."

"Now I am going to ask you, Mr. Cohn," Sacher told him sharply, "to desist from interrupting my questions. Will you bear that in mind, please?"

From that moment on there was little doubt as to who occupied the seat of authority.

Referring to specific charges Matusow had made in the Flynn case, Sacher asked Cohn to indicate the nature of the "very careful check" he claimed had been made of them. How, for example, had he confirmed the accuracy of Matusow's assertion that one of the defendants had been present at a certain meeting?

The precise memory Cohn had displayed during direct examination suddenly blurred. "I don't recall," he said, "whether we asked him what evidence he had to substantiate that. . . . I think we made some kind of independent check."

Did Cohn recall what form that "independent check" had taken?

Cohn didn't.

Perhaps, said Sacher, Cohn would specify some of the "independent checks" in connection with other of Matusow's allegations. Was there confirmation by other witnesses? If not, what was the evidence by which his testimony had been corroborated?

The vagueness of Cohn's answers was matched by their loquaciousness.

"Mr. Cohn," said Sacher, "you are talking too much. Just answer my questions, please."

Wasn't it true, Sacher asked Cohn, that certain of Matusow's accusations against Flynn case defendants had first appeared in Cohn's pretrial briefs and that there had been no mention of these charges in Matusow's previous statements to government attorneys and the FBI?

Cohn's answers became increasingly evasive and argumentative.

Finally, Sacher snapped: "Bear in mind, Mr. Cohn, you are in a court of law and not on the McCarthy committee!"

Judge Dimock intervened. "Mr. Cohn," he said, "you are a lawyer, and I know it is awfully difficult not to argue as you go along, but it would be a lot easier for all of us if you would pay strict attention to the question and simply answer it as a matter of logic and grammar."

It seemed symptomatic of a healthy change in the temper of the times that McCarthy's former chief counsel, before whom key government dignitaries had stood in fear and trembling, was now being instructed by a federal magistrate in the rudiments of thought and speech.

2. *Complications*

It is axiomatic that life's misfortunes tend to come in droves; and, as if the Justice Department had not enough on its hands with the Matusow scandal, new embarrassments of a similar nature suddenly materialized.

On February 11, the nation's press announced that another government witness had recanted.

The witness, a Mrs. Marie Natvig, had testified several months before at a Federal Communications Commission hearing that the Pennsylvania newspaper publisher and broadcaster Edward Lamb was a "Communist sympathizer." Now, reappearing before the same commission, Mrs. Natvig admitted that her testimony about Lamb had been false and charged that government attorneys had "coerced" her to lie.

"I was reciting a prepared speech," Mrs. Natvig declared. "I was scared to death. They told me what the truth was and what to tell. . . . We started to manufacture the evidence after Mr. Powell said, 'All right, kid, let's murder the bum'. . . . Only an idiot would have put any credence in what I said."

The *National Guardian* headlined its account of Mrs. Natvig's recantation: "Is Matusow Starting a Trend?"

An affirmative answer seemed indicated when, a few days later, a third government witness publicly announced that he too had been giving perjured testimony. He was Lowell Watson, a Kansas dairy farmer and former member of the Communist party who for some time had been one of the Justice Department's paid "expert witnesses" on communism.

Like Mrs. Natvig, Watson had testified against Edward Lamb at the FCC hearing. He now admitted he had deliberately lied in claiming that he had personally known Lamb as a Communist party member. Watson stated that his fabrications were "the result of constant coaching and conditioning" by members of the government's legal staff, and that he had been able to identify Lamb at the hearing only after a government investigator had secretly shown him photographs of Lamb and indicated where he was seated in the hearing room.[36]

"The sudden turn in the case of the Government against Edward Lamb," commented columnist Doris Fleeson, "finds the Government itself on trial."

The Madison, Wisconsin, *Capitol Times* editorialized, "There should be an investigation . . . into the conduct of responsible governmental agencies such as the Dept. of Justice and the FBI."

Senator Margaret Chase Smith of Maine told the graduating class at Temple University: "At long last, the shining truth about the false accusers, the half-truth artists, the professional fabricators, the prevaricators for pay is beginning to break through the dark and ugly clouds of doubt they have so evilly blown up."

At the office of Cameron & Kahn there was general agreement with Senator Smith's viewpoint.

True, our firm was still being investigated for its part in bringing the truth to light; and, besides Angus and me, the New York grand jury had now subpoenaed Ruth, Herb Tank, Nat Witt, and even the stenographers who had typed the manuscript of *False Witness*. Moreover, Attorney General Brownell had now convened two additional grand juries in El Paso and Denver to see what could be done in those regions toward proving Matusow had been bribed to recant by the "Communist-dominated" Mine-Mill union. But we could not help feeling that despite these earnest efforts on its part, the Justice Department had suffered a major setback in the admissions of Mrs. Natvig and Lowell Watson. There had to be a limit, after all, to the number of government witnesses who could be bribed by Communists to make false confessions of perjury.

"If any more witnesses recant," said Harvey, "Brownell is going to have to claim that the Justice Department has been taken over by the Communist party."

In our flush of optimism, however, we underestimated the resiliency and resourcefulness of the Justice Department. We were soon to learn that if the Department's problems were multiplying, it had by no means lost the capacity to create new ones for us.

One of these now loomed in an unexpected quarter.

On the day on which the plates of *False Witness* were due to be delivered at the printer's, one of the firm's top executives telephoned us. He was "very sorry," he said, but his company couldn't go ahead with the job. "We just can't fit it into our schedule. We don't have the presses available. . . ." He did not explain what had happened to the presses that had been previously set aside for the job.

I asked if his firm could take care of the binding.

"I'm afraid not," he said.

We immediately gave another printer the specifications on the book and asked for a bid that same day. His terms were satisfactory. The following morning he called us. He regretted, he said, that he could no longer handle the job. He had made "some miscalculations."

It was becoming clear that we, too, had made some miscalculations. Under the pressure of events we had given too little thought to the possibility of our not being able to get Matusow's book printed.

We called a progressive book manufacturer whom we had not previously contacted because we thought he lacked the equipment to produce the book as quickly as we needed it. Yes, he told us, he would be glad to handle the job. How soon could he get it done? He gave us a date that was three weeks later than the publication date we had already announced.

We got in touch with another printer. He had the reputation of being a liberal. When asked if he would print *False Witness* he replied with a categorical no.

Our staff held a council of war. It was agreed that Arthur Kahn would temporarily drop all other work and devote himself to the task of trying to find a printer.

For the next two days Arthur contacted printers, in and out of New York. None would print Matusow's book.

"I've looked over the galleys you sent me," one of them told Arthur, "and I think the book should be published. But I don't dare to do it. I'm ashamed to say it, but I'm afraid. I can't afford to lose my other accounts."

From another printer we learned that FBI agents were making the rounds of book printers to "inquire" about the production of *False Witness*. "They've got the printers really scared," he told us.

Angus and I promptly issued a press statement reporting what was happening. "We regard this effort to intimidate the book publishing community," we said, "as a continuation of the campaign on the part of the Justice Department to suppress the book, *False Witness*.

On the third day of his search, Arthur jubilantly announced he had found a printer who might take the job. His name was Harvey Satenstein, and he headed a new printing firm called Book Craftsmen Associates. That same afternoon Satenstein visited our office at the Chelsea Hotel. He was an impressive figure. When he entered the doorway, he completely filled it. Over six feet tall and built like a bull, he had coal black hair, a neatly groomed mustache, and a genial expression. With affectionate pride, he began describing the equipment in his printing plant.

"Before you tell us about that," I said, "there's a question I'd like to ask. Can you be intimidated?"

"Why?"

Arthur recounted our experiences to date in trying to get a printer.

"I don't scare easily," Satenstein said with a smile, his dark eyes gleaming behind his horn-rimmed glasses. One felt he was not overstating the case. I suggested he read a set of the galleys before committing himself to printing the book.

On his way out, he stopped. "You know, I'm just an ordinary businessman," he said, "but I don't like Senator McCarthy. And I do believe in freedom of the press.

Satenstein was back the next morning. "I've read the book," he said. "Stayed up last night and finished it."

"Well?"

"I'll print it. When do you need it?"

We told him.

"That's about twice as fast as it ordinarily takes to manufacture a book," he said. "But I'll get it done. It'll be a damn good job too."

He called the next day. "Well, the FBI boys have been here trying

to get me to cancel printing the book." He chuckled. "I had some fun
with them. I asked them "What's with you guys—are you Socialists
or something, interfering as you are with private enterprise?'"

Forty-eight hours later, Satenstein had the plates of *False Witness*
on the presses at his plant.

CHAPTER TEN

JUDGMENT ON THE HILL

1. *Cast of Characters*

The telegram which Angus and I had sent to the Senate Judiciary Committee on February 10, read:

> As publishers of the forthcoming book, *False Witness*, by Harvey Matusow, we wish to place at the disposal of the Senate Judiciary Committee all of the material in our possession relating to the writing and publication of this book. We believe that this material will aid in the conduct of a public investigation of the facts this book reveals regarding Matusow's testimony as a paid government witness and his fraudulent operations as an aide to Senator McCarthy. . . .

The telegram was addressed to the committee chairman, Senator Harley Kilgore. Copies went to all committee members. We had reason to believe that an investigation of the Matusow case by the Judiciary Committee might produce interesting results. Besides Senator Kilgore, the committee had four other members whose records on civil rights issues were among the best in the Senate—Senators Estes Kefauver, Thomas Hennings, William Langer, and Joseph O'Mahoney.

In the days when FDR was in the White House, and certain members of Congress were actually not afraid to associate with persons left of center, I had enjoyed a cordial acquaintanceship with the staunch and vigorous New Dealer Senator Kilgore. Now, however, the senator did not answer the communication from Cameron and me. Instead, to our somewhat pained surprise, we received a reply from Senator James Eastland, chairman of the Internal Security Subcommittee of the Judiciary Committee. Senator Eastland's telegram read:

> Regarding your telegram purporting to be a voluntary offer to furnish committee material in your possession relating to writing and publication of Matusow's book. It will be sufficient if you produce this material in accordance with Internal Security Subcommittee subpoena. . . . committee does not desire to interfere with grand jury proceedings or furnish refuge from grand jury subpoena.

On the heels of Eastland's message came subpoenas summoning Harvey, Angus and me to appear before Eastland's subcommittee in Washington.

Evidently, it had been decided that the Matusow case was too hot for the Judiciary Committee to handle. The subcommittee, moreover, had a rather special interest in the matter—Matusow had formerly been one of its own star witnesses.

There was a considerable difference between these two congressional bodies. The Internal Security Subcommittee was one of the most zealous of those congressional investigative committees which in the name of guarding the nation's security were diligently subverting its Constitution. As originally conceived, Congress' power of investigation was intended to facilitate the collection of data concerning contemplated laws, and to enable the legislative branch of government to scrutinize the operations of the executive branch. As applied in the Cold War, the power had become a major means of enforcing official dogma, spying on citizens, persecuting political heretics, and, last but by no means least, advancing the careers of the investigators.

While trials by legislative bodies were theoretically prohibited by the Constitution, such was in fact the nature of the hearings conducted by the congressional investigative committees. They were, however, trials of a very special sort, at which the committee members acted as prosecutors, jury and judges, and the accused were denied elementary rights under due process of law.

"It is," Walter Lippmann had noted, "a pillory in which reputations are ruined, often without proof and always without the legal safeguards that protect the ordinary tribunal; it is a tribunal before which men are arraigned and charged with acts that are, as a matter of fact, lawful."

In view of these circumstances we had little reason to expect an enlightened investigation of the Matusow case by the Internal Security Subcommittee. The composition of the subcommittee gave no added cause for optimism. Its chairman, the avowed segregationist, Senator Eastland, was now challenging McCarthy's position as the outstanding demagogue in the Senate.[37]

Another member of the subcommittee was its former chairman, Senator William E. Jenner. He was a devoted McCarthy disciple. He had demanded that President Truman be impeached as a tool of "a secret coterie directed by agents of the Soviet Union." He presently claimed that the United States had fought on the wrong side in World War II. Such was the measure of his erudition.

A third member, Senator Herman Welker, was, in the words of the *New York Times*, "a sort of floor manager for the pro-McCarthy bloc in the Senate."

Senator Arthur Watkins was a fourth member. He had been campaigning for reelection in Utah when the hearing on the Mine-Mill union, at which Matusow testified, had been held in Salt Lake City in 1952. Together with his close friend, the arch-reactionary Senator Pat McCarran, Watkins had presided over the proceedings. It was following this hearing that Matusow had toured several western states campaigning for McCarthy-endorsed candidates—including Senator Watkins; and the latter's office had paid part of Matusow's traveling expenses.[38]

Then there was the subcommittee counsel. When Matusow had been one of the committee's star witnesses, its chief counsel had been Senator McCarran's aide and confidant, Julian G. Sourwine. He still served the committee in that capacity. It was unlikely that Senators Eastland, Jenner, Welker, and Watkins and their counsel, Sourwine, would accord us a very sympathetic hearing. Matusow's recantation reflected upon them no less than upon the Justice Department.

Even so, I thought there might be a fighting chance of getting the committee to conduct an investigation different from that we were experiencing at the hands of the Justice Department. For one thing,

there were five new committee members who had never been involved in the use of Matusow as a witness. Four of these senators—
Thomas Hennings, John McClellan, Olin Johnston, and Price
Daniel—were Democrats, and conceivably might want to expose
Matusow's role in spreading fraudulent propaganda at McCarthy's behest against their Democratic colleagues. Senator Hennings had
headed an investigation of McCarthy's dubious financial dealings and
had been an outspoken critic of repressive security measures.

Angus was not at all persuaded by my wishful thinking. "As far as
I'm concerned," he said, "there won't be an iota of difference between the committee's approach and the Justice Department's. Every
Democrat on the committee is a Southerner. What you've got is a
microcosm of the Dixiecrat-McCarthyite combination that's been running the Senate. With the possible exception of Hennings, they'll all
see eye-to-eye on this thing."

Even if this was the case, I argued, we were in the paradoxical
position of having ourselves requested a Senate investigation. "We
can't very well now act as if we didn't want one. I think we ought to
wait and see how things shape up. Let's concentrate our fire on the
Justice Department and not go after the committee for the time being,
at any rate."

"What'll happen," Angus replied a bit gloomily, "is that they'll go
after us."

2. Return Engagement

The marble-columned Senate caucus chamber in which the Senate
subcommittee hearing on the Matusow case began on February 21,
1955, had become familiar to millions of television viewers as the
scene of the fantastic extravaganza of the Army-McCarthy hearings
the previous year. And when Matusow appeared as the first witness
in the subcommittee hearing, the setting seemed unchanged. There
was the same jungle of flood-lights, newsreel cameras, television and
radio tables, the same packed rows of spectators. But there were
other, different reasons why McCarthy's name came to mind. As reporter William Shannon wrote in the *New York Post*:

In that vast chamber where Joe McCarthy had scored so many of his triumphs . . . his ghost stalked again. Harvey Matusow, once one of McCarthy's favorite witnesses, and now the visible relic of his vanished power, returned . . . to tell the Internal Security Subcommittee that most of his former testimony had been lies and that most of the august senators who sat before him had been his silent accomplices in deceit. . . .

It was only two and a half years ago that several of the same senators had cowered before McCarthy's power and begged for his assistance. Some who couldn't get McCarthy had been glad to settle for Matusow.

Senator Eastland, porcine, bespectacled, and smoking a cigar, opened the hearing by reading a prepared statement. The investigation, he said, was to inquire into Matusow's recent "public statements . . . that he lied when he testified before this subcommittee and on other occasions." The fact the inquiry was just starting did not prevent the chairman from indicating its probable outcome. Matusow's repudiation of his testimony, Eastland stressed, did not reflect upon those government agencies that had used him as a witness or upon other informer-witnesses. The latter were performing a great service not only to American democracy but also "in the world struggle to preserve human freedom." As an outstanding example, the senator cited the well-known professional witness Elizabeth Bentley, whose testimony had been found by the subcommittee to be "flawlessly truthful. . . ."

Eastland's tribute to informer-witnesses completed, the interrogation of Matusow got under way.

The committee counsel, Sourwine, promptly indicated the contemplated line of examination by stating it had been "charged in the press" that the Communist party was using Matusow's recantation in an "all-out offensive against the Government's effective campaign to expose the Communist conspiracy and prosecute its leaders." Did Matusow, asked Sourwine, have any comment to make on that charge?

"I do have a comment, sir," said Harvey in a voice that could be clearly heard throughout the caucus room. "I have lied in court. . . . When I testified in El Paso, Texas, against labor leader Clinton Jencks, I did not know whether he was or was not a Communist. . . .

If the government based its conviction on my testimony, my false testimony, then he should have a new trial. . . . If the conviction of the Communist leaders was based in any way upon my testimony, which was false, then these people should have a new trial. . . . They don't belong in jail, on my lies."[39]

Matusow added he had lied consistently as a government witness to prove himself "a good anti-Communist." "I was," he said, "a perpetual and habitual liar."

As the hearing progressed, the senators made every effort to avoid asking questions that might elicit proof of Harvey's admission of the falsity of his past testimony. They concentrated, instead, on trying to prove his testimony was now untrue, apparently operating on the theory that by impugning his present veracity they could lend credibility to his previous lies.

Increasingly, their questions took the form of crude taunts:

JENNER: You are telling the truth now?
MATUSOW: Yes, sir.
JENNER: You are not a habitual liar?. . . .
MATUSOW: I am not a perpetual liar now. . . .
WATKINS: You told us in unequivocal language, "I am a habitual and perpetual liar."
MATUSOW: I believe I said I had been a perpetual and habitual—
WATKINS: I think the record will speak for itself. If you said "I am," I think that is probably one of the true things you have said here today. . . .
McCLELLAN: You kind of intrigued me by a description of the kind of liar you are. Could you possibly be a congenital liar?
MATUSOW: Well, sir, there are many adjectives to describe liars. . . . And I think most of them would fit my past.
McCLELLAN: What I wanted to determine is whether this is a capacity or faculty that you have developed or did it come natural with you; was it congenital from birth?
MATUSOW: No, sir; I don't think it was congenital from birth.

A logical question which the senators chose not to explore was why they themselves had used Matusow as an expert witness if he were a "habitual," "perpetual," or "congenital" liar. But what their questions lacked in logic was more than compensated for in malice.

"No senator in the room," commented William Shannon of the

New York Post, "volunteered the thought that Matusow was doing the right thing in coming forward, even at this late date, to correct the record and undo the damage he'd done. They tried to 'rehabilitate' him as a witness. . . . They lightly suggested he should see a psychiatrist. When these tactics failed, they bluntly tried to intimidate him by warning they would send him to jail for perjury if they could. Thus, he would be punished not for his lies but for his present confession. . . ."

The fiercely hostile interrogation had no visible effect on Harvey. He seemed wholly undisturbed by the gibes, threats, and accusations of his examiners as he continued calmly to reiterate that he had lied as a government witness and was telling the truth now. "Actually," he later told me, "I was sore as hell when I thought how they'd used me and how they were going after me now because I was trying to do something decent. . . . But I made up my mind to keep cool and show them up. I guess they shouldn't have taught me to be such a good witness. . . ."

If Harvey maintained his composure, however, his interrogators became increasingly frustrated and enraged. As they undertook to depict Matusow as an unmitigated scoundrel who would sell himself to the highest bidder, they were apparently unaware they were simply disclosing their own standards for "expert witnesses." Flourishing the letter Matusow had sent McCarthy in the summer of 1953 saying he'd decided to give up being a professional witness and condemning his motives in becoming one, Sourwine asked, "Do you remember stating, sir, that you would do anything for a buck?"

"Yes, sir."

"Is that still true?"

"It is not."

Senator Jenner said with a smirk on his pale, hard-bitten face, "You are going to be paid for the publication of your book, *False Witness*. Could it be that you are lying again for money?"

"Sir," said Harvey, "I believe the legal fees in the proceedings that will be brought against me will more than cover the amount of royalties I will make on the book."

"You want us to believe," demanded Senator McClellan with the righteous tone and look of an unctuous deacon, "that you are now sincere, and that you are trying to purge your soul of the dastardly thing you have done?" His voice rose accusingly. "You are trying to capitalize on the crimes you have committed by publishing this book and having it sold to the American people."

For the first time, Harvey's air of serenity left him. "Right now," he shouted back angrily, "all monies that are not used in legal fees and defense of myself in relation to these charges, I will turn over to any charity in relation to scholarship for schools." He went on: "I would like to name the school, because I attacked that school—Antioch College in Yellow Springs, Ohio. If you like, sir, have any attorney ... draw it up and I will sign it and give it to the school."

Senator McClellan dropped the subject.

The subcommittee sought to rake up every possible sordid detail from Matusow's past. Had he stolen funds, they asked, from his former wife? Had he falsified his army record? Was it true he'd once tried to blackmail a subcommittee investigator into giving him money? Whether or not the charges and admissions in *False Witness* were true was a subject the senators and their counsel carefully shunned. They referred to the book only in an attempt to prove that while writing it Matusow had been surrounded by "Communists" and "fellow-travelers," as if the mere mention of these words would magically exorcise the book's disclosures.

"Isn't it true," asked Eastland, "that Mr. Kahn, Mr. Cameron, and Mr. Witt have been your closest associates for the past few months? And you have accused every one of them of being a Communist?"

"In one form or another, yes."

"In fact, you believe they are Communists, don't you?"

"No, sir, I don't," said Matusow, "I don't know and I don't care. . . . My relationship with these people is based on friendship, not political belief."

Supposing, asked Senator Daniel, Matusow were to learn his publishers were Communists, would he take his book away from them?

"The only publisher who offered to publish my book was Cameron & Kahn. . . ." said Harvey. "They were the only ones who had the courage. . . . If I knew they were members of the Communist party, I would continue to let them publish this book, yes, sir."

Toward the conclusion of the first day of the hearing, Senator Jenner recommended the whole inquiry be called off. "I just wonder about the feasibility of this committee taking up its time listening to such drivel and such testimony," he said. It had evidently dawned on the senator that the hearing was proving to be more of an indictment of the subcommittee than of Matusow.

His colleagues, however, were disinclined to heed his advice.

Harvey was to make five more appearances before the subcommittee and, before he was through, he would have been under examination for more than twenty hours. Even if his interrogation had been conducted with the utmost temperance and decorum, instead of the sustained vehemence with which it was, he might have been expected to show signs of tension and fatigue. But the very opposite proved to be the case.

With each day Harvey seemed to become more relaxed and invigorated. Not he but his examiners increasingly showed the strain as, unflustered by their irate accusations and insults, he repeatedly turned their attacks on him into disclosures of their own malpractices, chided them for the role of their committee, and made them the butt of his humor. "The consensus of opinion among reporters who covered the show," noted *I.F. Stone's Weekly*, "was that Harvey was in control of the proceedings."

Time and again, when the senators were excoriating him for his misdeeds, Harvey pointed out that they themselves were largely responsible for his role as lying witness.

At one point Senator Welker was questioning Harvey regarding his avowed distaste for the term "stool pigeon." "Notwithstanding that fact," said Welker, "you . . . went on crucifying people, is that right?"

"I joined with congressional committees," replied Matusow, "and crucified people. Yes, sir."

But how, persisted the senator, did Matusow account for the fact that he himself had become "a lying stool pigeon"?

"Because," retorted Matusow, "these committees of Congress, such as this one, forced me and many others to do it."

"We forced you?" demanded Senator Welker incredulously.

"Yes, sir, by creating a fear and hysteria which this country has never seen before. The people cannot turn around and talk with their neighbors without being called Communists—honest, decent people. You are the ones responsible for my role as a witness, not I!"

WELKER: There is no more low character in the history of the world
than a man who commits perjury and sends a fellow man to the
penitentiary.
MATUSOW: Why do you encourage it? . . .
WELKER: Have I ever encouraged you to commit perjury or to tell a
lie under oath?
MATUSOW: Sir, you encourage witnesses like Elizabeth Bentley and
Paul Crouch and the others to come before these committees and
tell many lies.

Harvey went on to say that Elizabeth Bentley, whom Senator Eastland
had singled out for special praise in his opening statement, had herself
indicated to him that she had given false testimony as a government
witness.

And under just what circumstances, asked Sourwine, had Miss
Bentley made this admission?

Matusow related that in the days when he had been a professional
witness, Miss Bentley had once broken down and wept while confid-
ing her woes to him. "She said that she had used up all the money she
had received from the publication of her book . . . that she was broke
. . . She said she didn't want to talk to the government any more. She
was sick of being used." She had bitterly complained that the government insisted on paying her periodic witness fees instead of a regular
salary as a witness. "You are a young man. . . ." Matusow quoted
Miss Bentley as saying. "You can go out and find a job. I can't. I
have to continue doing this sort of thing. It's the only way I can
work. . . . I just have to continue to find information to testify about."
He made it clear that the phrase, "finding information," as used by
Miss Bentley, was a euphemism for inventing it.

The subcommittee members listened glumly to Harvey's account of
this tête-à-tête with Elizabeth Bentley. When he had finished, Senator
Eastland announced in a challenging tone: "Mr. Matusow, this committee is going to call Miss Bentley as a witness."

The committee, however, would apparently decide that such action
might be indiscreet; and at no time during the hearing was Miss Bentley to be summoned to refute Matusow's charges.

When Harvey declared he also knew that the government witnesses
Matt Cvetic, Louis Budenz, Paul Crouch, and Manning Johnson had
repeatedly lied in their testimony, the senators made a spirited defense

of these protégés of theirs. Had Matusow, they demanded, incontrovertible proof of the lies these witnesses had told? Or was it simply a matter of his word against theirs? The senators' sudden concern for strict rules of evidence contrasted sharply with their ready acceptance in the past of rumors, hearsay accusations and downright lies as proof of the "subversive" character of hundreds of ordinary citizens.

Senator Welker asked Matusow to specify some "overt acts of perjury" by the witnesses under discussion.

"They are very clever at committing perjury," replied Harvey, "just as I was clever at telling falsehoods."

"Yes, sir," said Senator Welker, "indeed you are right on that."

"Yes, sir," said Harvey, "we had good training."

It was sometimes difficult to tell whether the ready quips and sallies with which Harvey punctuated his testimony were prompted mainly by the desire to disconcert his examiners or to exploit the national stage he now had for displaying his talents as an entertainer. Whichever the case, his performance was such that time and again he had the caucus room audience rocking with laughter and the subcommittee members reduced to a state of surly confusion.

Prior to one of his appearances the *Washington Daily News* noted: "Congressional entertainer Harvey Matusow is doing a matinee today at 2 p.m. at the Capitol."

Each day the press featured some new bon mot of Harvey's. One of the most widely quoted occurred when Senator Welker, who was continually getting his facts mixed up, addressed Harvey as "Mr. Matsu." Harvey shot back: "Sir, I don't lie in the Straits of Formosa . . ."

Following one session Harvey told me somewhat shamefacedly: "Maybe it's undignified of me to act that way at the hearing. But you know how I am. It's just me, that's all." He brightened up. "Anyway people like to laugh. And the main thing is that it's all in a good cause."

What was perhaps the most ludicrous moment of the whole proceedings came when Harvey was being questioned regarding his present sources of income. One prospective source, said Harvey, was a toy he'd invented which would soon be on the market. The toy became the subject of intensive inquiry. What kind of toy was it?

queried the senators. Harvey said it was "an entertaining, nondestructive toy for children." And who, he was asked, was the manufacturer? Harvey declined to identify the manufacturer on the grounds it might harm the latter's business. The committee members continued to press for the manufacturer's name, and Sourwine stated the reason for their concern. "The question," he said, "is whether the firm which is manufacturing or is to manufacture your toy is a Soviet or Communist firm."

"I think," remarked Senator Welker, "all of us are rather interested in this toy. Would you mind telling us what sort of a toy it is?"

There was a long pause. Then Harvey said, "Well, I call it a stringless yo-yo."

The laughter that swept the Senate caucus chamber spread across the nation that night as TV and radio news commentators regaled their listeners with the tale of Matusow's stringless yo-yo. Next day newspapers from coast to coast featured the picture of a wide-eyed Matusow catching an ordinary—not stringless—yo-yo that some enterprising photographer had tossed him as he left the hearing room. The *New York Times* soberly reported:

> Webster's International Dictionary defines the ordinary yo-yo thus: "A trademark applied to a spherical top attached to the finger by a cord looped around its middle groove. Run up and down by skillful jerks, the top does odd tricks and takes diverting positions."

Yet notwithstanding the many diverting aspects of the proceedings, and the frequent merriment caused by Matusow's agile wit, the drama of his appearance before the subcommittee was essentially more tragic than comic. It was tragic not only because his admissions concerned the waste and degradation of a gifted person, but also because ever present behind the glaring lights and amid the resounding laughter were the silent shadowy figures of a host of men and women— teachers with blighted careers, doctors with ruined reputations, workers dismissed from their jobs—who had been irrevocably wronged by the inquisitors and their lying witnesses. It was tragic, too, because the individuals conducting this hearing, who bore the proud title of senator and made daily decisions affecting the destinies of millions, were themselves revealed as men wanting in dignity and ethics, subverting the rights of the citizens they supposedly represented and shaming the nation as a whole.

For all these somber overtones, however, there was a triumphant note to Matusow's testimony. Truth had invaded the marketplace of lies. The inquisition had been dealt a devastating blow by a twenty-seven-year-old ex-informer who was seeking to redeem himself.

3. *Variations on a Theme*

With no particular reluctance I awaited my turn at the subcommittee hearing. To leave the impression that the proceedings were wholly without merit would be misleading. For all its defects, a public hearing of the subcommittee offered a major, and for progressives, a rare advantage—the opportunity to speak and be heard.

There had, I felt, been a tendency among "unfriendly witnesses" at congressional hearings not fully to exploit this asset. A frequent practice was to remain largely silent and refuse to answer numerous questions by invoking Constitutional privileges. I asked myself how best to take advantage of an appearance before the Senate subcommittee:

I had jotted down these notes:

> Keep in mind that every statement should be addressed not primarily to committee but to public.
>
> Assume offensive and keep committee on defensive.
>
> Stress responsibility and guilt of committee for Matusow's past.
>
> Meet red-baiting by positively stating own views but indicate that this is not supposed to be the subject of the investigation.
>
> Regard every question asked by committee members not as obstacle but rather as an opportunity to state facts.

In addition to this somewhat didactic advice to myself, I had listed a number of the most flagrant lies Matusow had told as a government witness. I intended to do my best to see that this data became part of the public record.

* * *

Riette and I decided to take our three boys to Washington to attend the subcommittee session at which I was to testify. We felt that the excursion would perhaps contribute more to their general education than the few days of school they might miss. Needless to say, Steven, Timmy, and Brian raised no vigorous objections to the idea of being temporarily absent from school.

We drove down to Washington the evening before my scheduled appearance. With the committee not due to convene until after lunch, we spent the morning sight-seeing. It was a cool, cloudless day. The mass of white granite government buildings conveyed a sense of the power of the state, fully arrayed against us. And yet, bathed resplendently in bright sunlight, the capital's serene vistas and majestic monuments summoned up memories of the nation's long and arduous struggle to achieve a way of life with liberty and justice for all.

Angus and Stanley Faulkner, who had come down from New York on a morning train, joined us at the hotel for lunch.

Afterward we all proceeded to the Senate Office Building.

The boys were in a high state of excitement. They scampered ahead of us down the long, shining corridors, to which they lent a sudden touch of life, chattering noisily to one another, pointing dramatically to the senators' names on the plaques on the doors to their offices.

The Senate caucus chamber was almost full when we arrived— full, it seemed at first glance, of strange and coldly curious faces. Then, here and there, I saw familiar countenances. One nodded in recognition. Another smiled a quiet welcome. A third winked. A Washington businessman I had known for some years walked over to me and shook my hand. His greeting was no mere casual formality. It was an act of courage. Conspicuously, he was declaring himself. While Riette, Angus and the boys went to find seats in the crowded caucus room, Stan and I took our places at the conference table facing the subcommittee members, who sat with regal aplomb amid the klieg lights, microphones, and television cameras. I noted with regret that Senator Hennings was not present. Besides the subcommittee counsel, Sourwine, my interrogators would consist of the three southern Bourbons—Senators Eastland, McClellan, and Daniel—and the two McCarthyites, Senators Jenner and Welker.

My examination began with the following colloquy:

EASTLAND: You wrote a book called *The Great Conspiracy*, did you not?

KAHN: Yes . . .

EASTLAND: Now, did you know that *The Great Conspiracy* was required reading for American prisons of war who were in Communist prison camps in Korea, and it was part of the brainwashing process they had to endure?

KAHN: It seems to me there are several questions there, Senator, one relating to whether or not I knew the book was read there.

EASTLAND: I want you to answer my question. Was it required reading for American prisoners of war?

KAHN: I have no way of knowing that, Senator. I was not there.

EASTLAND: Isn't that your understanding, sir?

KAHN: No. I believe another book of mine was read there.

EASTLAND: Well, now, what book was that that was read there?

KAHN: I saw a newspaper report to the effect that *High Treason* was read there.

EASTLAND: Who wrote *High Treason*?

KAHN: I wrote *High Treason*.

EASTLAND: It was part of the brainwashing process, wasn't it?

KAHN: That phrase is somewhat obscure to me. Perhaps you would explain it, Senator.

EASTLAND: Well, now, Mr. Kahn, you know the meaning. Was it required reading by the Communists for American prisoners in their hands? Wasn't it?

KAHN: You are telling me that, Senator.

The precise connection between the Matusow case and the reading matter of American prisoners of war in North Korea was perhaps a little obscure. Presumably if it could be shown that writings of mine had served as an ingredient in the black magic of "brainwashing," I could be that much more easily identified as a Communist sorcerer who had charmed Matusow into a false confession.

Senator Eastland's small eyes squinted at me over his glasses. One could sense the painful effort of his mind at work. In what countries, he asked, had my books been translated and published?

"In twenty-five or thirty countries," I told him.

He asked me to name the publishers.

I proceeded to list some of them.

Before long he interrupted impatiently, "Who in the Soviet Union?"

I gave him the name of the Soviet publisher.

Was it my opinion, he asked, that Soviet readers who bought my books did so because they were "in sympathy with the point of view expressed" in them?

I assumed, I said, that the Russians who bought my books, like the Americans who bought them, did so because they found them of interest.

My examination continued:

EASTLAND: Now I will ask you this question: are you a member of the Communist party, U.S.A.?

KAHN: I would decline to answer that question, Senator, on the grounds of the First Amendment and on the grounds of the Fifth Amendment, and would like to make a comment.

EASTLAND: We don't recognize the First Amendment.

KAHN: Well, I recognize the First Amendment, Senator Eastland, even if the committee doesn't.

EASTLAND: I know, but for the purpose of declining to answer, that is not a valid ground. If you are going to rest on the First Amendment, I order you to answer the question.

KAHN: I decline to answer, then, on the grounds of the Fifth Amendment.

EASTLAND: Yes, sir.

KAHN: And I would like to make a comment.

EASTLAND: Go ahead.

KAHN: My comment is this: I do not decline to answer this question with any shame whatsoever.

I might say that I proudly decline to answer it on the grounds of the Fifth Amendment, which I regard as an amendment protecting the rights of the innocent as well as the rights of the guilty; and it is my understanding that the wording does not include anything about self-incrimination, but protects any American citizen from bearing witness against himself. . . .

I understand that many people have been attacked for using the Fifth Amendment. I would simply say this, Senator; that he who attacks me for using the Fifth Amendment does not slander me but slanders the Constitution of the United States.

"Of course," sneered Senator Eastland, "that is the ground that Communists use when they don't want to state whether or not they are Communists."

"You mean," I asked, "that only Communists use the Constitution?"

Senator Welker spoke up. "You have before you," he said gravely, "a group of senators who have defended the defenseless and the oppressed for vicious, serious crimes, and I do not know one of them— one of them, including the interrogator—who has ever used the Fifth Amendment. The truth is always much better. Do you agree with me on that?"

"I agree with the framers of the Constitution and I assume they put that clause in for a very good purpose."[40]

"Is it true that you are a left-winger?" asked Senator Welker.

"I believe," I said, "that the implication of my remarks and my general conduct would indicate that I could be characterized, without injustice, as a left-winger." However, I added, I didn't think that the left wing should be given all the credit for bringing to light the facts in the Matusow case. "I think that is showing prejudice in favor of the left." There were, I pointed out, conservative elements, too, like the *New York Times*, that had played an important part in publicly exposing the informer-witness racket. And the credit should certainly be shared with them.

The proceedings had been under way a comparatively short time when an unexpected visitor entered the caucus room. It was none other than Senator Joseph McCarthy. Flashbulbs popped and newsmen scribbled hastily on their pads as the senator ostentatiously made his way up to the dais where the subcommittee members were seated. As if giving the hearing his benediction, he stopped briefly to shake hands with Senator Eastland, smilingly exchanged a few whispered words with another member of the committee, and sat down beside Senator Jenner. Since Matusow's charges against McCarthy should theoretically have fallen within the province of the committee's investigation, the senator's action was not lacking in arrogance and bravado. Soon he got up and started to leave the room.

I addressed Senator Eastland. "Is Senator McCarthy leaving already? I thought he was going to take my seat." I gestured toward the witness table.

Senator McCarthy halted, as if to speak. For once, however, he had no microphone. Flushing angrily, he left the room.

Senator Eastland rapped with his gavel to restore order in the caucus chamber. "I don't like cracks like that," he said angrily.

As my examination progressed one would hardly have suspected that it had anything to do with the matter of Matusow's recantation. Question after question concerned my political beliefs, the organizations to which I had belonged, the publishers of foreign editions of my book, my participation in peace congresses abroad, the trade unions that had purchased books issued by Cameron & Kahn. After a while I took the liberty of calling the subcommittee's attention to the fact that very few of the questions I had been asked "related to Matusow or our dealings with Matusow."

"We don't propose to be lectured by the witness," said Senator Eastland.

I was, I explained, interested in having the facts in the case investigated.

Senator Daniel leaned forward in his seat. "Well," he said, "I certainly give the Communists credit for bringing out what Matusow now says the facts are."

"And whom do you give credit for using him before this committee?" I asked. "Senator, who gets the credit for his appearances before this committee in the past and the lies he told here?"

"No, I do not take credit for that," Senator Daniel hastily replied.

"Or the slanders against your colleagues in the western states, sir?"

"I do not take credit for any of that."

"Well, who gets the credit for it, sir?" I asked. "I didn't know him then."

Perhaps something in our colloquy sufficiently irked Senator Daniel so that he momentarily forgot what he was saying. At any rate, he now made a most remarkable admission. "I will say to you," he declared hotly, "that I think that much of the evidence he gave heretofore was true. It has been checked and corroborated. And before these hearings are over . . . it is going to be shown that he was telling the truth then on much of his testimony, and that he is lying today while under the sponsorship of you and others like you who will not tell this committee whether or not you are members of the Communist party."

In other words, although the committee was still in the middle of its inquiry into the Matusow case, its members had already decided exactly what their findings were going to be![41]

It was, paradoxically enough, Senator Daniel who before long made it possible for me to get into the record proof of Matusow's having testified falsely as an "expert witness." "Do you feel," the

Senator asked, "that some of the Congressional committees were negligent in believing Matusow and using him?"

"I think," I said, "they were appallingly negligent." As an example of Matusow's "obvious lies," I cited the fact that at the Salt Lake City hearing conducted by the subcommittee in 1952 Matusow had given testimony "directly contradicting testimony he had given three months before under oath before the Un-American Activities Committee":

KAHN: When Mr. Matusow testified before the Un-American Activities Committee . . . he was asked if he knew of any specific instance in which a Communist had plotted to interfere with war production in the United States. He said he knew of no such instance in his sworn testimony. . . . If you will check the record, you will find that statement, and shortly afterwards a statement in your own record in which he not only says he knows of an instance, but gives the name of a person.

EASTLAND: Who was the person?

KAHN: The person was Clinton Jencks. . . .

EASTLAND: Did he take the Fifth Amendment at this hearing . . . in Salt Lake City?

KAHN: Senator Eastland, whether he did or not, the point I am making here is that you have before you—and I don't want to have the subject changed—you have before you two directly contradictory statements by Mr. Matusow—

EASTLAND: Yes.

KAHN: Proving that he lied on one of these two occasions. And your counsel should have caught it. I will give you another instance. . . . Mr. Matusow testified while Mr. Sourwine was counsel that there were more than 100 members of the Communist party on the *New York Times*. This was quite casually accepted, and he was invited to come back and testify again.

Turning to the committee counsel, I asked: "Now, why did you permit such things, Mr. Sourwine?"

"Wait a minute, please, sir," admonished Senator Eastland. "Mr. Sourwine is not under investigation."

"No, but he is investigating me," I said.

* * *

The lengths to which the senators were willing to discredit an "un-friendly witness" were indicated with particular vividness at one point during my examination.

Senator Jenner inquired whether my father had been the American industrial architect, Albert Kahn, who had acted as consulting archi-tect to the Soviet Union during the early 1930s. When I answered that the architect was my uncle, and that my father, now deceased, had been a member of my uncle's firm, Jenner asked whether any money I had inherited from my father had been used by me "for financing Communist books." Sourwine then inserted into the record a number of newspaper stories—some of them twenty-five years old—report-ing that the architectural firm of Albert Kahn, Inc., had supervised the building of "billions of dollars'" worth of Russian factories during the first Five Year Program.

The obvious implication was that I had received through my father a vast sum of money from the Soviet Union which somehow—two decades later—had been used to finance Moscow propaganda in the United States.

I requested of Senator Watkins, who was acting as chairman during Eastland's temporary absence from the room, that the committee strike from the record "all reference to my father, who . . . died eigh-teen years ago and can have no possible connection with the proceed-ings now under way."

Senator Watkins replied that the matter would be given considera-tion by the subcommittee.

It is perhaps superfluous to mention that the printed record was to contain all the references to my father.

Riette and I might have questioned the wisdom of having brought the children along if their experiences in the nation's capitol had been limited to what they observed of my two-day examination by the Senate subcommittee. It was the first time they had ever seen members of the U.S. Congress in action, or, for that matter, in the flesh; and the sight could hardly have been called inspirational.

The boys' gentlest comment regarding the senators came from Brian. "They talk too much," he confided to me during a recess in the proceedings, "and what they say is so boring." However, he had had the foresight to bring with him several volumes from his collection of books on animal life in the western hemisphere, and when the tedium of the hearing became intolerable, he found relief in the perusal of his *Field Guild to the Mammals*.

Fortunately, the contrast between the senators on the subcommittee and the citizens they supposedly represented was amply demonstrated to the boys during their stay in Washington. They struck up cordial acquaintanceships with all sorts of people—spectators at the hearing, newspapermen, TV technicians, persons at the hotel where we were staying and, with the keen discernment of children, they were not unaware that many of these individuals went out of their way to show them warm attention and make them feel at home.

By no means the least memorable of their experiences happened to Timmy. Although we had told the boys not to get separated from us, Timmy at one point during my testimony got up from his seat and, unnoticed by Riette, wandered from the hearing room. In the corridor he was stopped by a burly man.

"Do you know who that guy is who's testifying in there?" the man asked. With some pride because he was, after all, speaking of his father, Timmy cheerfully responded: "Why, yes. His name is Albert Kahn."

"That's right," snarled the man, "and he's nothing but a dirty Commie bastard!"

At that moment a Senate guard appeared, like the good jinni in a fairy tale. Seizing the man by the lapels of his coat, the guard hissed, "Do you know you're talking to Mr. Kahn's son? Get out of here!"

After recounting the story to us with wide-eyed delight, Timmy said, "Wasn't that a nice thing for that guard to do?"

4. *"Let Us Have Peace and Quiet"*

It was with a good deal of anticipation that I looked forward to Angus's appearance before the subcommittee. I had previously had the opportunity of witnessing a performance of his before the same committee. That was in May 1952, when Senator Jenner, then chairman of the committee, conducted a one-man hearing in Boston on "Communism in education,"[42] and Angus was summoned for questioning on the "Red literature" published by Little, Brown & Company

while he had been the firm's editor-in-chief and vice president. The
tone of Angus's testimony on that occasion was set the moment he
had entered the packed hearing room. Glancing about with an exasperated expression, he demanded of Senator Jenner in a loud imperi-
ous voice, "And where is *my* chair, Senator?" At the realization that
there actually was no empty chair for the witness, Senator Jenner
flushed with the embarrassment of a host who has neglected to set a
place for the guest of honor and stammered to an aide, "Get a chair, a
chair for Mr. Cameron...." Throughout the hearing, Angus sharply
chided Jenner for the "prejudice, obscurantism, and intellectual flum-
mery" of his committee, and lectured him sternly on matters of literature, politics, American history, and freedom of the press.
Afterwards, Boston newspapers carried such headlines as these: "PUB-
LISHER BLASTS COMMITTEE"—"EDITOR DEFIES RED PROBERS"—"CA-
MERON FLAYS WITCH-HUNT...."

If Angus's appearance at the Matusow hearing was to prove somewhat less impressive than his previous encounter with the committee,
it was perhaps primarily due to the fact that he now had to cope with
half a dozen senators instead of one. By sheer weight of numbers they
were able to smother his indignation or, at least, prevent him from
fully articulating it. However, if their constant interruptions stopped
him from saying much that was on his mind, his untiring outbursts
kept them from expressing much that was on theirs.

Typical was the exchange that occurred when Angus declined to
discuss his political beliefs and affiliations on three constitutional
grounds and designated as the first of these "freedom of the press
under the First Amendment":

EASTLAND: You think—
CAMERON: May I finish?
EASTLAND: You think that the First—
CAMERON: I would like to finish.
EASTLAND: Wait just a minute.... You say it is an abridgment of
freedom of the press?
CAMERON: That is correct.
EASTLAND: You think if you ask a man if he is a Communist and
engaged in a conspiracy against his country—
CAMERON: You didn't ask that question.
EASTLAND: As a matter of fact, now, you know that being a member

of the Communist party is a crime, don't you?

CAMERON: No, I didn't know it was—is it?

EASTLAND: Well, you certainly ought to know. I cannot tell you. I am not a Communist. I am not a Fifth-Amendment case.

CAMERON: Well, now, just a minute, am I a Fifth-Amendment case?. . . .

EASTLAND: Well, but wait a minute; we will see in a minute.

CAMERON: All right. . . .

EASTLAND: Now, I am not going to recognize your first ground.

CAMERON: I know you are not. . . . But I do recognize it.

As his second ground, Angus quoted the Ninth Amendment: "The enumeration in the Constitution of certain rights shall not be construed to deny or disparage others retained by the people."

EASTLAND: Yes, but that does not—

CAMERON: I also—

EASTLAND: That does not justify a man engaging in a conspiracy against his country.

CAMERON: Are you accusing me of engaging in a conspiracy?

EASTLAND: What is your third ground?

CAMERON: Are you accusing me—

EASTLAND: What is your third ground?

CAMERON: Please, don't put words in my mouth—

EASTLAND: What is your third ground?

CAMERON: My third ground is the privilege of the Fifth Amendment, having to do with testifying against oneself.

EASTLAND: That is right. Now you are a Fifth-Amendment case, then, are you not?. . . .

CAMERON: Just a minute. Everyone here knows that you had prejudged the matter before I even said so.

Joining the fray, Senator Welker asked Angus whether he had any literary dealings with the Communist publisher Alexander Trachtenberg. "Come on, now," the senator instructed, "tell us what you know about it."

"Don't talk to me that way," snapped Angus.

"Well, all right," said Welker. "I don't want to be impatient. . . . I am sorry if I offended you."

"Well, you did."

"Well, I am sorry, sir."

Mr. Cameron had admitted, said Senator Jenner, that the firm of Cameron & Kahn cooperated with "left-wing labor organizations" in publishing "pro-Communist and left-wing books."

"Don't put words in my mouth," Angus told the senator.

"I am not. I am asking you a question."

"You made an assertion. . . ."

"Is it true—answer it 'Yes' or 'No,' and then explain. . . ."

"Look, Senator—"

"I am entitled to an answer," declared Jenner.

Angus pointed at his own microphone. "You have one of those in front of you. . . . Don't yell at me."

"Just a minute," said Senator Welker. "Let us have peace and quiet."

"You don't gain anything," said Angus, "by this second-rate brow beating."

Senator Eastland rapped with his gavel. "Wait just a minute, wait. I am presiding as chairman, Mr. Cameron. . . ."

"Are you, Mr. Cameron," asked Sourwine, "a member of a conspiracy seeking to overthrow the government of the United States by force and violence?"

Angus smiled without answering.

"Why do you hesitate and smile?" asked Senator Welker.

"I smile at the insolence of the question."

Perhaps because the subcommittee members had been wearied by the heated debate, Angus was finally permitted to answer the question in full without interruption. "I am not part of any conspiracy," he said. "I am a publisher and a citizen who believes that the whole smelly cult of the conspiracy in this country has very badly needed airing, and believes that the revelations that Mr. Matusow made in this book ought to be investigated, and that other people like Mr. Matusow ought to be investigated. I have a feeling, however, it is the people who began these investigations, who first made the revelations available, namely, the publishers, who are the ones being investigated."

Angus added that in his opinion neither the Justice Department nor the Internal Security Subcommittee was competent to conduct a proper investigation of the Matusow case.

Following our appearance before the subcommittee, Angus and I submitted to Senator Eastland a written memorandum stating that an investigation of the Justice Department's former dealings with Matusow was essential to establish the truth in the Matusow case. Senator Eastland said that he questioned whether such an investigation came "within the jurisdiction" of his committee.

It was not until some time later that material would become available revealing that the Eastland committee and the Justice Department had entered into a secret arrangement at an early date in the joint endeavor to brand Matusow's recantation a "Communist conspiracy."

The very week that Angus and I were testifying before the Senate subcommittee, Attorney General Brownell appeared at a closed session of a House Appropriations subcommittee. When subsequently published, the transcript of this hearing included the following significant bit of dialogue.

"With regards to this fellow Matusow," asked Representative John Rooney, "what are you going to do about it?"

"The day he announced he had lied," replied Attorney General Brownell, "I instructed Assistant Attorney General W.F. Tompkins to make a thorough investigation of Matusow. They served a subpoena on Matusow. . . . We will have to wait for Judge Dimock's decision before we can know what our next step will be. In the meantime, we are cooperating with the Senate Subcommittee on Internal Security of the Judiciary, which is also examining Matusow."

CHAPTER ELEVEN

TALE OF TWO CITIES

1. *Lesson in Manhattan*

Since early February, with mounting frustration Angus and I had spent the major portion of our time answering subpoenas, testifying before the grand jury and the Senate Internal Security Committee, shuttling back and forth between New York and Washington, and fulfilling a seemingly endless variety of related tasks which contributed little or nothing to the issuance of Matusow's book. And now, following my final appearance before the Senate subcommittee, I was to spend three full days on the witness stand at the Flynn retrial hearing in Judge Dimock's court in New York.

I had been called as a witness by the government, and my direct examination was conducted by U.S. Attorney Lumbard. In retrospect, even after reviewing the transcript of the proceedings, I find it difficult to understand how Lumbard managed to make my interrogation last so long. But I must say the fault was not wholly Lumbard's. If he wasted a great deal of time with his questions, so did I with my answers. Following days before the grand jury and Senate subcommittee, I had developed a loquacious style of testifying ill-suited to courtroom procedure, in which one's answers should be succinct, to the point and without lengthy dissertations on matters of personal opinion. This fact was forcibly called to my attention by Harry Sacher during a court recess. With a look of infinite disgust he told me:

"You're talking too damn much. Why don't you just answer the questions and let it go at that? You know, you're in court, not on a lecture platform."

Lumbard's examination covered every aspect of my relationship to the Matusow case, in copious and repetitive detail, from the time I first read the newspaper account of Harvey's visit to Bishop Oxnam until the day when *False Witness* went to the printer. While the specific purpose of his questions was often obscure to me, and perhaps also to him, certain of his general objectives were clear. He wanted to show that Cameron & Kahn was financed with "Communist party funds," that the "Communist-dominated Mine-Mill union" had plotted with our firm to bribe Matusow into recanting, and that I, not Matusow, had actually authored his book.

Lumbard stressed that Matusow had a bodyguard while working on the book. Possibly, inquired Lumbard, the real purpose of the bodyguard was to keep Matusow under "protective custody" and make sure he didn't double-cross us or get "out of line"?

No, I said, Cameron and I wanted to avoid the sort of misadventures that sometimes befell key witnesses in criminal cases. "I also had in mind," I went on, "the case of Andrea Salsedo, who was kidnapped by Department of Justice agents and killed in the early 1920s, and I didn't want anything like that to happen to Mr. Matusow."[43]

Lumbard, who perhaps had never heard of the Salsedo case, looked thoroughly shocked. "Are you implying that they killed him?" he demanded.

"I believe that they did, yes." If he wished additional data on the subject, I said, Lumbard might consult the writings of Louis D. Post, then Assistant Secretary of Labor, and a report entitled *Illegal Practices of the United States Department of Justice*, which had been published at the time by a group of twelve noted American jurists, including Felix Frankfurter.

Lumbard chose to drop the subject.

There was, however, one phase of Lumbard's examination that not only had me at a distinct disadvantage but taught me an important lesson. It occurred when Lumbard questioned me regarding the advance royalties Cameron & Kahn had paid Matusow, and the money our firm had received from the Mine-Mill union for the books they had ordered. First, Lumbard wanted to know how much money we had sent Matusow before he came from Taos to New York.

"No funds whatsoever," I replied. We had made a plane reservation for him, and bought the ticket, but that was all. I added that I had heard the government witness, Riley Taintor, testify that Matusow had received one thousand dollars from us before coming east. "That," I said, "is an unmitigated falsehood."

And precisely how, asked Lumbard, had Matusow been paid his advance royalties when he did reach New York?

He had received cash payments from me of $50 a week, I said, the amount we agreed upon in our original letter-contract.

Why hadn't I paid him by check?

Cameron and I, I said, had at first taken precautions not to let it be generally known that Matusow was writing a book for our firm, because we thought attempts might be made to keep him from finishing it. "I felt that payments by check to Mr. Matusow would become known to the FBI, and that the Department of Justice would bring pressure on Mr. Matusow to prevent him from telling the full details about his relationship with them."

Did I have signed receipts for the payments I had made to Matusow? And had they been entered at the time in the Cameron & Kahn ledgers?

All at once I realized my inexcusible stupidity in not having kept such records, despite all my other elaborate precautions. "No, there were no records of that nature."

What about the funds Cameron & Kahn had received from Mine-Mill?

The $1,000 on their initial order of 2000 books, I said, had been paid to me in cash installments by Nat Witt.

And what current record had I kept of these payments?

With mounting embarrassment and stumbling over my words I said I couldn't recall having kept any records of them at the time. Mr. Witt, however, had recorded them. "I have respect for his integrity. He is more businesslike than I am, and I have much more confidence in his figures about this sort of thing. Subsequent entries of all of these financial transactions between Mine-Mill and Cameron & Kahn, as well as those between Matusow and us, had been made in our firm's books by Mr. Cameron and our accountant. "I am not very knowledgeable about bookkeeping matters. My profession is mainly writing."

I felt that with every sentence I was adding to the impression that I was either an utter idiot or an obvious conspirator.

In other words, emphasized Lumbard, I could not produce any contemporaneous records whatsoever of the financial transactions on Matusow's book?

Suddenly, with immense relief, I realized I could! "I now remember," I declared loudly, "that I did keep some records, and, in fact, I have them with me." I searched my wallet, finally found what I was looking for, and lifted it out triumphantly. It was a scrap of paper on which I had jotted down each of the payments to Harvey. The paper was about two inches square.

Lumbard took the crumpled little piece of paper from me and held it aloft between his thumb and forefinger. "You mean to say," he asked with withering scorn, "that this is what your initial financial records consisted of?"

"Yes," I feebly rejoined, "that's it."

Sacher finally came to the rescue. "It's clear," he dryly told Judge Dimock, "that Mr. Kahn, as he indicates, isn't much of a businessman. I would suggest that whatever other information is needed in this regard can be obtained from Mr. Cameron, who has charge of the Cameron & Kahn books. Mr. Kahn isn't exactly an expert on bookkeeping."

A rather more critical evaluation was made at the close of that day's session by Riette, who had been present during my testimony. "You've always been careless with money," she said. "Possibly you used to think it was cute or bohemian or the way an author is supposed to act. This should be a lesson to you. There was nothing cute about today's performance. It was careless and irresponsible, and you're lucky if you haven't convinced Judge Dimock that the whole thing was a plot!"

2. *"Law West of the Pecos"*

While I was testifying at the retrial hearing on the Flynn case in New York, Harvey had been called to testify at the retrial hearing on the Jencks case in El Paso, Texas.

Just one year had elapsed since Harvey's last sojourn in El Paso when, as the government's chief witness at Clint's trial, he had given testimony which the local U.S. attorney had characterized as "absolutely essential to a successful prosecution." Of that previous visit, Harvey had written in *False Witness*: "I was in my glory. . . . I was the star. . . . When I arrived in El Paso, there were banner headlines screaming about the Jencks trial." Now, in a statement to the press, Jencks declared: "It will be interesting to see if the newspapers give as much coverage to the repudiation as they did to his testimony against me at the trial."

Jencks's skepticism proved groundless. Once again, the Jencks case dominated the news in El Paso. Every day there were front-page stories and lead editorials about the retrial hearing.

Not all the dramatic aspects of Harvey's return to El Paso, however, were reported in the press. It was now that Harvey and Clint met for the first time since the lies of the one had resulted in a five-year jail sentence for the other.

"It was wonderful—the way Clint acted," Harvey told me afterward. "If I'd had any doubts about whether I was doing the right thing, the way he treated me would have made me forget them. Virginia was wonderful to me too. Maybe more so."

The strange reunion made no less of an impression on Clint and his wife, Virginia. "I didn't know just how to act at first," Clint told me. "In spite of everything he'd done to make amends, it was still hard not to think of him as sort of a phony, you know. Basically, I felt sorry for the guy; it was much easier to be in my position than his. But before the hearing was over, I came to really respect him because of the courage he showed. He understood what he was up against, you know, and he knew they'd give him the works for what he was doing."

One thing about Harvey's testimony disturbed both Virginia and Clint. "He still had to show how clever he was," Virginia said. "You had the feeling he was constantly trying to get the better of the government attorney. I told him he was only alienating people by acting like a smart aleck. He said he knew and was trying to get over it, but it was hard because it had become so much a part of him."

* * *

There were a number of similarities between the retrial hearings in the Flynn and Jencks cases. At both proceedings the Justice Department sought to prove Matusow had been bribed to make a false recantation. Much of the testimony given at both hearings was identical. Moreover, in the courthouse in El Paso, as in New York, a federal grand jury on the Matusow case was simultaneously in session; and, as Clint later told me, couriers were constantly hurrying between the grand jury room and the courtroom, keeping the government attorneys at the hearing supplied with supposedly confidential grand jury data.

But there was one striking difference: the judge in New York was interested in upholding the law and the judge in El Paso was interested in upholding the authority of the government.

Judge E.R. Thomason, who presided at the El Paso hearing, as he had at the Jencks trial, was a plump, bespectacled, ruddy-faced man in his early sixties who formerly had been a U.S. congressman. His approach to juridical matters was graphically depicted in a character sketch of him by the Washington correspondent Bascom Timmons. According to Timmons, the judge's handling of the Jencks case "brought back to Thomason's congressional colleagues some of the stories Thomason used to tell of Judge Roy Bean." Bean had come to Texas as "a bearded adventurer . . . in the 1880s, built a log cabin with the sign, "Roy Bean—Barrel Whiskey—Justice of the Peace—Law West of the Pecos," and "for many years dispensed a reasonably satisfactory grade of liquor and a grade of justice which was sometimes very exact and sometimes very unique." One of Thomason's favorite anecdotes about Judge Bean, related Timmons, was this:

> Into Bean's shack . . . one day marched a culprit charged with a grave crime. He had hired a lawyer from San Antonio to defend him.
> Bean sat down behind his bench, improvised from an empty whiskey barrel, unholstered a six-shooter and laid it atop the barrel.
> The lawyer introduced himself and objected to the whole procedure. "I demand Constitutional rights and protection of my client."
> Judge Bean summoned his assistant to the bench. "Oscar, in about eight minutes I expect to find this here defendant guilty and order you and the boys to take him out and hang him. . . . What'er you intend to do?"

"Take him out and hang him, of course," Oscar replied.

"Supposin'," Bean continued, "I decided you had better hang his lawyer with him. Then what would you do?"

"Why, hang 'im, Judge. It ain't much more trouble to hang two than one."

Bean now addressed the young lawyer: "Now you set down. I'm the law west of the Pecos. I run my court the way I see fit."

Timmons wrote that in Judge Thomason's court "the law west of the Pecos" was "still administered with firmness" comparable to that in Roy Bean's shack. The validity of that observation was to be clearly established at the Jencks retrial hearing.

Two of the most prominent attorneys in the Southwest, A.T. Hannett, a former governor of New Mexico, and Harold L. Bigbee, a former assistant attorney general in that state, had been retained by Mine-Mill to act as co-counsel with the union's regular lawyers, Nat Witt and John McTernan, in representing Jencks at the hearing. The participation of Hannett and Bigbee, which would have been hardly conceivable at the time of Jencks's trial, was one more sign that Cold War tensions were slackening.

Harvey was Jencks's only witness. His direct examination by Bigbee lasted less than two hours.

Paragraph by paragraph, Bigbee read aloud Matusow's testimony at the Jencks trial and asked him to state what was true and what was false in it. It was true, said Harvey, that he had met Jencks at the San Cristobal Valley Ranch in the summer of 1950. Jencks and he, however, had never discussed Communist party activities, as he had testified. Nor had Jencks ever said that he was a member of the Communist party or that he and "fellow party members" in the Mine-Mill union were plotting to slow down copper production to obstruct the Korean war effort. Harvey said he had fabricated these charges.

Harvey's cross-examination was conducted by one of Attorney General Brownell's special assistants, a Justice Department lawyer named David L. Harris, who had been dispatched from Washington to present the government's case. After U.S. Attorney Lumbard's performance in New York, the Justice Department higher-ups had evidently decided not to rely on their local talent in El Paso. Harris's interrogation of Matusow, however, was hardly more effectual than Lumbard's. True, its pace was a bit swifter—it lasted four days instead of five; but the ground it covered was essentially the same and the effort to confute Matusow equally fruitless. Like Lumbard, Harris displayed a special fascination for Harvey's bicycle trip through Texas and New Mexico in the fall of 1954. He devoted almost a day and a half to the subject and, in the words of the *El Paso Herald-Post*, "covered virtually every mile of the trip." Harris made explicit the reason for the government's consuming curiosity about Harvey's peregrinations:

> HARRIS: I put it to you, sir, that somewhere along that route you were put in touch with somebody from Mine-Mill.
> MATUSOW: That is a lie.
> HARRIS: I put it to you, sir, that somewhere along that route you were put in touch with somebody who persuaded you to write a book called *False Witness*.
> MATUSOW: That is a lie. It never happened.
> HARRIS: I put it to you, Mr. Matusow, that either in Taos or in the vicinity, and before you took that ride from Albuquerque to New York, you received a thousand dollars for which you promised to swear falsely here.
> MATUSOW: The biggest lie I ever heard. . . .
> HARRIS: I put it to you, Mr. Matusow, that you are sitting in that witness chair paid by the Communist party.
> MATUSOW: That is not a fact.[44]

There was another point on which Harris also placed much stress. Referring to the transcript of the final tape-recorded talk between Matusow and me in December, Harris pointed out that Matusow had told me he "knew Jencks was a party member." Harris quoted Matusow's statement: "I can't say here that Jencks wasn't a party member after he signed the (Taft-Hartley non-Communist) affidavits because I know that he was." How then did it happen, challenged Harris, that in his book Matusow had subsequently declared he had never had any grounds for accusing Jencks of being a Communist party member?

Perhaps because he was getting a bit weary after fourteen days of testifying in New York, Washington, and El Paso, Harvey's answer was less effective than it might have been. He said that since he had still been apprehensive about the use to which his admissions might be put, and because he wanted his book in print before any legal action was taken about his lies against Jencks, he had deliberately "held back information" from me. Harvey could, of course, have added that when I had asked him in the very same tape-recorded talk how he "knew" Jencks was a Communist, he had evasively replied: "Jencks legally, according to the law, might not have been a member of the party. . . . But to my mind then, in my thinking, it made him no less of a Communist. . . ." Harvey might also have mentioned that there was a noteworthy difference between his telling me he had had intuitive knowledge of Jencks' Communist party membership, and his testifying at Jencks' trial that the latter had personally admitted being a Communist to him.

There was a marked inconsistency in U.S. Attorney Harris's reasoning. As Harris had stated, it was the government's contention that before coming east from Taos in October, Matusow had accepted a thousand-dollar bribe for which he "promised to swear falsely" by recanting his testimony against Jencks; and to support this thesis the Taos gambler Riley Taintor was again called as a government witness to testify he had seen the money Matusow had received from his prospective publishers. But if Matusow *had* entered into this agreement "to swear falsely," how did one explain the fact that in a tape-recorded conversation with me in December—some two months after he supposedly received his bribe—he was still trying to avoid admitting he had lied at the Jencks trial?

As in the Flynn case, the defense attorneys at the Jencks hearing requested that Matusow's FBI reports be made available so that their contents might be checked with his subsequent trial testimony. The matter first came up when Harvey stated during cross-examination that prior to Jencks's trial he had dictated a statement at the Sante Fe FBI office asserting he didn't want to be a witness, as he had "testified dishonestly" in the past. Immediately, Bigbee asked Judge Thomason to instruct the government to produce Matusow's statement to the FBI.

"I take it that this is part of the private files of the FBI," Judge Thomason replied. "So that request is denied."

During redirect examination Bigbee asked Harvey if he had ever claimed in his contemporaneous reports to the FBI that he had "conversations with Jencks that established that Jencks was a Communist." When Harvey said he had not, Bigbee told Judge Thomason that the FBI reports went "to the very vital point in this case as to whether or not his testimony was fabricated." Would the judge, inquired Bigbee, reconsider his prior ruling and instruct the government to produce Matusow's FBI reports?

"The request is denied," said Judge Thomason. "The Court has ruled and adheres to its former ruling."

On the last day of the hearing, after oral arguments by government and defense counsel, Judge Thomason handed down his ruling. Picking up a sheet of paper, the judge read: "In January of 1954, Clinton E. Jencks was tried in this very courtroom. In the opinion of the Court then and now, he had a fair trial before a fair and impartial jury. That jury found him guilty of the crime with which he is charged.... There has been nothing developed here ... that has changed the Court's opinion ... about the correctness and justice of that trial and of the verdict that was then returned by the jury. Therefore ... the motion for a new trial is in all things overruled and denied."

Judge Thomason summoned Matusow to the bench. Again, the judge read from a prepared statement:

> I am thoroughly convinced that you are in contempt of this Court in that you, alone or in conjunction with others, deliberately and maliciously and designedly schemed to obstruct justice in this Court.... By recanting your former testimony given in this Court ... which, I believe, in substance, was true, you have ... deliberately shown contempt for this Court by attempting to set aside the conviction heretofore had in this regard and obtain a new trial for Clinton E. Jencks.

There was an Alice-in-Wonderland flavor to the judge's concluding comment: "Before sentencing you, I will give you a hearing in this regard and permit you to present evidence in your behalf if you desire to do so."

If Judge Roy Bean of "law west of the Pecos" fame could have witnessed this episode, he would doubtless have been enchanted at the idea of first finding a man guilty and then granting him a hearing to present his side of the case.

Four days later, on March 16, Judge Thomason sentenced Matusow to serve three years in prison for criminal contempt of court. The judge set bail at $10,000.

"If Judge Thomason," Harvey told reporters, "had decided I'd made a mockery of justice when I first testified against Clinton Jencks and had granted Jencks a new trial, one might have understood the contempt sentence." He would go to jail with pride, Harvey added, "because it will be for deciding to become honest and tell the truth."

"The judge threw the book at the varmints, and he didn't miss," exulted the *El Paso Herald-Post*, adding that Thomason was "the only judge in the U.S. who has taken direct action to punish one of the most notorious liars since Ananias.... Matusow had been lying with impunity for years—until he made the mistake of lying in Judge Thomason's court."

Attorney General Brownell cited Judge Thomason's ruling as "evidence" of the fact that Matusow was the "focal point" of a "Communist effort to stem the government's campaign against subversion." "Refreshing and wholly praiseworthy!" exulted Senator Eastland. "What Judge Thomason has done cannot help but add luster to the federal bench."

A somewhat more sober appraisal appeared as a lead editorial in the *Harvard Law Record*:

> If Matusow's affidavit that he lied in the Jencks case is the truth, then he is being wrongfully punished for attempting to bring an injustice to light. . . .
>
> On the other hand, if Matusow's affidavit is false, then it is perjury. If a perjury, the judge punished it as contempt of court. We agree with Judge Learned Hand that "this power must not be used to punish perjury."
>
> . . . We do view with alarm the fact that an American judge can, by summary action, send a man to jail for three years for attempting

to retract prior testimony. This is beyond all bounds of due process
of law.

... We, therefore, hope that the Fifth Circuit will allow Matusow's appeal and reverse this dubious judicial proceeding.

I.F. Stone's Weekly summed up the broader implications of the verdict
in these words:

> Judge Thomason's action against Matusow must be seen in the
> context of frantic efforts by the government to protect its system of
> informers from full public examination. ... To hold Matusow in
> contempt is in effect to punish him for recanting without having to
> take the trouble of proving a charge of perjury. The three-year sen-
> tence, imposed on a judge's fiat without jury trial, is a brutal warn-
> ing to other informers.

As if to confirm Stone's analysis of the outcome of the Jencks retrial
hearing, the Justice Department now announced that a federal court
jury in Washington had indicted the self-admitted liar and former government witness Mrs. Marie Natvig on the charge of perjury. She was
not, however, indicted for the false testimony she had confessed giving against publisher and broadcaster Edward Lamb. She was instead
charged with lying in her recantation in stating she had been coerced
by government attorneys into giving perjurious testimony.

CHAPTER TWELVE

OFF THE PRESS

1. Peculiar Circumstances

It is doubtful whether the publication of any book was ever attended by circumstances more peculiar than those under which Harvey Matusow's *False Witness* went on sale in the bookstores on March 15, 1955.

Government agencies had done everything they could to obstruct the issuance of the book. They had attempted to seize the manuscript, had intimidated printers, had investigated the publishers and kept them under constant FBI surveillance. One member of the publishing firm had been given a six month contempt sentence by a federal judge; both members of the firm were still under grand jury, congressional, and federal court subpoenas; and one day after the book's publication its author began serving a three-year prison term for having made the revelations it contained.

By no means the least peculiar of the circumstances surrounding the appearance of *False Witness* was the effect of its extraordinary advance publicity upon its sale.

Publishers naturally like to have their books widely discussed; and the amount of advance publicity *False Witness* had received was perhaps unprecedented in the annals of book publishing. For six weeks the book had been the center of intense national controversy. From one end of the country to the other, politicians and editors, churchmen and jurists, educators and labor leaders, scientists and sociologists had joined in the public debate over its revelations. Not a day had passed without mention of the book or its author by the press, radio, and television. If it had been conceivably possible to purchase the newspaper space and radio-television time given to the subject, the cost would have run into tens of millions of dollars. A major section of the nation's population had become familiar with the name of Harvey Matusow.

It was not without reason that Angus and I believed this extensive publicity augured well for the sale of *False Witness*.

But we overlooked one contingency: that the book might have received too much publicity.

And such was to prove to be the case.

Countless persons by now felt they were familiar with the entire contents of Matusow's book. And, in a sense, they were. For there was scarcely a phase of its story which had not been told and retold to the whole nation. The publication of the book itself came as a definite anticlimax. Within a matter of days, it was clear that the sale of the book would fall far below our expectations.

Nor was excessive publicity the only sales problem. With our firm unable to afford other than token advertising, many prospective buyers were doubtless unaware that the book was finally available. Moreover, whereas regular commercial publishers maintained efficient sales forces for canvassing the nation's book stores, our own sales apparatus at the time consisted of one part-time salesman.

There were, of course, other factors hampering the distribution of *False Witness*. The widespread disintegration of progressive organizations under Cold War pressures had eliminated a large potential market for the book. Then, too, many progressives had little desire to augment its sales. Repeatedly, such persons were to tell us they had no intention of promoting the writings of an ex-informer. Some vehemently declared they wouldn't buy the book themselves since Matusow would get part of the money in royalties. "What guarantee do we have he won't become an informer again?" was a frequent refrain.

While abhorrence of Matusow for his past activities was not difficult to understand, I felt a limited patience with the protests of these individuals. For one thing, it should have been clear to them that Harvey's book was a potent weapon not only for righting the wrongs he had done but also for counteracting the far-flung repressions in which his wrongdoing had played only a minor part. For another thing, the attitude of these individuals was a little too self-righteous. According to their own lights, they were persons dedicated to the betterment of the world in which they lived; but how did they believe society could change if they so rigidly doubted the ability of a single human being to do so?

And precisely in what way did they expect Matusow to prove himself? He had recanted and was doing his best to make restitution. With all the power of the government arrayed against him, he had stood up to and defied his former paymasters in the Justice Department and Congress. He had shown himself ready to go to jail for his crimes. What else did they demand of him? Surely, if Matusow could be forgiven by Clinton and Virginia Jencks, whom he had so grievously wronged, others could afford to show some clemency toward him.

Most liberals and progressives, it should be said, recognized the value of Matusow's book. Typical of the letters pouring into our office from all parts of the country was one from the venerable sociologist and civil rights champion, Dr. John A. Kingsbury: "I must tell you and Angus Cameron," Dr. Kingsbury wrote me, "how profoundly impressed I am by the message conveyed in *False Witness.* . . . You have rendered a service of first significance in the struggle to restore the liberties our forefathers established. . . . It is an amazing story. The book should be read by every citizen who ventures to lift his voice in these critical days. Every leader of thought should aid in its distribution."

"I am . . . happy beyond measure," wrote my friend Olin Downes, noted music critic and fervent partisan of human rights, "at seeing this book, which they tried so hard to suppress, actually in circulation. I think it is going to be one of the most decisive blows struck for freedom and against present indecencies in government that have appeared in the tortuous late years."

Having failed to prevent its publication, the Justice Department— with the continued aid of the Senate Internal Security Subcommittee —was energetically disseminating the warning that Matusow's book was Communist propaganda and that reading it was practically tantamount to an act of treason.

"Grave officials of the federal government," noted John Van Kamp in a review of *False Witness* in the *Baltimore Evening Sun*, "have hinted that one would be aiding the enemy by owning a copy."

Van Kamp made this wry suggestion to his readers: "Presumably, this difficulty could be solved by wrapping it up in an old dust jacket from *Mein Kampf*."

2. *Pro and Con*

For the most part, the reviews of *False Witness* fell into three categories: those that readily embraced the government's thesis that *False Witness* was part of a Communist conspiracy; those expressing doubt as to whether its author had lied in the past or was lying in the present, and those that recognized the validity of Matusow's disclosures and regarded his book as a document of major social import.

Exemplifying the reviews in the first category was one, signed with the initials "HAF," in the *Omaha World-Herald*. "This book," wrote HAF, "can be boiled down to a very concise synopsis. Matusow says he is a retired liar. He claims that he lied for several years while he was testifying against a long list of people he then identified as Communists. . . . But this reviewer could find no proof that Matusow is telling the truth now or that he was lying during his previous life as a witness."

Of a different genre were those reviewers who, while condemning Matusow for his role as an informer-witness, announced their inability to decide if he was now telling the truth. In the *Dayton Daily News*, for example, Walt McCaslin wrote:

> Those who doubted Matusow's integrity from the very beginning of his career—and this reviewer is one of that group—will, of course, be attracted to the possibility that he is now telling the truth. Yet one cannot avoid the man's own admission that he would 'do anything for a buck.' And one recalls that Matusow's publishers were once called Communists by him. . . .

Such an observation was perhaps less of a comment on the book than on the reviewer, who was revealed as a man with enough decency and good sense to distrust Matusow as a government witness. At the same time, he had been sufficiently victimized by what he himself called "the confusion and distrust . . . planted in the minds of Americans" to find it hard to reject the propaganda myths of the informers and their mentors.

A considerable percentage of the reviewers of *False Witness*, however, found little ambiguity in its import. They saw in the book a damning indictment of the informer-witness system and the political environment in which it had evolved.

Such a reviewer was Chester S. Davis, whose thoughtful analysis of the book appeared in the Winston-Salem, North Carolina, *Journal & Sentinel*. Davis wrote:

> In the postwar hysteria over Communism, this country has been infected by a fear that has caused men to adopt a sort of ends-justify-the-means in dealing with Communists. The philosophy has been summed up in one word: "McCarthyism."
>
> Although McCarthyism has been attacked many times and for many reasons, no one has struck at it harder or with more telling effect than this opportunistic, calculating, psychopathic liar known as Harvey Matusow.

False Witness, Davis went on to say, was essentially a "tragic story."

> And there is tragedy in the fact this young man was encouraged to take the witness stand for the purpose of: (1) character assassination; (2) casting doubts on the patriotism of the press, radio, the schools, the labor unions . . . and, worst of all, (3) deliberately putting certain men and women into prison on the strength of lies and distorted half-truths.
>
> This man emerges from his story as the symbol of the low moral ebb in the administration of American justice.

What was perhaps at the time the most penetrating evaluation of Matusow's revelations appeared in the form of a full-page editorial by John Steinbeck in the *Saturday Review of Literature*. The famous novelist wrote:

> The Matusow testimony to anyone who will listen places a bouquet of forget-me-nots on the grave of McCarthy. The ridiculousness of the whole series of investigations now becomes apparent. . . .
>
> Now a wave of hysteria has swept over the investigators. Sena-

tors who are personally involved cry out that Matusow lies now but
didn't lie when he testified for them and against their enemies. . . .

Steinbeck went on to point out that Matusow's "flamboyant charges"
had been the stock in trade of government informers during the postwar years in the United States. "Such were the winds of the time that
certain basic nonsense was allowed to pass unnoticed. . . . I put all of
this in the past tense because I believe it is nearly over. I suspect that
government informers . . . can't survive Matusow's testimony. He has
said that it was a good racket. Well, Matusow has ruined the racket. It
will never be so good again."

The title of Steinbeck's editorial was: "Death of a Racket."

CHAPTER THIRTEEN

THE MATTER OF BAIL

1. *Anxious Days*

The constitution of the United States not only guarantees that a person accused of a crime "shall enjoy the right to have a speedy and a public trial" and "the assistance of counsel for his defense," but also stipulates: "Excessive bail shall not be required."

That justice can be a costly commodity was a fact of which I had not been unaware in the past. But since my involvement in the Matusow case the multiple demands that justice can make upon the pocketbook had revealed themselves with ever-growing urgency. The costs of litigation and attendant matters included such diverse items as: the counsel's fee during appearances made by Harvey, Angus, me and members of our staff before the federal grand jury in New York; the counsel's fee and traveling expenses during appearances before the Senate Subcommittee in Washington; the counsel's fee for Harvey in El Paso; the cost of transcripts of court proceedings in New York and El Paso; the cost of filing an appeal motion and printing the counsel's brief for submission to the Appellate Court. These expenses had run into thousands of dollars. While Harvey was helping defray his share with royalties from his book, the firm of Cameron & Kahn was paying most of the bills. Or, rather, trying to pay them. The income from the sale of *Fales Witness* was proving barely enough to cover production costs (greatly increased as they had been by the rushed publication.) Our firm, despite the congratulations of well-wishers on our having a highly publicized book on the market, remained in its perennial state of near-pauperism. Some of the legal costs Angus and I paid out of our own pockets, which, in the process, had been quickly emptied; some we had met with loans and contributions from sympathetic friends; and a sizable portion of them were still unpaid.

Now we were faced with the task of raising $10,000 for Harvey's bail.

Where to get it?

Since Harvey's testimony in El Paso had been on behalf of a Mine-Mill leader, Jencks, it seemed reasonable to expect the union to help with Harvey's bail and to contribute something toward the cost of his appeal. In fact, having anticipated that Harvey might face legal problems from testifying at the Jencks hearing, Angus and I had previously raised with Nat Witt the question of the cost of such litigation. It was our impression that Witt had indicated the union would halp defray these expenses. Apparently, from what Witt now told us, we had misunderstood him. He said he would find out what the union was willing to do.

A few days later we had the answer. The Mine-Mill leadership was opposed to advancing any funds for either Matusow's bail or his appeal. Such action, they felt, would give the Justice Department ammunition to bolster its charge that the union had bribed Matusow to recant.

If the news came as a blow, it was not only because Angus and I had no idea where next to turn for the bail. Of equal concern was the question of the effect of the union's decision on Harvey. He had, we knew, been counting on this aid. Might he not feel that now he had done all he could to make amends in the Jencks case, the union was washing its hands of him? If he believed this, how would he react?

I wrote to the Mine-Mill president, John Clark. Referring to his column praising Matusow for trying to rectify the harm he had done, I told Clark:

> There is, it seems to me, a vital need for Matusow's deriving strength from decent and honest people who make apparent by their actions their appreciation of his present efforts . . . to undo the harm done through his former lies. I am, however, afraid that the recent decision of the union to give no aid to his defense will not make any such attitude clear to Matusow. I am afraid it may have the opposite effect.

I said that Angus and I did not share the Mine-Mill leadership's view that helping with Matusow's bail might lend weight to the spurious charges of the Justice Department. It was "quite proper, ethical and legal for the union to act in Matusow's defense." Aside from all other considerations, their decision not to aid Matusow might result in the very situation they wanted to forestall:

It is my personal belief, as I have stated on a number of occasions, that Matusow will continue to mature as a fundamentally decent human being. However, I by no means dismiss the chance of the opposite. And should Matusow under pressure now retrogress and become a liar again, the harm not only to your union but to the whole cause of progress and decency would be immeasurable.

The decision of the Mine-Mill leadership remained unchanged.

Nor did it seem to me that the reason for the decision was entirely the one given. It was not improbable, I felt, that Matusow's recantation had stirred up much more of a hornet's nest than the Mine-Mill officials had anticipated; and that, with the union already under attack as "Red-dominated, they had become increasingly troubled by the government's widely publicized charge of a "Communist conspiracy" to get Matusow to recant. Hence, instead of continuing on the offensive in the Matusow case, they were now going on the defensive. To my way of thinking, this new orientation was as self-defeating as it was short sighted.[45]

With the Mine-Mill eliminated as a potential source of bail money, Angus and I drew up a list of individuals who might conceivably help. Having already approached most of them for aid on the Matusow case, neither of us was very hopeful about the prospects.

The next few days confirmed our worst expectations. The loans available amounted to a small fraction of the amount needed.

Our spirits were temporarily raised by one most welcome development. In the mail there came a communication from the Bill of Rights Fund, which had been established by the militant libertarian and author-educator Corliss Lamont to aid in legal cases involving key constitutional issues.[46] The letter informed us that the Fund's executive committee, "having before it the editorial of the *Harvard Law Review* on the Harvey Matusow case, believes that the legal issue here is important, and that a grant of $1,000 should be made . . . toward the legal costs in the appeal of Mr. Harvey Matusow from his conviction in Texas for contempt of court." We now, at least, could afford to proceed with Harvey's appeal.

We were, however, no nearer to a solution on the question of his bail. Stan Faulkner suggested our approaching a bonding company and made an appointment for us with a bondsman.

The bondsman was a stout, jovial man who wore a loose-fitting woolen waistcoat. "In a case like this one, you know," he told us, chewing vigorously on a cigar, "where there's been such a rumpus, most bonding companies won't touch the thing with a ten-foot pole. But I got connections. . . . Of course, you'll have to put up security. What sort of security have you got?"

Angus and I catalogued our worldly possessions. It did not take long.

The bondsman's hearty chuckling jarred ashes from his cigar onto his vest. "Lord, that's no security, my friends. You'll have to come up with something better than that." He rattled off various types of security that would be acceptable: stocks, bonds, real estate, business property. . . .

"You mean," said Angus, "that if Matusow had committed murder, there'd be a better chance of getting bail from a bonding company?"

"Lord, yes. This case is political. I don't need to tell you fellows that."

"Maybe we should simply join Harvey in jail," I said. "At least the government would pay our living expenses."

The bondsman bellowed with laughter. "I swear," he gasped, "you're a couple of characters."

The humor of the situation, however, had its limitations.

As the days went by and Harvey remained in jail, our apprehension mounted. It was not lessened by the fact that while we were sending frequent letters to Harvey in an effort to keep his spirits up there were no replies from him.

According to Harvey's lawyer in El Paso, his client was becoming increasingly restive. "Mind you, I wouldn't say he's despondent," he observed. "But the sooner you get him out, the better."

Finally, after ten days, we received a letter from Matusow. It read:

Dear Al—
This letter is also for Riette and the boys.

Here I sit where I've been sitting for the past 10 days. I've been alone and silent. They call it maximum security, but it is a form of solitary confinement. . . .

You know how much I like to talk! So just picture me here with 10 days of silence and God knows how many more in the offing.

I know you're doing your best on the bail question. I just hope it's soon.

Regards to all,
Harvey

Angus and I found nothing especially consoling in the tone of the letter. Riette's reaction was more philosophical. "What did you expect him to write?" she said. "That he's having a simply marvelous time and relishes every moment?"

2. *American Heritage*

Harvey had been in jail for two weeks when I drove to South Norwalk, Connecticut, to see my friends Henry and Anita Willcox. Theirs were the only names left on my list of bail prospects. The retired sixty-five-year-old building contractor and his artist wife made one mindful of the true American heritage. Henry was a direct descendant of some of those left-wing Puritans who emigrated from England on the *Mayflower* in 1620. His progenitors included that intrepid Pilgrim leader, William Bradford, governor of the first New England colony. Anita traced her lineage to Roger Williams, rebel founder of the colony of Rhode Island and passionate exponent of the brotherhood of man. Ancestors on both sides of the family had fought in the War of Independence and the Civil War. And for continuing in the tradition of such forebears by espousing a wide variety of democratic causes, the Willcoxes had been branded as "un-American" and harried by the bigots of their own day.[47]

In the bright airy living room of their small house overlooking an estuary of the Long Island Sound, Henry and Anita listened attentively as I told them of the bail situation. Henry's gentle, deeply lined face expressed his sympathy. "There's no question about the importance of the case," he said. "But, you know, so many cases deserve help today. And the amount of bail needed for Matusow is a good deal out of line with what we've done in other cases." He added, almost apologetically, "As a matter of fact, it's a good deal more than we can actually afford."

Anita, a small, vibrant woman with birdlike features and silvery hair, said, "What about publicity? If we did help, would it be all over the papers? I hate that sort of thing."

Sooner or later, I said, the press would undoubtedly find out who had loaned the bail money.

We talked a while longer.

All at once Anita said, "Henry, I could put up some real estate as security. Why don't we do it that way?" It was more of a declaration than a question. He shrugged. "Perhaps we should talk it over a little more. We can let Albert know."

Anita telephoned me that same night.

"I'm going ahead on the bail," she said.

The following day I met the Willcoxes at Faulkner's office. Anita handed Faulkner a cashier's check for $10,000.

"I don't suppose Matusow will skip the country," she remarked with a slight smile.

Faulkner shook his head soberly. "I don't think there's any likelihood of that. Of course, we can ask his parents to assume some responsibility for the loan."

"I wouldn't think of it," Anita said emphatically. "They've had enough trouble as it is."

Within forty-eight hours, Harvey was released on bail.

Later, he showed me these notes he had made during the airplane flight from El Paso to New York:

> I have had many thoughts while spending my 20 days and 19 nights in the El Paso County Jail. I frequently asked myself, "Why did you show up for sentencing, why didn't you—when there was no bond posted—skip to Mexico or some other country?" And still another frequent companion in my thought was, "To hell with what you are doing. Ask the government if they will vacate the sentence if you will agree to leave the country." Very natural when you are in jail for a crime you know you didn't commit, but even more natural

are the thoughts and motivations which caused me to be in jail, the conscience which moved me to tell the truth about my past false testimony—for every day and hour made me realize more than ever that I was free and that what I was doing was going to help this nation regain some of its recently lost freedom. . . .

Something I read on my first Saturday there stuck with me and helps me keep going on my present course—a position I know to be right. "Nothing is ever lost until it is abandoned, and then everything is lost. Don't let anything take away your hope, faith, dreams, and courage. Then life is always worth living."

I know the quote is all screwed up, but so is the prison system that deprives a man of a pen.

And on his arrival in New York, Harvey gave me a poem which, not without a certain pride, he told me he had composed in jail. It read:

Dear Friends—
and what is more dear than friends?
a minute of silence please . . .
Al,
who organized the air
knowing that some day it would be free,
a minute of silence please . . .
Riette,
the house that is a home,
her soft smile that is its heart,
a minute of silence please . . .
Steve,
young athlete,
your strength will conquer hate,
a minute of silence please . . .
Timmy,
a poet's cry singing tomorrow's song,
a minute of silence please . . .
Brian,
who traps the woods
for love of life,
a minute of silence please . . .
A minute of silence please . . .
yes. thank you.
silence,
it roars like thunder.

Before a week was up, a *New York Herald Tribune* reporter had found out the source of Matusow's bail money and interviewed Anita Willcox regarding her reasons for providing it.

The *Herald Tribune* front-paged the scoop. Anita was quoted as saying:

> I put up bail for Harvey Matusow because I believe that however he may deserve jail for the wrongs he has done, he should not be jailed for trying to right those wrongs. I have never seen Matusow but I have read his book, *False Witness*, which is a devastating portrait of a paid informer. The book is also an even more appalling, and, unfortunately for our country, a very convincing picture of how the Department of Justice and Congressional committees nourish such phenomena.

A day or so later Anita telephoned me to say she had been served with a subpoena by the Senate Internal Security Subcommittee. "I can't abide all that fuss and those circus effects," she told me tensely. "I don't know if I'll have the slightest notion of what to say."

It turned out that she knew precisely what to say. Throughout her testimony, Anita made it clear that she had no patience with the attempt of the committee members to pillory her for advancing Matusow's bail money. Periodically she scolded them with brisk irritation, as if they were misbehaving children.

"Have you, Mrs. Willcox," asked counsel Sourwine at one point, "ever taken any action in opposition to the Communist party, U.S.A.?"[48]

"Listen," Anita snapped, "I'm an artist."

When the committee members started to question her about the political affiliations of her children, and the acting chairman, Senator McClellan, solemnly explained that the committee had the duty "to ferret out those elements . . . promoting a conspiracy that would overthrow this government," Anita sharply demanded to know whether the senator was suggesting her children were involved in such a conspiracy.

"Nobody has expressed that," Senator McClellan hastily replied.

"What are you bringing it up for, then?" said Anita. "Look now, I want to tell you a blanket statement on all of my children. They are all married; they are all of age; and, as far as I know, not one of them is now or ever has been a member of the Communist party." Nor, she added, were any of her nine grandchildren members of the Communist party. "They are," she said, "all under five."

Toward the end of her testimony, Anita made this statement:

> When I was a little girl, over half a century ago, I was so proud of our country. I believed without question in the reality of the freedom my forebears had fought to establish; freedom to do; freedom to explore places and people and ideas. I believed in the wisdom, the justice, of our courts. Ours was a country where all the downtrodden of the earth could find a haven, could know that with hard work they would have an expanding future for themselves and their children. . . .
>
> But something has happened to this beautiful country of ours. Today experts and scholars are afraid to voice their opinions if they do not agree with the dogma of the government; scientists may not serve if they speak to the wrong people; men and women are in jail for thoughts, not acts. . . .
>
> Harvey Matusow is a symbol of a sickness that is blighting our beloved country. We must not lock him up or forget him. We must carefully exhume the truth. We must be in fact what we boast to be—the land of the free and the home of the brave.

Shortly after Anita's appearance, the Senate subcommittee concluded its protracted hearing on the Matusow case.

The hearing had dragged on over a period of some nine weeks. More than half a million words of testimony and "documentary evidence" had been recorded. The final transcript of the hearing would be 1,300 pages in length. The witnesses, however, had not included a single Justice Department official or any of the other government personnel who had hired Matusow's services as a lying witness. Instead, with the exception of five "friendly witnesses," three of whom were FBI informers, all of the persons examined by the subcommittee had been put on the witness stand for the purpose of establishing their involvement in a "Communist conspiracy" around Matusow.[49]

Senator Eastland announced that within a few days the subcommittee would send a report of its findings to the Justice Department. He hoped, he stated, that it contained "grounds for jailing Matusow . . . on some charge."

The subcommittee voted to cite Matusow for contempt. The citation was based on the fact that in his testimony at the hearing Matusow had refused to reveal the name of the manufacturer of his "stringless yo-yo."

CHAPTER FOURTEEN

CROSSCURRENTS

1. *"Which Was the Lie?"*

April 22, 1955, was a memorable date in the annals of the Matusow case.

Harvey telephoned late that afternoon. "Congratulations!" he shouted. "Did you hear the news?"

"What's up?" I asked.

"We've won! Dimock's decision is in. Trachtenberg and Charney get new trials. . . . By God, I feel good! I don't care now if I lose the appeal in Texas and go to jail!"

It is doubtful that anyone had ever before displayed so much enthusiasm over a court ruling affirming the fact he had committed perjury.

The opinion rendered by Judge Dimock on the retrial motion in the Flynn case was a document of major import. As the first reversal of any Smith Act conviction and as a federal court finding that one of the government's "expert witnesses" was a perjurer, it represented a turning point in judicial decisions on political cases during the Cold War period. It forecast other, similar rulings in the federal courts. In contrast to Judge Thomason's opinion in the Jencks case, Judge Dimock's twenty-four page opinion detailed the evidence for finding that when Matusow testified for the government at the Flynn trial in 1952 he had been "a completely irresponsible witness . . . a man without regard for the truth, with a passion for the limelight, and with the need for a few dollars."

Judge Dimock posed the question: "Which was the lie—the original story or the recantation?" It was the government's contention, he said, that the retraction was the lie, and that "persons acting in the interest of the defendants here and of one Jencks . . . paid for the recantation in the guise of paying Matusow for work on the book, *False Witness*. . . ." He demolished this argument:

> The fact is that it was news of a statement by Matusow that he had been giving false testimony that led these persons sympathetic to the defendants to seek his aid. Matusow had made that statement to Bishop G. Bromley Oxnam, of the Methodist Church, on April 27, 1954. Bishop Oxnam disclosed it in a speech on June 7. Undoubtedly the financial assistance given Matusow was a factor in inducing the actual execution of the affidavit on which this motion is founded, but Matusow's admission that he had been lying came first. That was not induced by friends of these defendants. . . .

Judge Dimock went on to state "the internal evidence all points to the original story as the lie." Not one of Matusow's "damaging statements" in court had been made by him when he was first questioned by government attorneys before the trial. Matusow had then failed to designate a single instance of any defendant having advocated "the forcible or violent overthrow of the government." Only during his preparation as a witness, as a study of the pretrial briefs of the government attorneys revealed, had Matusow gradually introduced into his discussions with these lawyers "embellishments indicating advocacy of force and violence":

> In every case the effective thrust was finally given in connection with something about which Matusow had first given his interrogators a comparatively innocent statement. . . .
>
> It is incredible that, with the search for advocacy of force and violence uppermost in his consciousness, Matusow's memory would first recall a matter to his mind in an innocuous form and, on some later occasion, recall the damaging feature indicative of the advocacy of force and violence.

Judge Dimock also pointed out that in none of the reports Matusow had written as an FBI informer before becoming a government witness, was there a "statement of any advocacy by the American Communist party or any of its members of the duty of overthrowing the government of the United States by force and violence."[50]

By the time, however, that Matusow took the stand at the Flynn trial his "memory had gone so far as to recall" a whole series of specific instances in which various of the defendants had supposedly not only advocated the forcible overthrow of the government, but indicated they were acting toward this end as agents of the Soviet Union.

The jurors who believed Matusow's testimony, the judge pointed out, did not have at their disposal "the history of the development of Matusow's testimony" or the "evidence . . . now for the first time available throwing light on Matusow's character."

On the other hand, Judge Dimock stated he could not give credence to Matusow's claim that his false testimony had been encouraged by government attorneys and that Roy Cohn had deliberately suborned portions of it. Mentioning that the government attorneys had categorically denied these charges, Judge Dimock declared:

> I cannot accept the word of a proved perjurer against theirs and the circumstantial evidence is in their favor. I find that all of Matusow's fabrications were his own suggestions. By hindsight we see that the government attorneys were credulous but that they did not have the benefit of the knowledge of Matusow's character that the developments of the years have brought.

The conviction of two of the defendants, George Charney and Alexander Trachtenberg, had been based primarily on Matusow's perjured testimony, said Judge Dimock. Therefore: "The motion to set aside the verdict and for a new trial is granted as to defendants Trachtenberg and Charney."

Notable as was Judge Dimock's opinion, it was not without flaws. To characterize the government lawyers as merely "credulous" was euphemistic; and to say they lacked "the knowledge of Matusow's character that the developments of the years have brought" was to overlook what they did know about his character when they used him as a witness. As Judge Dimock had pointed out, "the history of the development of Matusow's testimony" was not available to the trial jurors, and they therefore could not know Matusow was lying. That history, however, *was*, available to the government attorneys: all of it—Matusow's FBI reports and the pretrial briefs exposed the evolution of his testimony. The government lawyers were intimately acquainted with the transformations in Matusow's stories while they were preparing him as a witness. If this later made it obvious to Judge Dimock that Matusow had lied at the trial, surely that fact should have been no less obvious to these attorneys at the time of Matusow's testimony. And if the trial jurors lacked the evidence that Matusow was lying, was it not precisely because the government attorneys had kept it from them?

The government attorneys in the Flynn case, moreover, were not as unfamiliar with Matusow's character as Judge Dimock assumed. They were acquainted with the patent lies he was telling in his appearances before congressional committees.

Furthermore, these government attorneys had in their possession evidence of Matusow's emotional instability. The evidence consisted of a confidential report about Matusow which the U.S. attorney's office in New York had received from FBI Washington headquarters before Matusow testified at the Flynn trial. Written in the form of a letter from FBI chief Hoover to U.S. Attorney Myles Lane, this report stated in part:

> For your further confidential information the Veterans Administration file on MATUSOW . . . contains the following information:
> . . . On April 21, 1945, while still in service . . . he reported spells of headaches and dizziness, which were diagnosed as psychoneurosis of a mild but acute form. . . .
> It was . . . conjectured by the interviewing psychiatrist that much of his difficulty, at this time, might be due to the fact that his

brother DANIEL MATUSOW had been killed in action . . . near Nuren-
burg, Germany, and that he was having difficulty facing up to the
task of visiting his brother's grave and identifying some personal
belongings of this brother.[51]

Not until after the conclusion of the Flynn retrial hearing would the
existence of this secret document become publicly known, and then
hardly because of any suddenly awakened sense of honor in the Justice Department. On March 1, 1955, Assistant Attorney General
Tompkins appeared before a closed session of a House Appropriations
subcommittee. The subcommittee chairman Representative John
Rooney, had learned of the confidential FBI report on Matusow's
"psychoneurosis" and questioned Tompkins about it. Tompkins admitted the existence of the report. He claimed, however, that he had
only recently come to know about it. "I then asked Mr. Lumbard
about it," said Tompkins, "and he told me that the United States
Attorney's office had received the letter in January 1952."[52]

"How many cases have come up where you have used Matusow?"
asked Representative Rooney.

"The Communist Party case, the three front cases, the Flynn case
in New York, the Jencks case in Texas. . . ."

"Are we to understand," queried the congressman, "that all during
this time the matter of the question of his mental equilibrium has
never been brought to the attention of the Attorney General's office . . . ?"

"As far as we know, sir," said Tompkins, "that is true. . . . I am
going to be very frank with you. With that information, I would have
used the witness. . . . In other words, that medical description
wouldn't have had any impact as far as I am concerned . . . on his
credibility."

Tompkins added: "If we are just going to get somebody of absolutely impeccable and unassailable character, it is going to have a
terrific impact upon our prosecutions. You use the best you have."

No less significant than the Justice Department's failure to divulge
this information about Matusow at the time of the Flynn trial, was the
failure of Assistant Attorney General Tompkins and U.S. Attorney
Lumbard to bring it to Judge Dimock's attention during the retrial
hearing.

This was no obstacle to political advancement for Lumbard. President Eisenhower subsequently appointed him to fill a vacancy on the New York Federal Court of Appeals.

2. *Comedy Sketches*

In the light of Judge Dimock's ruling, one might have expected a prompt indictment of Matusow for perjury at the Flynn trial. His admission that he had testified falsely had now, after all, been substantiated by the findings of a federal magistrate. Anyone, however, who believed that Matusow would now face trial for this offense was simply unfamiliar with the workings of the Justice Department.

Within a week after Judge Dimock's decision, Assistant Attorney General Tompkins informed the press that the Justice Department would move "as expeditiously as possible"—not to arraign Matusow on a perjury charge, but to try Charney and Trachtenberg again for violation of the Smith Act. Simultaneously, the U.S. Attorney's office in New York announced that the federal grand jury would continue to investigate "Matusow's claim that he perjured himself at the Communist trial" and the possibility that he had been bribed by Communists to make this claim.

Regarding the continuing grand jury inquiry, columnist Murray Kempton wrote:

> Last week, Judge Dimock . . . ordered new trials for the two main victims of his (Matusow's) testimony. Despite this decision and the shadow it casts on the Department of Justice, Brownell proceeds on the premise that Matusow told the truth then and is lying now.
>
> In its zeal to prove this point, the local grand jury has spent weeks investigating everyone who ever dealt with Matusow. This week, it began calling people who had never met him.
>
> Since Monday, it has called and questioned 10 printers and production men who handled the mechanics of publishing Matusow's *False Witness*. They range from contractors down to pressroom workers.

Their "sin" said Kempton, was that of printing "material which shames the Department of Justice." He added:

> The grand jury consumes its time in a useless search. . . . But the effrontery of its search is more important than its futility, for the effect has to be the intimidation and harassment of men whose only function is the production of the word. . . .

One of the witnesses now summoned before the grand jury was Harvey Satenstein, president of Book Craftsmen Associates, the firm that had printed *False Witness*. I saw him shortly afterward.

"They asked me if I was a Communist!" he snorted. "Can you imagine that? Damn it, what right did they have to drag me down there anyway? And think of it—yanking my men off the presses to answer their fool questions! I told them I print what I want to print and that no one's going to stop me, either!"

Besides interrogating the men who had manufactured the book *False Witness*, the grand jury now, at long last, undertook to examine its author.

On the advice of Faulkner, who stressed that the Justice Department's paramount concern was to indict Matusow on a spurious charge and that there was no reason to aid in this endeavor, Harvey decided to invoke the Fifth Amendment on all questions relating to his book and his affidavits of recantation.

"It was fabulous!" Harvey told me following his grand jury appearance. "When I refused to answer any questions about my previous testimony, someone asked what I did for a living. So I said I was an entertainer and did comedy routines. One of them said, what sort of routines? So I showed them! For about half an hour!" He chortled gleefully, shaking his head, as if he found it hard to believe. "You know, my regular stuff. Monologues, imitations . . . stuff I've written for nightclub and TV shows. They enjoyed it too. They were all laughing . . . God, I wish I had a tape recording of that scene!" He paused. "I made some of my pipe cleaner animals for them too. One of them was my French poodle. I told them that the poodle had emigrated to the United States and had been called before a grand jury and asked if he'd attended a Communist cocktail party. The poodle refused to answer the question—on the grounds of the Eighteenth Amendment. . . ."

To some observers it appeared that the knowledge the grand jurors were now gleaning was not overly germane to the purpose of their inquiry.

As the Springfield, Ohio, *Sun* editorialized:

> According to Manhattan newspapers, Matusow exhibited to the grand jurors some "comedy sketches" he has written, and he also performed "a nightclub routine" for their benefit. We are not told what, if anything, this has to do with a federal grand jury hearing; but perhaps the jurors, or the courthouse reporters, died laughing before they could explain. . . .

3. *Straws in the Wind*

Notwithstanding the comic interlude of Matusow's grand jury appearance, the Justice Department was moving ahead to offset the ramifications of the Matusow scandal and shore up the creaking structure of its informer-witness apparatus. On May 16 Mrs. Marie Natvig, the former government witness who had repudiated her testimony in the Lamb case, was found guilty of perjury by a federal court jury in Washington, D.C. She was convicted not for the crime to which she had confessed but for allegedly lying in her confession. After commending the jury on its verdict, Judge Alexander Holtzoff sentenced Mrs. Natvig to eight months in jail.[53]

Meanwhile, with the obvious aim of discouraging other government witnesses from admitting their lies, Attorney General Brownell was sponsoring in Congress a bill to revise the federal perjury statute so as to facilitate the prosecution of witnesses who recanted. A spate of official pronouncements was pouring from the Justice Department charging that "Communists" were behind the mounting criticism of its use of paid professional witnesses.

"It is becoming increasingly apparent," stated Assistant Attorney General Tompkins, "that the current attack against government witnesses and informants of the Federal Bureau of Investigation has its roots in a Communist effort. . . ."

Commented a *New York Times* editorial:

If Mr. Tompkins' words mean anything, they mean that the nationwide protests against the repeated use of totally unreliable paid professional informers by the Department of Justice and other Government agencies are Communist-inspired. They imply that only Communists or Communist dupes would make such protests. They suggest that the very purpose of such protests, and protests against secret, star-chamber procedures, is "to stem" the Government's campaign against subversion. . . .

To hear one of the highest officials of the Department of Justice suggest that the doubts cast on present procedures must stem from pro-Communists is almost incredible.

Despite the government's frantic efforts to turn the tide, the scathing criticism of its "security" measures and informer system was gaining volume on all sides. "We have seen our public life debauched," wrote former U.S. Ambassador to Moscow George F. Kennan in an article in the *Christian Register*, "the faith of our people in great and distinguished citizens systematically undermined. . . . The most subtle sort of damage done to our intellectual life. . . . A pall of anxiety thrown over our entire scientific community; our libraries and forums of knowledge placed on the defensive before the inroads of self-appointed snoopers and censors. . . . We have seen our people taught to distrust one another, to spy, to bear tales, to behave in a manner which is in sharpest conflict with the American tradition."

"What would be useful right now," declared Reverend James A. Pike, Dean of the Protestant Episcopal Diocese of New York, "would be a congressional investigation of the paid informer system."

With every day, church groups, trade unions, and associations of teachers, lawyers, and other professions, were making new demands for a review of so-called anti-subversive legislation and an end to the use of paid informer-witnesses.

In the middle of April, in an effort to assuage the mounting furor, Attorney General Brownell announced that the Justice Department had decided to discontinue the employment of informer-witnesses as full-time "consultants." Instead of being on regular salaries as in the past, he said, they would henceforth be paid only for their specific services as witnesses. It was, however, difficult to see how the government's paying informer-witnesses "by the job" would change their mode of employment or the dubious nature of their testimony.

Perhaps most distressing of all from the viewpoint of the Justice Department was the initiation of other federal court actions that boded ill for the government's "internal security" program. On May 23 the U.S. Supreme Court set aside the convictions of two union officials and the general manager of the *Daily Worker*, who had been prosecuted by the Justice Department on contempt charges for refusing to answer questions at a congressional inquiry relating to their political beliefs and associations. "The power to investigate..." declared Chief Justice Earl Warren, "cannot be used to inquire into private affairs...."[54]

Three weeks later, following a series of adverse federal court rulings, the Justice Department announced it was dropping the perjury case against Owen Lattimore because of "insufficient evidence"—a genteel way of conceding that Matusow and other government witnesses against Lattimore had lied. In a deportation case in Los Angeles, a federal magistrate refused to accept the testimony of a government informer-witness appearing as an "expert" on Communism. "This is a court of law," said the judge. "I won't take his opinion on what the Communist party taught. And I won't take the opinions of such big name experts as Paul Crouch, Louis Budenz, Harvey Matusow...." A U.S. Circuit Court of Appeals decision held that seamen and longshoremen being "screened" by the Coast Guard with the aid of anonymous informers, were being denied their constitutional rights.

As if the combination of these events was not sufficiently onerous for the Justice Department, still another government informer, David Brown, chose this moment to confess that he had been a habitual liar while employed as an undercover agent by the FBI. A former organizer for the Mine-Mill union and ex-secretary of the Civil Rights Congress in Los Angeles, Brown admitted at a hearing of the Federal

Subversive Activities Control Board that during his four years as an FBI informer he had repeatedly falsified lists of "subversives" he included in his Bureau reports.

"Did you ever put names in of persons you didn't see?" he was asked on the witness stand.

"Oh, very often," he said. "I picked many names at random— hundreds of names that had no significance to me."

"And are you now admitting you lied to the FBI?"

"All during my association with the FBI, I lied—from 1950 to January, 1955," said Brown. "That's what I was paid to do by the FBI."[55]

CHAPTER FIFTEEN

SIGNS OF SUMMER

1. *Again the Grand Jury*

Early in June I was summoned back before the grand jury in New York. Four months had elapsed since my last appearance. Then the weather had been inclement, cold and blustery. Now a balmy warmth embraced the city, lovers sat in the parks and children played baseball in the streets. The climate in the jury room, however, had undergone no comparable spring. The atmosphere was even chillier than before.

After Judge Dimock had confirmed the fact that Matusow had lied at the Flynn trial and had not been bribed to recant, one would have thought the jury would be less suspicious of Matusow's publishers and would perhaps even acknowledge they had helped uncover the facts in the case. But for nineteen weeks the jurors had been functioning under the solicitous tutelage of the Justice Department; and if at the outset they had contemplated the government with awe and respect, they had since come to regard themselves as virtually a branch of it. For them, Judge Dimock's ruling represented no vindication of the truth but rather a serious complication in their task of proving a Communist plot against the Justice Department.

Acting as new counsel to the grand jury was an assistant U.S. attorney named Thomas Bolan, a self-possessed, sandy-haired young man who went about the job of interrogating me in a methodical, business-like manner. His influence over the jurors was manifest in their hushed attentiveness to his questions. Equally apparent was the antagonism with which they received my answers.

My examination had not been long under way when an incident occurred that crystallized the atmosphere prevailing in the jury room. All at once, one of the jurors addressed the foreman in a loud, irritable voice. "Will you instruct the witness," he said, "to stop making notes."

"You will desist from making notes, Mr. Kahn," the foreman ordered.

I said that my brief notes were for use for later discussion with my lawyer, and that there had been no objection to my making notes during my previous appearances before the jury.

"We were very lenient then," snapped the foreman. "We allowed you to make speeches.... Things have changed." The foreman, too, had changed. Formerly, his timidity had outweighed his officiousness; but in the intervening weeks his authority had given him a sense of power. His servility, however, was revealed in the frequent glances he darted at Bolan for approval of his remarks.

I said I would answer no more questions until a judge had ruled on whether or not I had the right to make notes.

Once again, as in a scene from an old film, the jurors and I reenacted the ritual of early February and marched down the hall. The magistrate before whom we now appeared listened with a grave expression as Bolan indignantly related that I had been constantly disrupting the grand jury proceedings and was now seeking to dictate the terms under which I would testify. Under Bolan's deft legerdemain, my sketchy notes assumed the dimensions of an exhaustive journal.

The judge reprimanded me for hampering the investigation, and ordered me to comply henceforth with the foreman's instructions on note-making.

I cannot truthfully claim, however, that my inability to make notes during the remainder of my examination was a major disadvantage. There was actually little worth recording.

For four protracted, wearisome days, Bolan labored to uncover some contradiction in my former testimony and to establish my involvement in a conspiracy. Outside, the sun shone temptingly. Soft breezes stirred through the open windows. A lethargic warmth permeated the room, through which an occasional fly buzzed inquisitively and then, as if even it could not stand the monotony, fled to the open air. As Bolan's questions droned on hour after hour, the jurors' heads nodded; they stifled yawns, and periodically a couple of them dozed off.

It was difficult not to feel a certain sympathy toward them. For me, at least, the ordeal would soon be over. But who could tell how long it would last for them? They had already consumed more time in their deliberations on the Matusow case than the Federal Convention had taken in 1787 to frame the Constitution of the United States. Yet from the occasional questions they put to me it was clear they were no nearer to the truth than they had been at the very start. Indeed, with possibly one or two exceptions, they were further from it. Before, at least, their minds had been more open and less cluttered with misinformation. In the intervening months, under the diligent schooling of the Justice Department, instead of acquiring knowledge they had amassed prejudice and built up defenses against reality.

This was a sad and somewhat frightening thing to see, because these were ordinary, decent people, who decried injustice and wanted to do what was honorable. They were, in fact, a microcosm of a large section of the population, and, as such, offered vivid proof of the way in which the collective mind can be duped by the devices of officialdom.

Perhaps, I thought, the jury could be shocked, if only momentarily, into a recognition of the truth. I waited for what seemed an appropriate moment and then declared: "I have reason to believe the Justice Department is keeping vital information from this grand jury and is seeking to charge me with a crime of which I'm innocent. In other words, I believe they're trying to frame me."

An uneasy stir went through the room.

Bolan did the only thing he could under the circumstances. "How long would it take you, Mr. Kahn," he inquired coldly, "to tell the jury what facts are being kept from them?"

I could indicate some of them, I said, in a few minutes. I reminded the jury that when I had last appeared before them early in February, I had submitted a memorandum recommending that the Justice Department produce for their examination certain data from its files. "If you'll check that memorandum, you'll find that among the items are the FBI reports on Matusow, and the Justice Department pre-trial briefs on which Judge Dimock largely based his findings that Matusow had lied at the Flynn trial. Unbiased attorneys, seeking to get at the truth in this case, would have pursued the same line of inquiry as

Judge Dimock. They would have placed all this material at your disposal, so that you might have been enabled to reach the same conclusions as the judge."

"And how do you know, Mr. Kahn," Bolan demanded, "that the Department didn't provide the jury with this material?"

"Well, did it?"

Bolan did not answer.

The mere fact of his having spoken, however, had the effect of reminding the jurors whose was the voice of authority.

One of them said with pronounced sarcasm, "Apparently you and Mr. Cameron are quite proud of what you've accomplished."

"Yes, I suppose you might say we are. We're proud of having published Matusow's book because we think it's rendered a real public service. We're also gratified that as a result of Matusow's recantation two individuals who were unjustly imprisoned have now been set free."

No juror was willing to voice a similar opinion. The two persons who had been vindicated were, after all, Communists, and if Communists personify all that is inquitous, what right have they to share in the safeguards of justice?

2. *Strange Interlude*

One evening during the second week of June, Harvey telephoned me at Croton. "Can you stand a shock?" he asked in a strangely elated tone.

"What's up?"

"Al," he said, "I'm getting married."

"When in the world did all this happen?"

He laughed. "I figured you'd be surprised. I've known her for a couple of months, Al. She's a wonderful person, really wonderful! You'll see. Her name's Helen. We want Riette and you at the wedding. We want you to be best man. . . . And, Al, can you do me a favor? We want a Jewish ceremony. Can you get a rabbi for us?"

I called a rabbi who was an old acquaintance and asked him if he would perform the ceremony.

"You mean *the* Harvey Matusow?" he said with surprise.

"None other."

"So he's getting married, eh? Well, what do you know! Certainly, I'll be glad to do it." He added cheerfully, "You can't tell. Maybe it's just what he needs."

My own feelings on the matter were mixed. On the one hand, I was inclined to share the rabbi's opinion that marriage was perhaps what Harvey needed. Considering the problems and struggles that doubtless lay ahead of him, he could surely benefit from the affection and stability that a home of his own might bring. But all of that, of course, depended on the nature of the marriage. And I could not help wondering how many marriages would stand up under the strains likely to beset this one. Moreover, it was easier to understand Harvey's wanting to get married than someone's eagerness to marry him. Aside from his sordid past, notoriety still hounded his every move, and a jail sentence hung over his head. What sort of person was ready to share this cloudy future with Harvey?

A day or so later Riette and I went into New York to have lunch with him and his bride-to-be. Helen was a slender, attractive young woman; she had a placid manner in which cool reserve and shyness seemed strangely mingled. Throughout the meal she remained as reticent as Harvey was garrulous. Occasionally, she glanced at Riette and me with a slight, enigmatic smile, as Harvey ebulliently undertook to convince the three of us how much we liked each other at first sight.

Helen, Harvey proudly told us, was a talented painter. She had been married before and had a six-year-old daughter, Judith. They would move immediately into his apartment. It would be crowded but would do until they found something better.

"But I haven't even told you how we met," he exclaimed. "Listen to this. It's quite a yarn. For some time I'd been walking the little girl of a friend of mine to school, and it happens that Judith goes to the same school. One day Helen saw me there. She recognized me from my pictures. So she goes to the principal and says she doesn't think my being around the school is a good influence on the children. Then it turns out that the mother of the child I'm walking to school is a friend of Helen's, and she introduces us." He laughed gaily. "How's that for the start of a romance?"

As he chattered on excitedly, I realized I had never before seen him so spontaneous and truly at ease. It was as if, suddenly, for the moment at least, all artificiality had dropped from him. His effusiveness was without brashness, and he made no attempt at witty phrases.

More than once he began a sentence, floundered, and broke off in the middle. "I guess I'm all mixed up," he said with a foolish grin.

After lunch, he took me aside. "Al," he said, hesitantly, "I don't know just how to put this, but . . . well, there's something I want you to speak to Helen about."

He groped for the right words. "Look . . . oh, hell, you'll understand. There's one thing I'm worried about. It's about Helen's friends. She's progressive, you know, and most of her friends are too. And how are they going to feel about her marrying me? Christ, Al, you know how they feel about an—" He could not bring himself to say the word "informer."

In the mail next morning there was a letter from Harvey:

Dear Al,

Today was not unusual, in that I enjoyed lunching with you and Riette. During lunch I remarked that you looked depressed. You said you were thinking about your book, and that you always looked that way when you were thinking about a book, etc., etc. That may be. But I still think you looked depressed.

You made other comments today about the grand jury, and the possibility of an indictment. If such an indictment comes down, I want to be on the record to you, in this letter, prior to any such action. I want the record of our friendship—unsoiled and unspoiled by lies and distrust—to go on, as in the past. I don't have to say it, you already know it, I'll never let you down.

You more than any other man have made me realize that I could still be a human being. . . . You've helped me when none would. But you did even more important things than that. You opened your priceless treasures to me. You brought me into your home, and let me taste the rarest of foods—knowing your wife and boys. All of these gifts and treasures of the past seven months have brought me to the event of this coming Monday—my marriage to Helen, which would not have been possible if you had not taught me how to live with myself. I consider you my best friend. . . .

My conscience convinced me to tell the truth. . . . But you showed me the trust which enabled me to believe my conscience. For this you've lost much. Oh, I know you gained much, too. . . .

I'm just rambling now. All I meant to say when I started this letter was THANKS. Helen thanks you too.

Harvey

The wedding took place in a suite in the Chelsea Hotel.

"Remember how I didn't want to work there at first because I connected it with my past?" Harvey said. "Well, now, because of the book and everything else, I guess, I connect it with the future."

Other than Angus, Riette and me, the only guest at the wedding was one of Helen's friends, a tall, preoccupied young man, who seemed ill at ease and had little to say to anyone.

Harvey, harried-looking but faultlessly attired in a dark suit and immaculate white shirt, bustled back and forth between the kitchenette and the living room, serving refreshments. Helen, looking very pretty in a sunny organdy dress, sat tensely in a large armchair, distractedly watching Harvey, while we waited for the rabbi. Her daughter, Judith, hovered at her side, a forlorn child with olive skin and dark, tormented eyes. She periodically clutched her mother and wailed, "I don't want you to get married! I don't want a daddy!"

Before long the rabbi arrived, and the ceremony got under way. With a businesslike air the rabbi intoned some sentences in Hebrew, periodically explaining their significance. On his instructions, Harvey and Helen drank from the same glass of wine. The newlyweds embraced while Judith clung to her mother's skirts and wept.

There was a poignant symbolism to the disconsolate weeping of the little girl. A wedding should be an occasion to celebrate with one's closest friends. But how many friends had this bridegroom to invite? And which of the bride's friends would have been willing to attend? The past could not be wiped away like chalk from a blackboard. Unsummoned and undesired, it reached into this room, infecting the present and shadowing the future.

Later, I went to see Harvey's parents at their cigar stand. Mrs. Matusow shrugged away her hurt at not having been invited to the wedding. "Harvey wanted to keep it as small as possible," she said. "He felt that if his father and I came, there would have to be other relatives—" She stopped to sell a customer a package of cigarettes. "Anyway, Harvey's happy. That's the main thing. You know, I haven't seen him so happy in years. Not since he was a little boy. He brought Helen up to the house the other day and spent the whole afternoon with us. She seems like a lovely girl." She paused and sighed. "But how's Harvey going to support a family? And what will the grand jury do?"

* * *

On July 13, one month after Harvey's wedding, the grand jury indicted Harvey on six counts of perjury. *Not a single one of the counts concerned any of the numerous falsehoods he had admitted telling as a government witness at the Flynn trial.* The only charge brought against him was that he had lied in accusing Roy Cohn of suborning his perjurious testimony.

At the same time, in an action which came as an utter surprise, the grand jury returned indictments against two lawyers for the *Nation* magazine and an assistant to the publisher. The *Nation* lawyers were charged with perjury and conspiracy to obstruct justice by allegedly falsifying memoranda concerning meetings they had had with Matusow. The assistant to the publisher was charged with obstructing justice by allegedly removing from the *Nation*'s files correspondence with the Mine-Mill union relating to Matusow. The magazine characterized the indictments as an effort by the Justice Department "to smear and silence a publication which has played a leading role in attacking the use of political informers."[56]

CHAPTER SIXTEEN

ACROSS THE LAND

1. *Westward Ho!*

For a number of years it had been our family's custom, when summer came and school was out, to squeeze into a car piled high with suitcases, fishing poles, picnic supplies, games, and other miscellanea, and head west for our vacation. By mid-May, several weeks in advance of departure, maps would be brought out and eager debate begin on possible routes of travel and places to be visited. This year our discussions had been of a different sort. I was still under grand jury subpoena and might be indicted any day, and there were obvious inconveniences in being arrested while traveling across country with one's family. Instead of our usual practice of listing motels at which to stop en route, Riette and I were cataloguing persons to whom we might turn, if need be, for my bail money.

Steven, Timmy and Brian were growing increasingly impatient with the influence of the Matusow case upon our lives. As Steven put it: "Okay, so we've put off moving west because of Harvey, but, gosh, can't we even have a vacation!"

By the end of June, Riette and I had been won over to the boys' viewpoint. Come what might, indictment or not, we would take a trip to California and, while there, seek our future home site.

On the trip I could combine business with pleasure. I had been asked by progressive organizations in several midwestern and western cities to lecture on the Matusow case. In the middle of July, with the ever-reliable Faulkner in possession of our day-to-day itinerary in the event of my indictment, our family departed on its westward trek.

As a specific for curing mental myopia, as well as for general invigoration of the spirit, few remedies are as efficacious as a trip across the giant span of the United States. To travel across New Jersey, Pennsylvania and Ohio through woodlands, meadows and tunneled mountains; to traverse the Great Plains past fields of wheat and corn, and cattle ranges; to come upon the sudden mighty wall of the Rockies and climb among their snow-capped peaks; to journey through trackless deserts; to drop from the High Sierras into the fragrant orchards of the Sacramento Valley and at last arrive where suddenly the gleaming city of San Francisco cascades like a white wave over the hills at the Pacific's edge—this is a tonic that clarifies the vision and sets things in true perspective.

That summer the Cold War seemed finally on the wane. The leaders of the four major powers had convened in Geneva to explore peaceful solutions to the antagonisms that had wracked the world for almost a decade. Returning from Europe, President Eisenhower told the tumultuous crowd that welcomed him at the Washington airport: "There is evidence of a new friendliness in the world. . . ." Proof of that new friendliness met us as we journeyed west. Our arrival in Iowa coincided with that of a delegation of Soviet farm experts who had come to America on the initiative of the *Des Moines Register*. In every town and hamlet in the Hawkeye state, newspapers carried editorials radiating goodwill toward the Russian guests, photographs of banquets in their honor, front-page stories of their visits to factories and farms.

The proprietor of a small shop in one town showed us a newspaper photograph of four men in shirt-sleeves walking down a street. "Two of them are Russians, and two of them are our fellows," he said. "You tell me which is which. . . ." He smiled with satisfaction. "Of course, you can't. They're really just the same as we are."

Such events would have been inconceivable a year before. Even now they seemed strangely incongruous, like an anachronism plucked from our wartime alliance with Russia.

There was a feeling of relaxation in the air. Everywhere, people seemed readier to speak their minds. It was as if after a long, harsh winter, democracy was venturing forth from hibernation.

"We are," wrote Walter Lippmann in his syndicated column, "in the early stages of a great popular reaction against the hysteria and demagoguery, the lawlessness and cruel injustice which we rightfully call the era of McCarthyism. . . ."

Unfortunately, Lippmann was overly optimistic. There was little promise of any "great popular reaction," since no great popular movement existed to sustain it. The Cold War years had done their work too well. The democratic forces which had marched together under the banners of the New Deal were now scattered. The tragedy of the situation was that while the fortress of reaction appeared ready to fall, the forces of progress were not on hand for the assault.

If talk of peaceful coexistence had partially replaced dire prophecies of war, military expenditures were soaring to new heights and schoolchildren still crouched under desks during atom bomb drills; and if the malaise of McCarthyism seemed considerably assuaged, the federal loyalty-security inquisition was far from defunct.

At the various meetings at which I spoke on the trip, the contradictions of the times were amply evident. Each meeting was concerned in part with recent Smith Act indictments, prosecutions, or convictions: and, at the same time, mention was always made of encouraging local developments. "Since Matusow's confession things have changed quite a bit here," I was told by the chairman of the meeting in Detroit. "For one thing, you read a lot more in the papers about constitutional rights, especially free speech." That the right of free speech was not yet wholly without restriction in Detroit, however, was indicated by a subsequent Federated Press dispatch which reported:

> The 250 guests at the recent banquet of the Michigan Committee for the Protection of the Foreign-born did not know that Detroit police were tape-recording every word. . . . But the management (of the banquet hall) had given the cops permission to tape the public address system and get a tape recording of what publisher and author Albert Kahn had to say as a guest speaker. . . .
>
> The guests did not know that a camera mounted in an apartment across the street was photographing everyone as he left the banquet hall. It was manned by the police.

The day we arrived on the West Coast, a federal judge in San Francisco dismissed denaturalization proceedings brought against labor leader Harry Bridges by the Justice Department as part of its twenty-year-old campaign to deport him. In rendering the Bridges decision, the judge scathingly rebuked the government for its use of informer-witnesses, whose testimony he characterized as "inherently flimsy . . . unsubstantial . . . incredible. . . ."

"A lot of things have happened in this country this summer," wrote Murray Kempton in a column dealing with the Bridges case, "and I think we owe most of them to Harvey Matusow. There is a sudden sense that judges no longer trust the Dept. of Justice. A witness . . . walks into court . . . and the judge sees only Harvey Matusow. The face haunts . . . every courtroom in this country. . . . As long as the memory of Harvey Matusow lasts, the government will call the next witness, and the judge will retch."

"To sum it up," wrote Hyman Lumer, former professor at Fenn College, in a pamphlet entitled, *The Professional Informer*, "the distrust of the professional informer is mounting on all sides. And this is not merely because a Matusow seemingly was afflicted with pangs of conscience. Basically, it is due to the fact that with the easing of international tensions and growing prospects of peaceful co-existence, people . . . are far less affected by anti-Communist hysteria."

2. Trailing the FBI

As we headed homeward from the Pacific Coast late in August, strangely contradictory motives took us off the main route and into Taos, that old and lovely Spanish town set like an antique jewel in a ring of mountains in northern New Mexico.

On the one hand, we wanted to see friends in the nearby village of San Cristobal. On the other, I had heard that Justice Department representatives had visited Taos several times during the past months, seeking proof of conspiratorial dealings between Matusow and Cameron & Kahn prior to his coming east the previous fall. I thought it possible these government agents might have left telltale traces of their activities.

On arriving in Taos we drove out to San Cristobal to visit Craig and Jennie Vincent, our erstwhile hosts at the San Cristobal Valley

Ranch. The ranch, which had been known as a resort where guests of all colors and creeds were welcome, no longer belonged to the Vincents. It had been one of the casualties of Matusow's lies as a professional witness. At various congressional and court proceedings, he had charged that the ranch was a "secret rendezvous" for Communists and "Soviet agents." The lurid headlines had done their work. The continued operation of the ranch soon became impossible, and the Vincents had been compelled to sell it.

Yes, said the Vincents in answer to my query, they had heard about the FBI visits to Taos. They suggested several persons in town who might have additional information on the subject.

So thorough, in fact, had been the search conducted by the FBI agents that they had discovered exactly what they had not wanted to.

Instead of finding evidence that Matusow had surreptitiously received funds from the Mine-Mill union or Cameron & Kahn before coming to New York the previous October, they had uncovered substantial proof of the fraudulence of this theory. At all ensuing judicial proceedings in the Matusow case, however, the Justice Department had not only concealed from judges and jurors what the FBI learned in Taos, but had sought to convince them of the very opposite.

Among the persons questioned by the FBI were two who had seen perhaps more of Matusow than had anyone else during his brief visit to Taos: Mrs. Ruth Fish, secretary of the Chamber of Commerce and local correspondent for the Associated Press; and "Doughbelly" Price, a former rodeo rider who now operated a real estate agency.

To both Mrs. Fish and "Doughbelly" Price, it had been apparent that, far from being affluent at the time, Matusow was practically penniless.

"But he didn't seem too troubled about it," Mrs. Fish told me. "As a matter of fact, he was very excited. He kept talking about collecting material for a television show and his plans for writing a book. He said he thought he'd found a publisher."

Mrs. Fish said she had told this to the representatives of the Justice Department when they questioned her.

And what, I asked, had been their reaction?

"I can't say they seemed impressed one way or the other. They did indicate they thought Matusow had been given some money by the Mine-Mill union."

She leafed through the Chamber of Commerce guest book and

handed it to me. The page to which it was opened was dated October 23, 1954, the day on which Harvey had first telephoned me. On the page was scrawled his signature.

"I never could understand," she mused, "why the government believed his lies about the Vincents's ranch. People around here didn't take his stories seriously. But I guess other people believed them."

The fact that Matusow had been in dire financial straits during his stay in Taos was corroborated by "Doughbelly" Price, a gnomish weatherbeaten man wearing cowboy boots and a black Stetson, which he kept cocked on the back of his head as he sat at his desk.

"Sure, Harvey was broke," said Price. "Flat broke. He phoned me before he pulled in. . . . we'd met when he stayed at Vincents's ranch. Said he wanted to spend the night in my office. I told him he was welcome and that he'd find the key where it always is." Price pointed to a key hanging conspicuously from a nail outside the street door to his office. "Anybody's welcome to use my office that wants to. Some fellows, you know, get a bit too much under the belt and need to sleep it off before they go home."

He rolled a cigarette and stuck it in the corner of his mouth. "Harvey touched me for a ten-spot when he got here. That's okay. He needed it more than I did. He traded his bicycle for a room at the inn."

Had Harvey told him anything about writing a book?

"Sure. Said a publisher called him from New York and that's where he was heading."

I asked Price if he'd given this information to the government agents who interviewed him.

"Hell, yes," he said.

It was easy to understand why neither Mrs. Fish nor "Doughbelly" Price had been summoned by the Justice Department as witnesses at any of the court or grand jury proceedings in the Matusow case. Their testimony would have served only to disprove the government's contention that Matusow had been bribed prior to coming east, and to corroborate our account of how we had first contacted him.

The Justice Department had therefore sought out in Taos a witness who was better suited to its purposes. He was Riley Taintor, the gambler, who obligingly testified at the court hearings in New York and El Paso that Matusow had displayed a "roll of a thousand dollars" and that he said he'd received it from his prospective publishers.

I asked Price what he thought of Taintor's testimony.

Price grinned. "Hell," he said, "everybody knows Taintor's reputation. You can quote me on that."

Before leaving Taos, Taintor had told acquaintances that he had been wanting for some time to visit New York anyway. "So he got himself a free trip," said Price.

3. Year's End

That fall Harvey and Helen moved into a new apartment. It was a marked improvement over Harvey's former one. True, it needed renovations badly, but it had spacious sunlit rooms. Harvey applied himself with enthusiasm to scraping floors, painting walls and plastering ceilings. He took great pride in these improvements, as in his other handiwork—a large bookcase and table for Helen's use in her art work, a desk for Judith's bedroom, shelves for her toys, a big storage cabinet. . . .

I was reminded of the way he had gone about fixing up his Greenwich Village apartment one year before. But if his labors then had seemed to me a compulsive effort to create a make-believe home, I now felt he was in the process of building a real one.

He was, he told me, happier than he had ever been before. "Things are working out wonderfully," he said. "Of course, we've got problems. I mean, Helen and I don't fool ourselves about the future. We know there's a good chance of my going to jail. But we're both prepared for it, and we're making plans accordingly." He derived particular gratification from his relationship with Helen's daughter, Judith. "I really feel good about that. You know, she already thinks of me as her father."

Only one thing about his marriage worried Harvey. "I've got to find a regular job," he said, "I've a wife and child now. I've got to make enough money to pay off those legal bills and see that Helen and Judith are left with something if I do go to jail."

But getting work was not easy. At first, when he applied for jobs

through employment agencies and ads in the *New York Times*, he was
turned down as soon as he mentioned he was Harvey Matusow.

He began using his old "stage name." "I don't feel right about it,"
he said. "I feel people ought to know who I am if they're going to
hire me. But I've got to do it, that's all."

Finally, he landed a job with the *Encyclopedia Britannica*. "They
say I'm the best new salesman they've ever had!" he exulted. He
decided to tell them his real name. Shortly afterward, he was asked to
resign.

At the year's end, the name of Matusow was again in the nation's
news.

On December 31, almost nine months after the conclusion of its
hearings on the Matusow case, the Senate Internal Security Subcommittee finally made public a 104-page report on its findings.

Somewhat cryptically entitled, *Strategy and Tactics of World Communism—Significance of the Matusow Case*, the report offered no
major surprises since the subcommittee members had indicated from
the start of their inquiry what their findings would be. According to
their report, Matusow's recantation was

> a collective product of the Communist conspiracy ... to discredit
> Government witnesses, the Department of Justice, the courts, the
> FBI, and congressional investigative committees, and thus immobi-
> lize the prosecution and investigation of the Communist conspiracy.

Besides these far-reaching objectives on the home front, stated the
report, the plot had sought to provide "new fuel for the Kremlin's
anti-American campaign in the Cold War."

The Senate subcommittee asserted that this conspiracy had been
"masterminded ... by Nathan Witt, Albert Kahn and others." Eleven
pages of the report, divided into sections with such intriguing titles as
"Who Is Albert Kahn?" "Kahn, Matusow's Literary Watchdog," and
"Kahn's Communist Friends," were devoted to comments on my writings and my work in various civil rights and peace organizations.
There was reason to believe, opined the subcommittee, that in addi-

tion to being a "pro-Soviet propagandist," I had been "an integral part of the international Soviet espionage and intelligence apparatus."

Of the report's myriad misrepresentations and glaring distortions, perhaps the crudest concerned the court proceedings to date in connection with the Matusow case. While it quoted at length from Judge Thomason's ruling denying Jencks a retrial and depicting Matusow's recantation as part of a Communist plot, the body of the report contained no mention whatsoever of Judge Dimock's contrary findings in the Flynn hearing. The sole reference to the Dimock decision was a single-sentence footnote in microscopic type stating that a new trial had been granted one of the Flynn defendants. The authors of the report apparently could not bring themselves to mention that actually two of the defendants had been granted new trials.

The committee recommended that the Justice Department seek an indictment of "Matusow, Witt, Kahn, and others for conspiracy to obstruct justice."

Noteworthy was the fact that one committee member, Senator Hennings, declined to sign the report. It had, he announced to the press, been released without his knowledge and without his having an opportunity to express his disagreement with it.

If the authors of the committee report had delayed its publication another month, they would have had to rewrite a considerable portion of it. On January 27, the Court of Appeals for the Fifth Circuit unanimously reversed Matusow's conviction by Judge Thomason for contempt in connection with the Jencks retrial motion.

CHAPTER SEVENTEEN

CRIME AND PUNISHMENT

1. *The Law's Delay*

One year after Matusow's recantation had first made national headlines, no action whatsoever had been taken, or was apparently contemplated, against any of the government officials who had repeatedly used Matusow as a lying witness. The two Flynn defendants whose convictions under the Smith Act had been reversed were about to be tried again on the same charge. The Appellate Court which had reversed Matusow's contempt conviction had upheld Judge Thomason's ruling denying Jencks a new trial, and Jencks was now appealing his case to the Supreme Court. Harvey himself, seven months after his indictment on the charge of lying in his recantation, was still awaiting trial.

From our viewpoint, time was on Harvey's side. The longer his trial was delayed, the better seemed his chances of a fair verdict. "The decline of Mr. McCarthy," editorialized the *New York Times*, "is indicative of . . . the gradual return of equilibrium to the American people. . . ." The most auspicious sign of the changing climate was the increasingly clear-cut position of the Supreme Court on basic constitutional questions. Then, too, with every new disclosure of the Justice Department's use of perjurious witnesses, the possibility grew of a jury's realizing that some government lawyers might have encouraged witnesses to lie.[57]

The Justice Department's interest in postponing Matusow's trial was naturally of a different sort. As long as there was a chance of bagging bigger game, they preferred not to try Matusow for allegedly lying against Roy Cohn. What they still wanted was a conspiracy indictment charging Matusow had been bribed to recant.

However, by the spring of 1956, after a small army of FBI agents had spent months futilely scouring the nation for clues of a plot, the Justice Department seemed at last resigned to the unlikelihood of obtaining a conspiracy indictment and had begun to press for Matusow's immediate trial on the charge of perjury.

On April 30, the U.S. Supreme Court handed down a decision that was a significant indication of the political current of the times and had a direct bearing on the Matusow case. The high tribunal ruled invalid a Subversive Activities Control board order that the Communist party register with the Justice Department as a "Moscow-controlled" organization. There was evidence, noted the Court, that the board's findings might have been partly based on the "tainted testimony" of three government witnesses accused of perjury. Named as one of the three witnesses was Harvey Matusow.

When I telephoned Harvey after the Supreme Court decision, he said, "I suppose you're going to congratulate me on being exposed again as a liar."

"No," I said. "I'll congratulate you because the Court's ruling confirms that you've been telling the truth."

For a moment he was silent. Then he said, "You know something, Al? I'd just as soon never read the name Harvey Matusow in print again."

I was not seeing much of Harvey at the time. Each of us was engaged in his own personal affairs.

Although the New York grand jury had not yet concluded their proceedings, and there was still the possibility of their contriving my indictment, Riette and I had decided we would no longer postpone moving to California. We had sold our house and were already immersed in the myriad tasks connected with transplanting a family across the continent.

Toward the end of June, a day or two before we were due to start out for California, Harvey visited us in Croton for the last time.

Strangely silent, he wandered through the almost empty house, idly inspecting the furniture gathered together for loading on the moving van, the crates ready for shipment by freight, the stacks of cartons filled with books.

"I'm going to miss all of you, Al," he said. "I wonder when we'll see one another again."

Actually, it would not be long before we did. In less than two months I would be returning east to attend Harvey's trial.

2. *Cul-de-Sac*

It was in the last days of September 1956, after twenty months of federal court proceedings, grand jury inquiries, congressional hearings, and nationwide FBI sleuthing that Matusow finally went on trial in the federal courthouse in New York City. The crime for which he stood accused was not, of course, one he had confessed to in his various affidavits, court and Senate testimony and the book *False Witness*. He had never been indicted for lying as a government witness, for helping railroad people to jail, for blacklisting and ruining the reputations of scores of citizens. Instead, the might of the law was now aligned against him for allegedly lying in accusing Roy Cohn of persuading him to testify falsely.

However, while there were grounds for questioning the justice of Harvey's being tried for his alleged offense, one could not deny the likelihood of his being convicted for it. Backing up Cohn's contention that he had never sought to influence Matusow's testimony were four other Justice Department attorneys and an FBI agent who had all worked on the Flynn case, and obviously any jury of twelve ordinary citizens would be more inclined to accept the word of six government spokesmen than that of a notorious, self-admitted perjurer.

Angus and I had periodically discussed with Harvey the conduct of his defense, and we had not allowed our amateur standing in the juridical field to keep us from relaying all our ideas to Faulkner who, to his credit, heard us out with unflagging patience.

My feelings in the matter were summed up in a memorandum I gave Faulkner:

It seems to me there's only one possible chance of winning the case. The trial has to be converted from a defense of Matusow into a prosecution of the Justice Department.

There is ample evidence to prove the Justice Department was aware of Harvey's true character at the time of the Flynn trial. There were (as Dimock has pointed out) the flagrant discrepancies between his trial testimony and his FBI reports and pretrial conferences with government lawyers; the obvious lies he told at congressional hearings; the confidential FBI memorandum in the Justice Department's possession revealing Harvey had been suffering from a "psychoneurosis of a mild but acute form". . . .

I think it's also important to establish that the Justice Department continued to use Harvey as a witness even after he had admitted he was a habitual liar, and had given his affidavits to the *New York Times* and *Time* magazine, admitting he'd lied about these papers.

I added:

Also, it can be shown that Matusow wasn't in any sense an exceptional sort of government witness. On the contrary, the Justice Department has made a practice of using informers and witnesses of that caliber. . . . In other words, the witting use by the Justice Department of a lying witness named Harvey Matusow fits into a pattern of conduct. . . .

If one takes all these facts into account, what reason is there to doubt Harvey's claim that he was occasionally encouraged to lie? And, more important, doesn't it become patently clear that in prosecuting Harvey the Justice Department is seeking not only to punish him for recanting but also to distract public attention from the growing revelations of its own malpractices?

Harvey's defense, however, was destined to be conducted in an entirely different fashion, and ironically enough, it was Harvey himself who made his own conviction a virtual certainty.

The one aspect of the Matusow trial which most impressed the newsmen covering it was the striking metamorphosis in Harvey's manner and appearance since the days when he had been a professional government witness. "Matusow looked like dependability itself in court...." commented the *New York World-Telegram* story on the opening day of the trial. "He is a trim 145 pounds.... All in all, defendant Matusow of today was a far cry from the fat, badly groomed wiseacre of yesteryear—when he was a government witness in a Communist conspiracy trial."

On my arrival in New York I was struck by the fact that Harvey showed hardly a trace of his old spirit. I sensed a great weariness in him. He was like a man overcome by exhaustion toward the end of a long race who no longer cares whether he wins or loses, but only wants the ordeal finished as soon as possible. Above all he was sick of his past, sick of reviewing its sordid details, sick of participating in the autopsy of his previous corruption.

Ironically, the only possibility of winning his trial lay in exhuming once more the sordid facts about his past.

"No," said Harvey, "I've gone over the whole thing with Stan and we've agreed how the case is to be handled. We're not going to rake up any of that stuff about my record as an informer and as a witness. We'll just discuss my affidavit and the fact I told the truth about Roy Cohn in it, and that's all."

Didn't he realize, I asked, that he couldn't prove the truth at the trial unless he did discuss his past?

"Look, Al," he said tensely, "there's no sense talking about it. My mind's made up.... The only thing I'm concerned about now is how to make sure Helen and Judith are taken care of if I do go to jail."

"Wouldn't not going to jail be a better way of showing concern for them?"

"If the Justice Department loses this case, they'll simply cook up some other charge, and I'll have to go through the whole thing again. I might as well serve the sentence and get it over with." He burst out, "I don't want to discuss it anymore!"

I had a talk with Faulkner.

"I know how Harvey feels," he told me, "and I don't think much can be done about it. He says that all he wants is to be asked a few questions about his war record and whether or not he told the truth about Cohn." Faulkner shrugged helplessly. "There's a limit to what I can do. He is my client, you know, and I've got to respect his wishes."

3. *Code of the Gang*

On the first day of the trial, U.S. Attorney Paul W. Williams, a tall, mannequin-like figure with a neatly groomed mustache, held a quiet talk with members of the press. Because of the case's "special importance," said Williams, he was taking "personal direction" of it. He observed gravely: "The integrity of the United States Attorney's office and of the government itself is at stake."

With that statement it was hard to disagree. But the regrettable fact was that the question of the Justice Department's integrity would never be examined at the trial.

While Williams's august presence solemnized the proceedings, the actual prosecution was handled by Assistant Attorney Thomas Bolan. He tackled the job with a fervor that reflected less desire for justice than personal animosity against Matusow. By his recantation in the Flynn case and his accusation against Cohn, declared Bolan in his opening address to the jury, Matusow had sought by "a vicious and monstrous lie . . . to release from prison" the thirteen Communist defendants. "It took the government nine months of trial and over two years of appeal to have these people put in prison," said Bolan, without, of course, mentioning the two defendants who had been granted a retrial by Judge Dimock.

As if the Dimock ruling had in fact never occurred, Bolan continued throughout the proceedings to expound the government's thesis that Matusow told the truth as a government witness and had lied only "after falling into the clutches of the Communists," personified by Angus Cameron and Albert Kahn.

Matusow's examination by Faulkner lasted about fifteen minutes. Cursory and superficial, it was limited to those questions Harvey had designated as the only ones he wanted to be asked. Harvey stated that he had told the truth in his affidavit of recantation and that if again asked the questions put to him at the Flynn retrial hearing he would give the same answers. The jury was offered no picture of Harvey's role as a government witness, of the fact his complete untrustworthiness had been demonstrated prior to his testimony in the Flynn case, or of the development he had since undergone.

Only one point, in fact, was brought out by Faulkner's questioning which lent credibility to Harvey's claim that Roy Cohn had persuaded him to lie. In his affidavit, Faulkner pointed out, Harvey had stated that four other Justice Department attorneys and an FBI agent had been present when Cohn had first raised with him the subject of Vyshinskii's book. Hadn't Harvey known of the federal law stipulating that for prosecution purposes there must be two or more witnesses to an act of perjury? Yes, said Harvey, he had. Why then, continued Faulkner, had he specified the presence of *six* witnesses? Because, Harvey replied, it was the truth. He had realized at the time, he added, that he might be putting his head "in a noose."

One after another the government attorneys and the FBI agent named in Harvey's affidavit took the stand and flatly denied Matusow's claim that Cohn had mentioned Vyshinskii's book to Matusow in their presence. When Roy Cohn testified, Bolan was temporarily relegated to the sidelines. Protocol seemingly required that Senator McCarthy's former aide be treated with proper deference, and U.S. Attorney Williams arose to conduct the examination.

Once more Cohn indignantly denied all.

Williams summed up for the prosecution. Matusow, he said, had repudiated his "honest" testimony as a government witness and had falsely accused Cohn of subornation of perjury in a plot to "discredit the entire fight of the government . . . against the Communist menace." Matusow's recantation had caused the government immense expense and labor, including the investigative work of "literally hundreds of FBI agents."

After less than two hours' deliberation, the jury found Matusow guilty of perjury as charged.

Harvey's sentencing took place two days later. When I arrived the courtroom was vacant, quiet and lifeless as an empty stage after a drama has been played out. Then reporters began to straggle in.

Harvey's mother appeared briefly for the first time during the proceedings. She had been to see the presiding magistrate, Judge John McGohey, she told me, and had pleaded with him to be lenient in sentencing her son. "He was very understanding," she said. "He told

me he had a son of his own and knew what I felt as a mother. But—"
she hesitated, then went on—"But he said Harvey had committed a
very serious crime and would have to pay for it."

Judge McGohey sentenced Harvey to five years imprisonment and
denied him the right to bail.

Before leaving the courthouse in the custody of a U.S. marshal,
Harvey told Angus and me: "Look, I know the case might have been
handled differently, but that was the way I wanted it. A person who
has done what I did deserves to be punished. The pity is that I'm
being sent to jail for something I didn't do."

The *New York Times* reported: "A high-ranking government
official . . . expressed relief at the result. 'It will have a far-reaching
effect on informers everywhere,' he explained."

Like gangsters, government informers were not to be allowed to
quit the mob.

Not long after the Matusow trial, I learned that Thomas Bolan had
resigned as Assistant U.S. Attorney to become the law associate of
Roy Cohn.

CHAPTER EIGHTEEN

FINALE

"Do you think there's still a chance of Matusow's reverting?" a friend wrote me after Harvey had been in prison for two months. "I mean, now he's in prison for the better part of four years, do you think he might get sufficiently depressed and embittered so that he becomes willing to make some sort of deal with the Justice Department? Prison is a hell of a place, you know, and does all sorts of things to people."

"Long ago," I wrote in reply, "I learned the foolishness of saying that anything was impossible. So I wouldn't answer your question about Harvey with a categorical no. But I personally believe that Harvey would rather kill himself than go back to what he was. It's not that I'm unaware of the effects of prison life, or that I think Harvey is now without any serious weaknesses. But I also know how greatly he's changed. I believed he had the capacity to change when I first met him—repulsive as I felt him to be at the time; but I really never thought that he would change to the extent I've witnessed."

Inmates of federal penitentiaries were permitted to correspond with but three individuals, each of whom must be acceptable to the prison authorities; and, since my name was not allowed on Harvey's approved list of correspondents, I received no word directly from him during the weeks following his incarceration at Lewisburg Prison in Pennsylvania. Occasionally I would hear about him from his mother or from Faulkner.

Then, one day early in January 1957, there was a long distance call to my house in Glen Ellen, California. An unmistakable voice declared, "Hello, Al! I just scaled the wall at Lewisburg!" It was Harvey calling from New York.

The Appellate Court had granted his right to bail pending the outcome of the appeal of his conviction, and his parents had posted $5,000 bond.

"Remember," he said, "I told you once before you can't keep a good man down."

Both he and Faulkner, he added, had high hopes for the appeal, as Faulkner had now come upon what seemed to be a major flaw in the indictment.

Helen and Judith were fine. He was going to start looking for work immediately, he said. His cheerful, animated tone contrasted sharply with his attitude at the time of his trial. Perhaps, I thought, it was just the first flush of relief and elation at being free again, if only temporarily.

That his present mood had deeper roots, however, was indicated by the letters I began receiving from him.

"I'm job-hunting," he wrote a few days after his call, "and hope to become a breadwinner before the week's end. It seems that my three months in Lewisburg have only made me more determined to move forward, taking only from the past that which was good and honest." He spoke of his conduct at the trial. "I know you saw the lack of vitality I had toward the case. I was that way because I felt from the start that the cards were stacked and deep down I was tired and wanted to see an end to it." Now he felt very different about the case, as if he had gotten his second wind.

He mentioned that he was now getting rid of all of the newspaper clippings about himself that he had accumulated over the years. Only a "sick ego," he said, would keep them any longer. "I have to relate them to myself as I live this very day. You see, I've given much thought recently to what my role as father, husband, and member of society must be."

But now, in this area of his life, too, Harvey was in the process of having illusions stripped away. Writing "on a rain-filled Saturday afternoon" early in February, "filled with frustration and conflicting emotions," he told me that Helen and he were separating. It was, he said, no sudden development—they'd had differences before he had gone to jail. "When I returned home last month we agreed to give it a try. But it just doesn't seem to work. Who or what do I blame? Nothing specific. I'm not looking for you to take sides." Of Judith he wrote: "I'm going to miss her terribly."

Barely two weeks later Harvey telephoned to tell me of another loss he had suffered. His father had died of a heart attack. "He wasn't well, you know," he said haltingly, "but I'm sure my sentence must have helped shorten his life. I keep asking myself, Al—am I to blame?"

I thought of the frail, little man with the tired, sad eyes. "No, Harvey, you're not to blame. You did what was right. He wouldn't have wanted you to do anything else."

With the break-up of his marriage, the death of his father, and the possibility of his soon returning to prison, it would not have been surprising if Harvey had shown signs of despondency. But as the weeks went by, the opposite proved true.

He wrote that he had found a job with a printing concern—just the sort of job he was looking for. He had other good news. His "string-less yo-yo" had gone on the market and was meeting wth phenomenal success. Almost overnight, it had become one of the largest-selling toys in the country. And while he derived no financial benefit, having sold all his rights, he was getting "immense satisfaction from seeing this toy of mine entering homes throughout the country. Paradoxical as it may seem, this period since my release from Lewisburg on January 4 has been the most fulfilling of my whole life. You have no idea of the kind of freedom I now feel...I no longer have to try to be honest. I know I am and always will be honest."

When the Appellate Court unanimously confirmed Harvey's conviction on May 10, he indicated he intended to make the most of his freedom up to the last minute. "I guess some people who are facing prison," he wrote, "just dissipate. I don't see it that way. To me at this point every minute is precious. Perhaps I am learning to be a gourmet of time. I don't know. But I do know that if I go back to prison I will have spent the time preceding it in growth. In a sense I guess you could say this is my fling."

There was, however, one thing that continued to trouble him deeply. That was the possibility that the Supreme Court might hand down an adverse decision in the case of Clinton Jencks.

"Each Monday night," he wrote, "I rush out to get the *Times* to see if the Supreme Court has ruled on his case yet. I pray to God that justice is done. . . . If the Supreme Court were to uphold his conviction, his conviction based on my lies, I don't have words to express how I'd feel."

This was one victory Harvey was not to be denied.

On June 3 the Supreme Court handed down its long-awaited decision in the Jencks case. The members of the high tribunal ruled that Jencks's conviction in Judge Thomason's court had been unconstitutional in that the defense had been denied access to the FBI reports of the prosecution witnesses Harvey Matusow and J.W. Ford.

That same night I talked with Harvey by telephone. "Give my best to Clint," he said. "Tell him that if I do have to go back in now, the verdict is the best going-away present I could have had."

Exactly one week later, continuance of bail denied, Harvey was remanded to prison to serve the balance of his sentence.

Before he left I wrote to him:

"A long time ago, both of us agreed that it wouldn't be a bad thing if you served a sentence for the wrongs you committed, but what stuck in the craw was the idea of your being punished for the very righting of those wrongs. Today, I no longer feel the first part of that. As far as I'm concerned, you've more than righted those wrongs during the last couple of years. . . . The only way in which I can state what I feel about this whole matter, from the beginning to the end, is in the book I'm writing. There I'll try to set the record straight."

EPILOGUE

[Editor's Note: Thirty years have passed since these events took place. What follows is a brief synopsis of the lives of the main characters in the intervening years.]

Harvey Matusow

After his release from prison on August 8, 1960, Harvey Matusow obtained work in New York City at Academic Press. He was subsequently employed by Book Craftsman as an art director and book designer.

In 1963 Matusow began publishing *The New York Arts Calendar*, a fine arts magazine. Two years later he was one of the founders of the *East Village Other*, a pioneering underground newspaper of the counterculture, and published *The Art Collector's Almanac*.

Matusow moved to England in 1966, where he organized the London Film Makers Coop and helped establish *IT*, an early underground paper. Living in Europe in the late sixties, he worked for newspapers and in music. His first album, *Harvey Matusow's Jews' Harp Band* was followed by several others in collaboration with Anna Lockwood. He travelled extensively, giving concerts throughout Europe and in Australia and New Zealand. During the same period, Matusow worked for the British Broadcasting Corporation in comedy, news and current affairs.

Returning to the United States in 1973, Matusow toured the country in a renovated school bus, visiting communes. Settling in Tucson, Arizona, he founded *The Magic Mouse Theatre Companie*, an innovative children's theatre, and produced a series for KUAT-TV and Radio. While there, he initiated a program to feed the homeless.

Harvey Matusow currently serves as director of the Gandhi Peace Centre in Massachusetts, a non-profit organization which operates programs for Native Americans, the homeless, developmentally disabled citizens and rehabilitated prisoners, and coordinates community-based social action efforts.

Albert E. Kahn

In October, 1958 Albert Kahn was called again before the Internal Security Subcommittee, chaired by Senator Eastland. Witnesses for the committee accused Kahn of being a Soviet agent and a spy. He responded with a challenge:

> If I could sue your committee for defamation of character and interference with my work, I would. . . . Perhaps you will advise me whether each of your committee members is willing to waive his congressional immunity and assume full personal responsibility for spreading the charges made against me by your witnesses at this hearing.

Stating that the "inquisition" conducted by the subcommittee had "gravely harmed our nation's welfare . . . through witchhunting and character assasination. . . ." Kahn said: "The sole contribution your committee can make to our nation's security is to disband."

As McCarthyism ebbed, major firms were willing once again to publish Kahn's books. His published works of this period include:

Days with Ulanova (Simon & Schuster, 1962), a critically acclaimed biography of the great Soviet prima ballerina, Galina Ulanova, illustrated with Kahn's photographs.

Smetana and the Beetles (Random House, 1967), a satire in verse about the events surrounding the defection of Stalin's daughter, Svetlana, illustrated by David Levine.

Joys and Sorrows (Simon & Schuster, 1970), Pablo Casals' life story as told to Kahn, illustrated with Kahn's photographs, published in thirteen countries.

The Unholy Hymnal (Simon & Schuster, 1971), an exposé of the Credibility Gap during the Johnson and Nixon administrations.

Other published works included articles and photo essays in *Life, McCall's, Newsday, Washington Post, London Times, Paris Match, Pravda, Epoca.*

Kahn's photographs of Ulanova are housed in the Dance Collection of the New York Public Library at Lincoln Center, New York. Collections of his photographs of Pablo Casals are maintained at Dartmouth College, Stanford University and the San Francisco Museum of Art.

A founding member of the World Peace Council, between 1960 and 1978 Kahn participated in congresses in Moscow, Stockholm, Budapest and Warsaw. His papers, manuscripts and research materials are housed at the Social Action Collection of the State Historical Society of Wisconsin.

Albert E. Kahn died on September 15, 1979.

Angus Cameron

Angus Cameron continued the publishing house after Albert Kahn moved to California, with Carl Marzani as his partner, under the name Cameron Associates. This firm took over Liberty Book Club which had selections from other publishers, but at least half were published originally by Cameron Associates.

Mr. Cameron continued with the firm until 1959 when Mr. Alfred A. and Blanche Knopf invited him to join the staff of Alfred A. Knopf, Inc.

The blacklisting from regular commercial publishing had lasted for eight years, from 1951 when as Editor-in-Chief and vice-president of the Boston publishers, Little, Brown & Co., he had been forced to resign for being what he called a "premature anti-McCarthyite." Mr. Cameron served with Knopf, first as senior editor, then as Vice-

President, Editorial, until 1973 when he retired as fulltime editor. He continued as a full time consultant for five years, and part time consultant until his final and complete retirement in 1981.

Angus Cameron lives with his wife, Sheila, in Wilton, Ct. where he does freelance editing. He is author of *The Nightwatchers*, a book about North American owls (1972); and more recently was co-author of *The L.L. Bean Game and Fish Cookbook* (1983). He is presently working on another book, on smoking and smoke-grilling, again to be sponsored by L.L. Bean.

Clinton E. Jencks

In 1956, under the intense pressure of continuing inquisition, the International Executive Board of the Mine, Mill and Smelter Workers Union requested that Clint Jencks resign his union positions of organizer and representative. He did.

Jencks found himself blacklisted: when hired as a machinist based on his qualifications and skills, he was repeatedly discharged when his employer learned of his prior union activities.

In 1957, the United States Supreme Court announced its decision in *Jencks vs. United States*, overturning Jencks's conviction. On reading the *Time* magazine article on the decision, his job foreman terminated Jencks's employment.

The same year, Jencks applied for and was awarded a Woodrow Wilson Foundation Fellowship. Shortly after, he was summoned to testify before the House Un-American Activities Committee in Washington. The Foundation, despite pressure to withdraw the fellowship, refused, and Jencks was admitted to the Ph.D. program at the University of California in 1959.

In 1963 he was awarded the prestigious Newton Booth Travelling Fellowship in Economics and spent nine months researching working conditions in the coalfields of Great Britain. The results of his research were accepted as his Ph.D. dissertation and subsequently published by San Diego State University Press under the title, *Men Underground: Working Conditions of British Coal Miners Since Nationalization*.

In 1964, Jencks was awarded a Doctorate in Economics by the University of California. That same year, he was appointed as Assistant Professor of Economics at San Diego State University. When the *San Diego Union* headlined a story about Jencks's past, he was summoned to the University President's office and informed the president had received requests that his appointment be cancelled. The University, however, stood firm.

In 1970, Jencks was promoted to Full Professor. He served in that capacity until his retirement from full-time teaching in 1986.

Throughout the years, Jencks has maintained close contact with his associates from his organizing days with the Mine, Mill and Smelter Workers. In 1967, he organized the transfer of the Mine-Mill and Western Federation of Miners Archives to the Western History Collection at the University of Colorado.

Of the Matusow Affair, he says:

> The case diverted me and the Mine-Mill Union from our chosen work, improving the wages, working conditions and lives of our union families. The diversion was costly and long. Still, it did not succeed, and can never succeed, in halting my contributions toward a world where every human being has increased effectiveness in determining the conditions that affect his or her life.

APPENDIX   A

HERBLOCK'S EDITORIAL CARTOON
Available in 2 or 3 Column Size

"This Could Spoil The Whole Racket, Men"

---from Herblock's Here And Now
(Simon & Schuster, 1955)

APPENDIX B

13026 Henno Road
Glen Ellen, California
October 2, 1958

Senator James Eastland, Chairman
Senate Internal Security Subcommittee
Senate Office Building
Washington, D.C.

Dear Senator Eastland:

During my appearance before your committee on September 23, your chief counsel, Mr. J. G. Sourwine, and your acting chairman, Senator William E. Jenner, stated that other witnesses were to testify who might make reference to me and that, if I wished, I could comment on their testimony at its conclusion.

Since my attorney, Mr. Leonard Boudin, and I were unable to be present throughout the testimony of the three witnesses who followed me, it was agreed I would be sent a transcript of the proceedings, that any comments of mine were to be made in affidavit form, and that these comments would then be included in the record as a part of the hearing.

Having received from your committee the transcript of the September 23 proceedings, I am sending you herewith for inclusion in the record my comments in affidavit form on the testimony of the witnesses who followed me.

Since the September 23 hearing was public, I am releasing these comments of mine to the press.

Sincerely yours,
Albert E. Kahn

THE   UNITED   STATES   SENATE

BEFORE THE SUBCOMMITTEE TO INVESTIGATE THE
ADMINISTRATION OF THE INTERNAL SECURITY ACT AND
OTHER INTERNAL SECURITY LAWS OF THE COMMITTEE OF
THE JUDICIARY

UNITED STATES OF AMERICA   )
)
STATE OF CALIFORNIA   )   ss.
)
City and County of San Francisco   )

AFFIDAVIT OF ALBERT E. KAHN BEFORE
SENATE INTERNAL SECURITY SUBCOM-
MITTEE IN COMMENT ON TESTIMONY
GIVEN BY WITNESSES JOHN LAUTNER,
FEDOR MANSVETOV, AND KURT SINGER
AT SUBCOMMITTEE HEARING ON SEP-
TEMBER 23, 1958

ALBERT E. KAHN, being first duly sworn, deposes and says:

I wish to comment on the testimony of your three witnesses at your
September 23 hearing not because of anything that testimony reveals
about me but because of what it reveals about your committee.

In my opening remarks at your hearing, I charged that your committee was trying to frame me because I have just finished a new book
dealing in part with the seditious, anti-constitutional activities of your
chairman, Senator James Eastland, which have harmed our nation's
reputation throughout the world. I added that your committee had
tried to frame me once before under similar circumstances by calling
for my indictment on a fraudulent conspiracy charge when I was co-
publisher of Harvey Matusow's book, *False Witness*, in which Matu-

sow confessed among other things how he had lied as a paid witness for your committee. The testimony of your three witnesses at the September 23 hearing forcefully bears out my contention that the proceedings were a deliberate frame-up.

But having now read your transcript of that testimony, I must admit that my original charge against you was too limited in scope and too personal in character. The testimony marks your hearing not merely as an attempt to frame me but, far more importantly, as an integral part of your continuing efforts to perpetrate a monstrous hoax upon the American people.

The testimony of your three witnesses would of course have been inadmissible in any court of law. It was largely a mixture of rumors, hearsay, slanders, wanton allegations and outright lies, uttered under the protection of congressional immunity. Your committee cannot disclaim responsibility for these utterances. You share the guilt for them. You had conferred in private with your witnesses beforehand and knew what they were going to say. All of the members of your committee, I understand, were at one time practicing attorneys; and one would think that a sense of self-respect, if nothing else, would prevent men knowledgeable in the ethics of the law from the promotion and propagation of such testimony. The shameful fact, however, is that your committee has repeatedly foisted similar lies and lunacies upon the public as data of vital national import; and such testimony has served as the grounds upon which a host of citizens have been pilloried, stigmatized, persecuted and ruined.

Let me cite a few typical examples of the testimony of your three witnesses.

I refer first to the testimony of your witness, Fedor Mansvetov. Having identified himself as a Russian emigre and proudly boasted of what he himself called his "anti-Soviet activity" in the United States during World War II when Soviet Russia was our fighting ally, Mansvetov stated he had been unjustly dismissed from two U.S. Army agencies and a Government office on the charge he was "an agent of Hitler." He lost these jobs, he protested, because of material about him which had appeared in *The Hour*, an anti-Nazi newsletter of which I was editor during the war years. Your transcript records the following exchange between Mansvetov and your chief counsel, J. G. Sourwine:

Mr. Sourwine.	What was Kahn's function in denouncing you and your associates?
Mr. Mansvetov.	Because he is a spy. He is a Soviet agent, and just from what you heard today you may know this.
Mr. Sourwine.	How do you know that yourself?
Mr. Mansvetov.	During this hearing he never even told satellites because he is following party line.

Although Mansvetov's language is here somewhat obscure, I gather he is saying that he knows I am a "Soviet agent" and "a spy" because I failed to use the word "satellite" in my testimony before your committee.

No further comment, I think, is necessary on Mansvetov's testimony.

I might, however, point out that if witnesses at your hearings have been repeatedly encouraged to bandy about such grotesque accusations, it may be partly because your committee members have themselves shown a weakness for making similar charges. For example, your presiding chairman, Senator Jenner, once called for the impeachment of President Truman on the charge that the President was a tool of "a secret coterie directed by agents of the Soviet Union." This same carelessness in the use of language, both in the congressional resolution under which your committee claims authority and in your proceedings themselves, was discussed by Federal Judge Luther Youngdahl in his decision reversing the conviction of Seymour Peck, a *New York Times* reporter cited for contempt after appearing before your committee. Referring to the "vice of vagueness" for which the Supreme Court had condemned investigations by the House Un-American Activities Committee, Judge Youngdahl declared: "It seems manifest that the vices to be found in the House Un-American Activities Committee's authorizing resolution are equally present in the charter of the Senate Internal Security Subcommittee." Judge Youngdahl also stated that your committee "conducted investigations which are indistinguishable in scope or nature from those that the Supreme Court condemned."

If I dwell but briefly on the testimony of your witness, John Lautner, I am sure you will understand. While admitting he had never been personally acquainted with me, Lautner alleged he knew I was a Communist from something someone told him about me a decade or so ago and from the fact I was once president of the Jewish People's Fraternal Order (a branch of the International Workers' Order, an interracial fraternal benefit society headed by the famous American artist, Rockwell Kent, and having some 250,000 members). A renegade Communist, Lautner practices that trade which the *New York Times* has characterized as "the shabby business of the paid professional informer." Each time he testifies against someone, he gets paid a fee as an "expert witness"; and during the past few years he has garnered many thousands of dollars in this line of endeavor.

You of course know that the federal courts have branded as perjurious the testimony of a number of the government's paid professional witnesses; and that not a few of these witnesses—Harvey Matusow, Mrs. Marie Natvig, Lowell Watson, David Brown, etc.—have confessed to giving false testimony for pay. Yet you shamelessly continue to use professional witnesses as paid traducers at your hearings. And who, I must ask, commits the greater crime—these wretched souls who earn their sordid living at the business of betrayal, or you who hire them to do their dirty work?

Is it any wonder that innocent persons subpoenaed by your committee—knowing you have available a stable of lying stoolpigeons whose testimony might send them to jail—have repeatedly invoked their rights of protection under the Fifth Amendment? You will, I assume, recall that the trade union leader, Clinton Jencks, was sentenced to five years imprisonment as a result of false testimony first given against him before your committee by the paid professional witness, Harvey Matusow; and if Matusow had not later confessed his lies, it is quite possible that Jencks's conviction might not have been reversed by the Supreme Court and that Jencks himself might now be in prison. And, as you know, not a few other innocent persons sent to jail on the testimony of professional witnesses have now finally had their convictions reversed.

From such circumstances, I must say that I myself have acquired a heightened appreciation of the wisdom of the framers of our constitution in including the Fifth Amendment to protect citizens against governmental abuses.

Your third witness against me at the September 23 hearing was a writer named Kurt Singer. He testified to the effect that, having met me twice some fifteen years ago, he knew I was "under communist discipline." And how did he know? He stated that he and I had appeared together on a national radio program called, "Author Meets Critic," on which a book of his was reviewed by me, and that he could tell from the harshness of my criticism of his book that I was "under communist discipline."

Seriously, gentlemen, let me ask this question: how in the world can you bring yourself to spend the taxpayers' money on transporting such witnesses to Washington, staging such hearings, and recording such testimony as this? Don't you really think the money would be better spent on schools, libraries, hospitals, and other public needs?

Through your interrogation of me, and through the testimony of your witnesses, you sought to label as "communist propaganda" *The Hour*, the newsletter I once edited, and the books I have written. But you know as well as I do that *The Hour* was founded shortly before World War II by the American Council Against Nazi Propaganda, of which the former Ambassador to Germany, William E. Dodd was chairman and I was executive secretary, and that this Council included among its members and advisory board such persons as Albert Einstein, Thomas Mann, Monsignor John A. Ryan, Hendrik Willem van Loon, William Green, John Gunther, Bishop Edgar Blake, Conde Nast, Lawrence Tibbett, and Helen Keller. You know that *The Hour* was a newsletter devoted to exposing Axis fifth column operations in America, and that its material was used by scores of newspapers and radio news-commentators, as well as by the War Department, Justice Department, Office of War Information, and other Government agencies. You also know that several of my books have been best-sellers in the United States (one of them, characterized as "communist" at your hearing, was condensed in *Reader's Digest*); that my writings during the war years were widely described as helpful to the war effort; and that my books have been translated abroad into some twenty-five languages.

And if you know these facts, why do you propagate the nonsense that these writings of mine were "communist propaganda"? Is it not because I have repeatedly denounced anti-democratic intrigue in high places, such as the machinations of your committee? And do you not also particularly desire to obstruct the publication of my new book, which singles out your committee for special condemnation?

A more significant question is this: are you not basically opposed to freedom of the press and independence of thought; to the voicing of opinions that do not conform with yours; to public criticism of your operations as a governmental body? Do you not realize the mammoth effrontery of this whole inquiry of yours and the extent of your defiance of the First Amendment?

Through the testimony of your witnesses at this last hearing, as in your so-called findings in the Matusow case, you charge me with "taking orders from Moscow." I have never taken nor intend ever to take orders from Moscow. But let me add I am not disposed to take orders from anywhere. That includes your committee. I do not like to be pushed around or dictated to by bureaucratic politicians and government officials who collect part of their salary from me in taxes. I believe the government should be the servant not the master of the people. That also goes for your committee.

If I could sue your committee for defamation of character and interference with my work, I would. It might be a good lesson for you. Perhaps you will advise me whether each of your committee members is willing to waive his congressional immunity and assume full personal responsibility for spreading the charges made against me by your witnesses at this hearing. Perhaps just one of you—let us say Senator Eastland—will repeat in public without congressional immunity the accusation that I am a spy. There seems a peculiar aptness to that popular American saying, "Put up or shut up."

Let me, however make one thing clear. I find nothing slanderous in your apparent conviction that I am a radical. I heartily respect the radical tradition that has enriched our nation since we sent King George packing in 1776; and while I have an old-fashioned unshakeable allegiance to the U.S. Constitution, I do share some of the political views of Jack London, that former noted resident of the Valley of the Moon in California where I now reside.

Let me also state there is considerable truth in one charge implicit in your hearing. I have sought to promote friendship and normal relations between our country and the Soviet Union, such as those we enjoyed during the war years. I shall continue to do so. I believe that the lives of my three sons, and the lives of millions of other children in every corner of the globe, will be made secure by the establishment of such relations.

Your committee claims concern with matters affecting the nation's internal security. If so, you should investigate the leading role of your chairman, Senator Eastland, in a conspiracy to subvert the Supreme Court's ruling that school segregation is unconstitutional. Actually, of course, the inquisitions conducted by your committee have gravely harmed our nation's welfare and true security. Former President Truman has pointed out that one of the reasons the Soviet Union outstripped our country in launching the first earth satellite was that witchhunting and "character assassination" drove many American scientists from vitally important projects. There is scarcely a phase of our national life which has not suffered from similar depredations, in which your committee has specialized. The sole contribution your committee can make to our nation's security is to disband.

Our land is too big, its traditions too strong, its people too fine for you to have your way. McCarthyism is rapidly becoming a shameful part of the past. And although you seem not yet fully aware of the fact, so also is your committee.

Albert E. Kahn

APPENDIX C

MORE ON MYSTERIOUS MATUSOW

—from Drew Pearson's column, "The Washington Merry-Go-Round" on Saturday, February 5, 1955 for the *Washington Post and Times Herald*

THERE'S A LOT more than meets the eye behind the sensational statements of Harvey Matusow, former Communist informer for Senator Joseph R. McCarthy who has now revealed that he was told how to testify against Communists by McCarthy counsel Roy Cohn, and who states that he deliberately falsified testimony.

If Congress gets to the bottom of this it will also find some interesting things Matusow did to cover up secret contributions made to Senator McCarthy.

For Matusow, this column can reveal, was the man who whisked a key witness out from under the nose of the Senate Rules Subcommittee in the winter of 1952 when that committee was striking pay dirt regarding McCarthy's finances.

The key witness was Mrs. Arvilla Bentley, former wife of Congressman Alvin Bentley of Michigan, seriously wounded by the Puerto Ricans. He had advanced McCarthy $3000 to fight communism—though the committee found it was later used to speculate on the soy bean market. Mrs. Bentley had advanced McCarthy $7000 to fight communism, which also turned up on the soy bean market.

However, when Senate investigators got on Mrs. Bentley's trail, the McCarthy entourage deftly removed her from the U.S.A. to the British West Indies. The man who went with her was none other than Harvey Matusow.

Her Bank Account

Matusow tells friends that the reason for getting Mrs. Bentley out of the U.S.A. during the Senate probe was not the $7000 she had advanced, but much larger sums she had contributed to McCarthy for a radio broadcast.

At any rate, McCarthy did not want her cross-examined by Senate probers, nor did he want her checking account examined in the Riggs National Bank here.

So Mrs. Bentley, safe in the Bahamas, wrote her lawyer Joseph Rafferty and the Riggs Bank careful instructions regarding her bank records. Furthermore, she had Matusow handle the letters. If anyone doubts the authenticity of Matusow's statements, here are the exact texts of Mrs. Bentley's interesting notes to him instructing him to get a letter off to her attorney and to the Riggs Bank.

Scribbled on the letterhead of the Bahamas Country Club, Nassau, and dated 5:30 a.m., here is what Mrs. Bentley wrote:

"HARVEY—

"Will you please do Joe McCarthy the favors outlined in the two notes beneath this. The jobs are of utmost importance and must be done exactly as directed in the two notes under this—by typewriter. I'm dead tired and have a migraine—so I ask you to do these three things for me, for Joe, for yourself—immediately. If you feel unable to, waken me and I'll do it. When these things are done we can relax—golf, sun, dancing, etc.

"Don't worry about disturbing me by typing right here—I'll be dead asleep. But please awaken me for my signature on letter to Riggs. Keep the car until all is finished.

A. P. B.

"P.S. Leave sign outside my door and keep door locked— please."

Instructions to Bank

Mrs. Bentley then proceeded to give very explicit instructions as to what she wanted sent to Washington. This is what she wrote in her own handwriting, part of which was for Matusow to type:

"Tuesday-must
"I. Letter on plain white stationery, typed thus:
"Riggs National Bank,
Dupont Circle Branch,
Washington, D. C.   .
"C/O Mr. Joseph A. Rafferty,
Southern Building,
Washington 5, D. C.
"Gentlemen:
"Please honor letter of December 8, 1952, sent to you by my attorney, Joseph A. Rafferty, requesting information concerning my account. I will appreciate immediate action on your part.
"Thank you."

ARVILLA P. BENTLEY

"Letter must be sent air mail—enclosed in small, white blank envelope, unsealed, addressed to:
"Riggs National Bank,
Dupont Circle Branch,
Washington D. C.
"Enclose small envelope, unsealed, containing letter in large, white, blank envelope—addressed to:
"Mr. Joseph A. Rafferty,
Southern Building,
Washington 5, D. C.
"More than correct air mail stamps to be put on large envelope to Rafferty. Mark large envelope—personal and confidential. No return address on either envelope—or on letter in small envelope."

Assumed Name—

Mrs. Bentley also wrote an instruction for Matusow to have her name changed to "Mary Peterson" on the passenger list for the return airplane trip to New York. She was so intent on throwing Senate probers off her trail that she even ordered two tickets, one via Pan

American to Miami, another via British Overseas Airlines to New York. Here is the instruction she gave Matusow:

> "II. Please change name on my B.O.A.C. ticket (for Saturday to N.Y.) to Mrs. Mary Peterson and bring back ticket with corrected name.
> "Thanks.   A.P.B.
> "III. Please make reservation by phone downtown for Mrs. Mary Peterson to N.Y. for Thursday for Pan Am to Miami—connecting with National or Eastern to Wash., D.C. (Harvey—this is a blind.)"

This gives just part of the strange life of Harvey Matusow, the former Communist who became an informer for Senator McCarthy, went out to Utah to defeat Sen. Elbert Thomas, and tried to defeat Sen. Mike Mansfield in Montana; and who now says that he falsified his testimony in the trial of top Communists at the direction of Roy Cohn.

If Senators want to dig to the bottom of his extraordinary story, I'll be glad to give them originals of the correspondence.

Note—Afterward Matusow married the lady.

APPENDIX D

THE DEATH OF A RACKET

—by John Steinbeck in the
Saturday Review on April 2, 1955.

The Matusow testimony to anyone who will listen places a bouquet of forget-me-nots on the grave of McCarthy. The ridiculousness of the whole silly series of investigations now becomes apparent, even to what a friend of mine used to call peanut-munchers. Matusow will have a much greater effect than he knows. What follows cannot be worse and may be better. It will surely be funny.

Matusow, swearing he was a Communist, was employed by various parts of our Government to swear that hundreds of other people were Communists. And now, he says, he lied. He swears that other professional Government witnesses also lied. Now a wave of hysteria has swept over the investigators. Senators who are personally involved cry out that Matusow lies now but didn't lie when he testified for them and against their enemies. A certain Senator not notorious for telling the truth himself says very sharply that he pays no attention to liars. And yet this liar campaigned for this Senator in a happier time. Very serious men are trying to determine when Matusow lied and when he did not. And the conclusion seems to be that he was truthful when he testified in your favor, and a liar when against. No one has publicly suspected that he was possibly a liar all the time—even now.

Matusow's description of the life of an informer is a sad commentary but a believable one. It is the story of Titus Oates all over again. An obscure man or woman, unsuccessful or unnoticed, joined or claimed to have joined the Communist Party. Perhaps the joining itself grew out of the desire to be noticed. The subject then recanted and offered his services to the Republic for the purpose of denouncing its enemies. Instantly such a person had dramatic center. Attentions were showered on him. Not only was he paid as a Government expert but he was paid for lectures. Magazines fought for his articles. He experienced the headiest of all drugs. As Matusow says, his fear was that it would all be over and himself again reduced to obscurity. It is natural that he would cast about for means to maintain his lonely position by bringing larger and more flamboyant charges. Remember —when Titus Oates's first bill of charges was thrown out he countered with a second larger bill. The parallel is exact.

Not only was the peak position of public informer precarious, it was also highly competitive. If one didn't keep center there were many others waiting to step into your position. If one's information dried up one was finished. A very famous informer dribbled out his revelations over a period of ten years. He is the dean. None other has ever equaled his technique.

Such were the winds of the times that certain basic nonsense was allowed to pass unnoticed. For example, a man with a perfectly clear record had to undergo a security check before being allowed to serve the Government. Even a suspicion of his having been near to the Communist Party was enough to eliminate him. During this process he was subjected to the scrutiny of self-confessed ex-Communists. In other words, the candidate's fate was in the hands of men and women who under the law could not themselves have been trusted in a Government job. I put all of this in the past tense because I believe it is mostly over. I suspect that Government informers, even if they have told the truth, can't survive Matusow's testimony. He has said that it was a good racket. Well, Matusow has ruined the racket. It will never be so good again.

Now, in spite of the hysterical words of the investigators about when they believe Matusow was lying and when telling the truth, the fact is that every bit of the testimony of professional witnesses will have to be inspected in terms of the old-fashioned rules of evidence. It is possible that much accurate testimony will be thrown out because of the perjured.

All of this is important, but even more important is the quick and violent change in the public climate. In the theatre the other night a reference to professional witnesses was greeted with roars of laughter.

There is a great feeling of relief in the air. The man who six months ago nodded solemnly over the revelations of a menopaused virgin will now be able to believe and say that he never took it seriously. It will now become apparent that 165,000,000 people have been shuddering in terror at a problematic 50,000 Communists.

The pendulum swing is manifest in many directions. If Cohn and Schine should travel again they would frighten no one. The books are coming back on the shelves of our libraries. The price for one noisy Senator's speeches has dropped to very little, and his political support has become dreaded. It is interesting to see various Congressmen try to disassociate themselves from the whole thing.

It is inevitable that some officials caught with their pants irretrievably down must charge that Matusow is still a Communist and that his reversal is a part of a plot of the masterminds of the Kremlin. But the time for such reasoning has passed. No Communist tactician would destroy the climate of disunity and suspicion which has haunted us for the last few years by substituting a return to sanity. An effective Communist Party would much rather keep the investigations going with their harvest of fear and disruption than to produce laughter which, in my estimation, is what Communists have most to fear and against which they have no armor.

We cannot know for sure why Matusow did any of it; whether, as some say, it was a deep plot all along or whether—as he himself says—to make a buck. But his testimony and retestimony may well be the little push which causes the pendulum of common sense to swing back. It seems to be happening right now.

NOTES

CHAPTER ONE

¹ In announcing the formation of our publishing firm early in 1953, Angus Cameron and I had issued a statement which read in part: " 'The black silence of fear,' as Justice Douglas has described the product of the hysteria of these times, has engulfed many among both writers and publishers. . . . Cameron & Kahn hope to provide a rostrum for writers who have not accepted and will not accept the orthodoxies of the witch hunters."

² *The Hour*, founded in 1939 by former Ambassador to Germany William E. Dodd and myself, was a confidential weekly newsletter published primarily for the use of the communications media and devoted to exposing Axis intelligence operations in the Americas.

³ In March 1947 President Harry Truman had promulgated his Executive Loyalty Order decreeing investigation of government employees and dismissal of the "disloyal". First covering 2,500,000 citizens, the Order was soon extended to include 3,000,000 employees of defense contractors and 3,000,000 members of the armed forces.

"Thus," wrote Professor D. S. Fleming in *The Cold War and Its Origins*, "at least 8,000,000 Americans are always under the shadow of having to prove their loyalty, if any anonymous, protected informer questions it."

The extent of the "loyalty" mania by the early 1950s was indicated when the State of Indiana enacted a statute requiring professional boxers and wrestlers to take a non-Communist oath before entering the ring.

⁴ Illustrative of the prevailing atmosphere in the land were the results of an experiment conducted by John Hunter of the Madison, Wisconsin, *Capital Times*. On the Fourth of July, 1951, in a public park, Hunter circulated a petition containing portions of the Declaration of Independence and the Bill of Rights. Of the 112 persons he approached, one was willing to sign the petition. Almost all of the others admitted they were afraid to do so. A number of them demanded to know if the reporter was a Communist: Said one: "Get the hell out of here with that Communist stuff!" Said another: "That may be the Russian Declaration of Independence, but you can't tell me it's ours."

⁵ The details of McCarthy's dubious financial transactions were brought out in a 1952 report of the Subcommittee on Privileges and Elections of the Senate Committee on Rules and Administration. This report documented Senator William Benton's charge that McCarthy had "practiced calculated fraud and deceit on the United States Senate and on the people of the country."

In 1953, under the chairmanship of McCarthy's friend, Senator William Jenner, the parent committee pigeonholed the report.

⁶ By 1955 Louis Budenz was estimated to have garnered some $100,000 from lectures, book royalties, and so on, in addition to his witness fees and professor's salary, since leaving the Communist Party. Matthew Cvetic was paid $12,500 for the motion picture rights and $6,500 for the magazine rights to his book *I Was A Communist For The FBI*. Herbert Philbrick's income was indicated by the fact that in 1956 his lawyer sued him for $125,000 in legal fees and commissions allegedly owed on his various earnings.

⁷ Even in Nazi Germany, despite Hitler's having served as an informer for the Reichswehr following World War I, political informers were not publicly acclaimed as such and treated as heroes as they were in the United States after World War II. No doubt one of the reasons for this difference was the fact that under fascism, though spies and informers functioned on a vast scale, it was not necessary to employ them extensively in court trials and other public proceedings, in order to denounce and prosecute "enemies of the state"—the latter could be imprisoned and executed at will. In the postwar democracy of America, however, where an attempt was made to suppress political dissent by "legal" means, it was necessary to have formal trials of accused "subversives," and to use informers as witnesses against them. Under these circumstances, it became expedient to present such witnesses to the public in the most favorable possible light.

But despite all the intensive efforts of officialdom to glamorize paid informers and professional witnesses, a very considerable number of Americans were not inclined to take too kindly to them. In the words of a July 8, 1954, editorial in the *New York Times*: "The informer smacks of the police state; and we think that most Americans shrink instinctively from his use."

[8] In an article in the *Journal of the American Medical Association*, for example, Hoover urged doctors to inform the FBI of any subversive tendencies among their patients. "The physicians of America, like other citizens," he wrote, "can best help in the protection of the Nation's internal security by reporting to the FBI any information of this nature that might come into their possession."

In the periodical, *Woman's Day*, Hoover exhorted "the women of America" to inform the FBI of any suspicious activities among their "acquaintances, friends, and neighbors." Female communists, he alerted his readers, were "outwardly . . . ordinary citizens like the women in the next block, the wife of the local businessman, or the mother of little Bobby."

[9] Without exception, all of the witnesses listed had served as FBI informers and been subsequently recommended by the Bureau as witnesses at congressional hearings and federal trials.

Significantly, J. Edgar Hoover and other top Justice Department officials made a practice of keeping the criminal records of such witnessses from the courts and the public in government proceedings at which they testified. The practice was, of course, illegal.

[10] The Smith Act and the Taft-Hartley Law were two of the most repressive statutes widely implemented during the postwar years.

Of the Smith Act, the noted authority on constitutional law, Zechariah Chafee, Jr., wrote: ". . . this statute contains the most drastic restrictions on freedom of speech ever enacted in the United States during peacetime."

The Taft-Hartley Law virtually nullified the historic National Labor Relations Act of the New Deal.

The Smith Act was an anti-advocacy federal statute which made it a criminal offense to advocate the overthrow of the government by force or violence, or to form, join or assist any organization whose object was to advocate the violent overthrow of the government. Since the American Communist Party was held to be an organization which engaged in such advocacy, the Smith Act was an attempt to make Party membership a crime. It was ruled by the Supreme Court to be unconstitutional in 1957.

The Taft-Hartley Act contained provisions which denied labor organizations access to the facilities and protection of the National Labor Relations Board unless each of its officers had filed an affidavit stating that he or she had never been, nor were currently, a member of the communist party, or any other organization which advocated the overthrow of the government by force or violence. During the 1950s, labor leaders including Clinton Jencks were persecuted for having filed false affidavits.

This affidavit provision of Taft-Hartley was repealed in 1959.

CHAPTER TWO

[11] *Counterattack* was published weekly by American Business Consultants, Inc., a firm operated by three former FBI agents, Frank McNamara, Jack Keehan, and Ken Birely. The ex-FBI men also published the booklet *Red Channels*. Both publications provided subscribers with lists of "Communists, fellow travelers, left wingers or suspects" in the entertainment world and other professions. (As a special service, for $5000 a year, American Business Consultants supplied business firms with labor spies and dossiers on employees.)

The ex-FBI agents heading the firm maintained close contact with J. Edgar Hoover's headquarters in Washington. They also operated a spy network of their own.

[12] In his column in the *New York Daily Compass*, I. F. Stone commented that Cameron's enforced resignation had given "aid and comfort to those out to destroy freedom of publishing and freedom of expression in America.

"Are books, too," wrote Stone, 'to be guilty by association?... Will there be any limit to the blackmail of ignorance, illiteracy and obscurantism, if men of intelligence and substance can be frightened so easily? How can we keep America free if no one cares enough about freedom to fight for it?"

[13] Editor's Note: Ralph Rimar was a labor spy for the Ford Motor Company's Service Department, the aim of which was to disrupt union activities and to root out union sympathizers. In a sworn statement Rimar declared: "Prior to 1937 and the rise of the CIO, I once estimated that I was responsible for the firing of close to 1500 men. During the year 1940 alone, I turned in lists of over 1000 sympathizers, and they were all fired as a result of my report." The author obtained Rimar's confession which was published in *PM* magazine in 1941.

[14] Among my friends, besides Clinton Jencks, who by 1953 had already received prison sentences in the postwar witch hunt were: writers, Alvah

Bessie, Ring Lardner, Jr., Dalton Trumbo, Albert Maltz (all members of the Hollywood Ten), and Dashiell Hammett; Rev. Willard Uphaus, scholar and theologian; Dr. Edward K. Barsky, chairman of the Joint Anti-Fascist Refugee Committee; Rev. Richard Morford, director of the Council of American-Soviet Friendship; Steve Nelson, Communist leader and former commander of the Abraham Lincoln Brigade in Spain; and union leaders, Harry Bridges, Julius Emspak, James Matles and Maurice Travis.

Such was the situation by 1953 that I began a speech at the annual convention of the United Electrical Workers Union by saying: "I have to make an apology. Several of your officers face jail terms, and so many other friends of mine have already served theirs, that I really feel embarrassed. To date I've only lost my passport. I haven't been indicted—not even subpoenaed. Perhaps my writing simply isn't what it should be. But I promise to keep doing my best, and maybe the authorities will take some action." Actually, I didn't have long to wait.

CHAPTER THREE

[15] The *Denver Post* series (September 19–October 7, 1954) was entitled "Faceless Informers and Our Schools." The author, associate editor Lawrence Martin, summarized his findings: "Guilt by association, on the basis of anonymous information, without benefit of due process, confrontation by an accuser or supported evidence, is driving scores of American schoolteachers from their jobs, bearing the stigma of loyalty risks or actual subversives . . . During the last three years, anonymous, unevaluated, and unsupported information has put at least 1,000 teachers in public schools and colleges on 'suspect lists' as disloyal or subversive."

The articles revealed that while a variety of agencies was involved in the secret investigation of "subversives" in the school system, the FBI was conducting the most extensive operation. "Without possessing any detailed authority to do so," stated a *Denver Post* editorial, "the FBI is undertaking to volunteer information to governors of states and school authorities regarding the hiring of schoolteachers. . . . The FBI has become sort of a volunteer guardian of our school system. . . . Schoolteachers all across the country are operating under the all-seeing eyes of the FBI."

[16] Except where otherwise specified in the text, dialogue in this section is taken directly from the transcripts of the tape-recorded discussions between Matusow and me.

CHAPTER FOUR

[17] A year or so after giving this testimony at the Senate subcommittee hearing, as Matusow was to relate in his book he gave affidavits to the *New York Times* and to *Time* magazine admitting that he had testified falsely about the "Communist control" of their staffs.

[18] Matusow's serialized articles in the *Journal-American* were written in collaboration with the reporter, Howard Rushmore.

An ex-Communist who had once been a reporter for the *Daily Worker*, Rushmore had joined the staff of the *Journal-American* in 1939 and afterwards had worked simultaneously for congressional investigative committees and the paper, sometimes covering hearings at which he was the chief informer. He took a particular delight in his anti-Communist "exposés." According to the account of a *New York Daily News* reporter, Rushmore periodically exhibited to his colleagues a press clipping about the suicide of a school teacher who had been hounded from his job by the inquisition. "Rushmore," related the *News* reporter, "announced happily, 'I was responsible for that. That's the second one I testified against that committed suicide.'"

In the early 1950's, Rushmore resigned from the *Journal-American* and went to work for Senator McCarthy as his research director. McCarthy characterized the former Hearst reporter as "one of the greatest living Americans." Later, Rushmore became a member of the staff of the semi-pornographic scandal sheet, *Confidential*.

Rushmore's sordid career came to a gruesome end in a taxicab in New York City on January 2, 1958, when he shot and killed his wife and then turned the gun on himself.

CHAPTER FIVE

[19] Editor's note: In June, 1986, Roy M. Cohn was disbarred by the Appellate Division of the New York State Supreme Court on charges of dishonesty, fraud, deceit, and misrepresentation. He died in August, 1986.

[20] Fortas would later be appointed Associate Justice of the Supreme Court by President Lyndon Johnson.

CHAPTER SIX

21 Editor's note: Alsop apparently underestimated the political forces involved in the case, and the pressure they could bring to bear. Within a month he wrote two additional columns, each one labelling Cameron & Kahn as "pro-Communist". In one he wrote: "Was the recantation of self-confessed liar Harvey Matusow carefully stage managed by the Communists? There are signs that it was. For example . . . Cameron & Kahn, the publishing firm which is sponsoring the Matusow confession, has a decidedly pro-Communist coloration." Alsop's reversal characterized the Cold War dilemma of the "liberal" press: they could ignore the abuses inherent in the anti-Communist crusade, or they could defend the rights of Communists and "pro-Communists". The career penalties were swift and severe for those who chose the latter course. Alsop's retreat exemplified the prevailing fear of dissenting views.

22 On one occasion, Representative John E. Rankin of the House Un-American Activities Committee placed in the Congressional Record a lengthy report about my books, articles, lectures, trips and organizational associations. The report indicated, if nothing else of much interest, the extent of the surveillance I was being accorded by the Committee and other federal agencies.

At the time my name was included on the Un-American Activities Committee's blacklist, Representative Richard M. Nixon was one of the committee's most active members. Some twenty-five years later, something of a stir would be created by the fact that—as President of the United States—Nixon was still in the business of compiling political enemies lists.

Editor's note: The author was not aware of the full extent of FBI surveillance. After Mr. Kahn's death, his family applied under the Freedom of Information act to obtain the FBI's case file. In excess of two thousand pages, it revealed that in addition to having agents monitor Kahn's travel, speeches and family, his study had been illegally entered and documents photographed or stolen.

23 The press reported next day that a dozen FBI agents converged on the scene when Harvey was served his subpoena—an apparent extravagance for taxpayers footing the bill.

24 The dialogue throughout this section is taken from the stenographic record of the press conference.

CHAPTER SEVEN

[25] A number of these indictments were later dropped, or convictions secured through them reversed, as the hysteria of McCarthyism abated in the latter 1950's. (See Chapters XIV, XVI, and XVII.) In the meantime, however, the persons falsely accused had suffered onerous legal expenses and untold personal problems, including loss of jobs and grave harm done to their reputations.

[26] "Recent examination of the history and meaning of the Fifth Amendment," declared a unanimous opinion of the Supreme Court on May 27, 1957, "has emphasized anew that one of the basic functions of the privilege is to protect innocent men." The Court recalled a previous opinion to the effect that "the privilege serves to protect the innocent who might otherwise be ensnared by ambiguous circumstances."

In a concurring opinion, Associate Justice Hugo Black stated: "It seems peculiarly incongruous and indefensible for courts, which exist and act only under the Constitution, to draw inferences of lack of honesty from invocation of a privilege deemed worthy of enshrinement in the Constitution."

[27] The record of a grand jury proceeding is not publicly available except by court order. The dialogue from my appearance is therefore based for the major part on notes I made at the time and memoranda I gave my attorney. In those instances where portions of these proceedings were made public in court and where I quote from the court record, I so indicate.

CHAPTER EIGHT

[28] The dialogue that immediately follows is quoted directly from the transcript of the grand jury proceedings. This portion became available when it was later made part of the court record.

[29] In his book, *Grand Inquest*, Telford Taylor, distinguished attorney and former chief counsel for the prosecution of Nazi war criminals at Nuremberg, writes: ". . . the First (Amendment) has its roots in the eighteenth-century prosecution for seditious utterances and publications, such as that of the New York printer, John Peter Zenger, in 1735. Its historical purpose, however, was not so much to prevent inquisition as to liberate public discussion,

and especially criticism of the government and its officials, from the inhibiting restrictions of sedition prosecutions."

[30] The dialogue of the proceedings in Judge Clancy's court is taken from the court transcript.

[31] As uncompromising a nonconformist as he was renowned a painter, illustrator and author, Rockwell Kent had himself been a repeated target of denunciation by government informer-witnesses. In his autobiography, *It's Me O Lord,* Kent includes a chapter entitled, "The Liar," which deals in part with testimony given under oath by "the notorious apostate, Louis Budenz," to the effect that he knew Kent was a member of the Communist party. "When Associated Press asked me for my comments (on Budenz's testimony), I complied," writes Kent, "and although calling Budenz a liar is hardly to be classified as news, the AP wires carried it."

When Kent, like a number of other prominent dissenters, was summarily deprived of his passport by the State Department—on the grounds that his traveling abroad to paint European landscapes would be "contrary to the best interests of the United States", the director of the passport division wrote Kent a letter offering this unique explanation as one of the reasons for the State Department's action: "You are a sponsor of a four-page petition addressed to Attorney General Herbert M. Brownell criticizing the use of paid informers."

[32] Verbatim transcript of the court proceedings.

CHAPTER NINE

[33] In my book, *The Game of Death—Effects of the Cold War on Our Children,* I had referred to one of Judge Lumbard's rulings made while a member of the New York Supreme Court.

One chapter dealt in part with court cases in which, in keeping with the prevailing passions of the time, the right of parents to maintain custody of their children had been decided on political grounds. The case involving Judge Lumbard concerned an Armenian-American shoemaker named Cholokian who, after residing in the United States for thirty-five years had decided in 1947 to return to Armenia with his wife and five children. Two of Cholokian's sons, aged twelve and eleven, were in Catholic welfare institutions, where they had been placed a few years before when Mrs. Cholokian became too ill to care for them. When Cholokian sought their release and the welfare institution refused to return the children to their parents, Cholokian's lawyer

brought the matter before the New York Supreme Court. The presiding magistrate was Judge Lumbard. In his ruling on the case, he denied the parents
the custody of their two sons on these grounds: "It would not be to the best
interests of the children to be taken to Soviet Armenia, even though it results
in the temporary or even the permanent separation of these children from
their parents."

[34] This dialogue of the proceedings in Judge Dimock's court is taken directly
from the court transcript.

[35] In connection with the fact that the Justice Department continued to use
Matusow as a witness in security cases until the midsummer of 1954, it is
interesting to note that the Department's Immigration and Naturalization Service had previously discontinued using Matusow as witness because of his
obvious vulnerability. An Immigration memorandum concerning Matusow,
which came to light at a closed congressional hearing on February 25, 1955,
contained this passage: "On April 8, 1954, Mr. Noto instructed Mr. Flagg in
New York that subject was not to be used as a witness in Service proceedings. This action was taken on receipt of information that the subject had
written letters to his wife in which he stated that he had committed perjury in
testifying regarding Communism."

[36] Like many of his colleagues in the professional witness game, Lowell
Watson had a criminal record, to which the Justice Department genteelly
made no reference when putting him on the witness stand.

Subsequent to the Lamb hearing, it was revealed at a closed session of a
congressional committee that the Justice Department's files contained a
memorandum on Watson which included this comment: "Watson's criminal
records consists of a sentence of 90 days in 1924 at St. Mary's, W. Va., for
contributing to the delinquency of a minor; sentence of 30 days at Toledo,
Ohio, for petty larceny, and a charge of assault and battery in resisting an
officer at Toledo, Ohio, for which he was found not guilty after a jury trial
on October 31, 1932."

CHAPTER TEN

[37] That Senator Eastland should have been chairman of a Senate subcomm-
mittee purportedly investigating subversive activities in the United States
was not without a certain irony since the senator himself was a key figure in
a far-reaching seditious conspiracy. The chief purpose of this conspiracy was
to sabotage the U.S. Supreme Court's decision ruling public school racial
segregation unconstitutional. "You are not required to obey any court which

passes out such a ruling," declared Senator Eastland. "In fact, you are obliged to defy it."

On December 30, 1955, the *New York Times* was to report that Senator Eastland had recently addressed a secret meeting in Memphis, Tennessee, of the leaders of a newly formed organization which had the avowed objective of coordinating all efforts in the South to defy the Supreme Court's decision and prevent Black Americans from exercising other constitutional rights. The organization called itself, somewhat euphemistically, the Federation for Constitutional Government.

"We are about to embark on a great crusade," Senator Eastland told the clandestine gathering, "a crusade to restore Americanism... Defeat means the death of Southern culture and our aspirations as an Anglo-Saxon race. Generations of Southerners yet unborn will cherish our memory because they will realize that the fight we wage will have preserved for them untainted racial heritage. . . ."

The senator was elected to serve on the Federation's board of directors.

In 1956, Senator Eastland was to become chairman of the Senate Judiciary Committee.

[38] In all fairness to Senator Watkins, it should be stated that in the fall of 1954, as chairman of the Senate Select Committee to Study Censure Charges against the Wisconsin senator, Watkins helped bring to light a considerable number of facts about McCarthy's misconduct as a senator. In December 1954 the Senate voted 67–22 to condemn McCarthy for his contemptuous and obstructive attitude toward the Watkins committee.

[39] In this chapter all of the dialogue from the Senate subcommittee hearing is taken directly from the transcript of the proceedings.

[40] Following my appearance before the subcommittee, I sent Senator Welker a letter advising him that I planned to write a book about the Matusow case, and that in it I might make reference to his statement indicating that none of the subcommittee members had "ever used the Fifth Amendment" as practicing attorneys.

My letter read in part:

"It seems to me that this statement of yours gives rise to a couple of interesting and important legal questions. Is it to be interpreted as meaning that in every criminal case in which you or your colleagues have acted as defense counsel, you have invariably insisted that your client take the witness stand? And is it your contention that every defendant in a criminal case should take the witness stand?

"As you yourself know as a lawyer, it is the Fifth Amendment of the Constitution which forbids compelling a witness in a criminal case to take the witness stand: 'No person . . . shall be compelled in any criminal case to be a witness against himself.' And if in any such case a defendant for whom you have been acting as defense counsel has not taken the witness stand, then you have of course relied upon the protection provided under, and you have made use of, the Fifth Amendment."

Senator Welker sent no answers to my questions.

[41] Senator Daniel was not without company in making this extraordinary admission. Most of the senators on the subcommittee clearly indicated during the course of their inquiry into the Matusow affair that they had already determined what their findings would be.

Following Matusow's first appearance, Eastland told the press that Matusow's recantation was "part of a shrewd plan to get some folks out of trouble" and that "this is all part of a shrewd scheme of the Commies."

Interviewed on February 23 after the second session of the hearings, Senator Watkins informed newsmen that he believed Matusow was "trying to discredit" other government witnesses "without any real knowledge about them."

A few days later, Senator McClellan declared on the floor of the Senate that "since this investigation had been undertaken, it was my hope that the testimony of Matusow and other witnesses in the investigation would reveal that the book *False Witness* was inspired by a desire on the part of its author and its publishers to serve the Communist cause. . . . and that the evidence would further reveal that its publication is being sponsored and financed by individual Communists and Communist organizations. *These views, I believe, are shared by every member of the Internal Security Subcommittee.*" (Italics mine.)

[42] Several years later following the launching of the first earth satellite by the Soviet Union in October 1957, with extensive comparisons being made between American and Soviet scientific progress, there was a hue and cry in the United States regarding what was widely characterized as the "crisis in education." "All over the nation," stated *U.S. News & World Report*, "people are asking: What's wrong with U.S. schools?" President Eisenhower, in a national broadcast, urged parents and teachers throughout the country "to make one single project their special order of business: To scrutinize your school's curriculum and standards. . . ."

Not a few commentators pointed out that one of the contributory causes to the "crisis in education" had been the widespread witch-hunts in the school system, the "loyalty purges" of teachers and the rampant fear of "controversial issues." Needless to say, investigations of "Communism in education" conducted by the Senate Internal Security Subcommittee and other Congressional investigative committees had contributed their share to spreading fear and tension in the schools. It was also worth recalling that paid informers of the calibre of Harvey Matusow had been helping decide which teachers were qualified to educate American youth.

CHAPTER ELEVEN

[43] Verbatim dialogue from the transcript of the proceedings.

[44] The dialogue is taken directly from the court transcript.

CHAPTER THIRTEEN

[45] That the attitude of the Mine-Mill leadership was to become increasingly defensive is indicated by the fact that within a few months after Matusow's recantation, as controversy mounted over the Jencks case and government propaganda against the union intensified, the executive board requested and received Jencks' resignation as a member of the union.

The failure, however, of such measures to mollify attacks on the union became apparent when in the summer of 1956 the Justice Department brought proceedings against fourteen Mine-Mill officers on the charge of conspiring to violate the Taft-Hartley Law—the very law under which Jencks himself had been convicted.

[46] An eminent humanist, teacher of philosophy at Columbia University, and vice-chairman of the Emergency Civil Liberties Committee, which was formed in 1951 "to give uncompromising support to the Bill of Rights and the freedom of conscience it guarantees," Corliss Lamont had himself come under frequent attack for his espousal of unpopular causes during the Cold War. In the fall of 1954, as a result of his asserting his rights under the First Amendment and challenging the constitutionality of the McCarthy committee when summoned before this body, Lamont was indicted for contempt of Congress. In 1956 the U.S. Court of Appeals in New York dismissed Lamont's contempt citation.

[47] On their return from an international peace conference in Peking in 1952, both Henry and Anita had been summarily deprived of their passports by the State Department on the grounds that such peace activities were "contrary to the interests of the United States." Henry's business associates, after being visited by FBI agents, had voted him out of the presidency of their construction company. Later, when Anita offered to donate some murals she had

painted to Norwalk public schools, violent protests from local patrioteers had persuaded the school board to reject the paintings.

[48] The dialogue is taken directly from the Senate subcommittee transcript.

[49] What was perhaps the most meaningful statement of the entire hearing was made by lawyer Harry Sacher, who was summoned before the subcommittee for questioning regarding his connection with the Matusow case. Asked whether he was a Communist, Sacher declared:

"I refuse categorically, Mr. Chairman, to discuss my beliefs, religious, political, economic, or social. I do not do so on the grounds of the Fifth Amendment. I do so because it is inconsistent with the dignity of any man to be compelled to disclose his political, religious, economic, social, or any other views."

When Senator McClellan said he did not think it "beneath the dignity of a good citizen to answer the question," Sacher replied: "Medieval inquisitors also thought there was no impropriety in asking those whom they regarded as heretics to answer the question."

For taking this position, Sacher was tried for contempt of Congress, found guilty, and sentenced to six months in jail and a $1,000 fine.

CHAPTER FOURTEEN

[50] There were other highly revealing omissions in Matusow's FBI reports. Not the least of these concerned Matusow's testimony as a professional witness to the effect that he had personal knowledge of "Communist atomic espionage activities" in America.

In his appearance on October 8, 1952, at the Senate Internal Security Subcommittee hearing in Salt Lake City, Matusow charged that in the fall of 1950 a member of the Czechoslovakian U.N. delegation had approached him in New York with a proposal "to get any atomic secrets that could be obtained in and around Sandia Base in Albuquerque and Los Alamos." Matusow added: "... from the way he talked ... I knew that some espionage activity was being conducted by the Czechoslovak government through the United Nations staff."

Obviously, had an incident of this nature occurred, an FBI informer would have considered it worth mentioning to his superiors; but Matusow's FBI reports contained no reference to any such conversation or to his knowledge of Czechoslovakian "espionage activity."

In the light of such glaring discrepancies between Matusow's FBI reports and his subsequent testimony as a government witness, one can easily understand the Justice Department's marked aversion to having these reports made public at the retrial hearings before Judge Dimock and Judge Thomason.

⁵¹ This confidential letter from J. Edgar Hoover also stated: "Reports furnished by Matusow to our Albuquerqe office will be sent to your office in the immediate furture." These particular reports by Matusow to the FBI dealt in part with Matusow's visit at the San Cristobal Valley Ranch in 1950 and with his meeting Clinton Jencks. Significantly enough, despite Judge Dimock's request at the Flynn retrial hearing for all of Matusow's FBI reports that were in the possession of the U.S. attorney's office, the Albuquerque reports were not produced in Dimock's court by U.S. Attorney Lumbard.

⁵² The dialogue here is taken directly from the transcript of the House subcommittee proceedings.

⁵³ Prior to his appointment as federal magistrate, Judge Holtzoff had served as legal adviser to FBI chief J. Edgar Hoover.

⁵⁴ The union officials were Secretary-Treasurer Julius Emspak of the United Electrical, Radio & Machine Workers Union, and Thomas Quinn, an officer of the same union. The general manager of the *Daily Worker* was Philip Bart.

⁵⁵ This dialogue is taken from press reports of Brown's appearance before the Federal Subversive Activities Control Board.

CHAPTER FIFTEEN

⁵⁶ In April 1954 the *Nation* magazine had published a lengthy article by lawyer Frank J. Donner entitled, "The Informer," which was the first definitive expose of the government's informer-witness system to appear in any publication.

CHAPTER SEVENTEEN

⁵⁷ One of the most important of the increasing revelations about lying government informer-witnesses concerned Elizabeth Bentley, regarding whose perjurious proclivities Matusow had testified before the Senate Internal Security Subcommittee in the spring of 1955.

The testimony of no professional witness had been more widely publicized than that of Miss Bentley, who claimed to have been "a secret espionage courier" for the Soviet Union and who, in various of her appearances on the witness stand, had named several dozen former New Deal government officials as "Communists" and members of "Russian spy rings." Among the more prominent of the individuals denounced by Miss Bentley was the former Treasury Department economist, William Henry Taylor.

Late in 1955, Taylor's attorney, former congressman Byron Scott, made public a 107-page brief detailing evidence that Miss Bentley had repeatedly told "demonstrable falsehoods" in her writings and on the witness stand. Shortly afterward, a Washington loyalty board cleared Taylor of all charges of disloyalty. Taylor's complete exoneration, stated his attorney, not only substantiated the fact that Miss Bentley had committed perjury but also "raised some sharp questions for Attorney General Brownell and FBI Director J. Edgar Hoover, since they have both endorsed her unequivocally."

Memorable was the fact that, as a government witness at the espionage trial of Julius and Ethel Rosenberg in March 1951, Miss Bentley had given testimony that helped send the Rosenbergs to the electric chair and effect a thirty-year prison term for Morton Sobell.

INDEX